Laying the Bed:

The Native Origins Of
The Underground Railroad

To those who show up
when needed.

Cover design: Brenan Pangborn
Maps: James Campbell-Prager

Back Cover 'stencils': Reverend Jermaine Lougen and Chief Joseph Brant

Revised Edition
Elora, Ontario Canada

ISBN# : 978-1-896312-08-8

copyright 2011-2014

written and published by
Jerry Prager

prager_jp@hotmail.com
abolition-emancipation.blogspot.ca

Seven generations ago some of my Tuscarora ancestors were
still in North Carolina. Over the internet I located notarized
documents at the Tuscarora Reservation in New York State
that trace my grandmother Caroline Beaver's ancestry
through her grandmother
and great-grandmother's line in the 1700s
to Margaret Groat of North Carolina.

- Haudenosaunee Social Dancing: Who We Are
George Beaver, Six Nations writer, historian and
descendant of Abram Groat (1814-1901)

"That there are a number of Negroes in this part of the Country
many of whom have been Soldiers during the late *ware* between
Great Britain and America, and others who were born free with a few
who have come into Canada since the peace,
-Your Petitioners are desirous of settling adjacent to each other that they
may be enabled to give assistance (in work) to those amongst them who
may most want it.
Your Petitioners therefore humbly Pray that their situation may be taken
into consideration, and if your Excellency should see fit to allow them a
Tract of Country to settle on, separate from the white Settlers, your
Petitioners hope their behaviour will be such as to shew, that Negroes
are capable of being industrious, and in loyalty to the Crown they are
not deficient."
Jack Baker, Jack Becker, John Cesar, John Dimon, Tom Frey, John Gerof,
Peter Green, **Michael Grote**, *John Jackson, Adam Lewis, Peter*
Ling, Richard Pierpoint, Pompadour, John Smith, Saison Sepyed, Simon
Speck, Robert Spranklin, Thomas Walker and Jack Wurmwood

Petition of Free Negroes, Upper Canada, 1794

Table of Contents

Centre Insert Maps

Images

A Guide to Names in the Book

Michael Groats

Mike Sr. ie. Michael Grote 1794 free negro petitioner, presumed father of all early
19th century black Groats/Grotes original owner of Nelson township farm

Michael of Nelson ie Michael Groat, son of Mike Sr., Dundas Road Patroler
inheritor of Mike Sr.'s farm, father of William of Guelph.

William Groats

William of Guelph 1820-1900 son of Michael of Nelson, m. Elizabeth Adams

William of Tuscarora 1783-4, son of Mike Sr., Tuscarora warriour, Road Patroler,
father of Abram Groat by Margaret, a Tuscarora, fathered other children with
Emily Smith.

William the Younger, son of William of Tuscarora and Emily Smith,
also a Tuscarora warriour.

William Groat-Mike Son of John and Caty, a Credit River Mississauga,
lived on New Credit reserve.

Abram Groat

Son of William of Tuscarora and Margaret of North Carolina, Tuscarora warriour,
husband of Sarah Williams of SC, father of Lydia and Levinia etc
Kansas Land settler, lived on Six Nations and Caradoc Reserves.

Pete Groat

Presumed son of Mike Sr. Dundas Road Patroler, Nelson township settler.

Peter Groat

Son of Michael of Nelson as per 1846 will.

Peter-Groat Mike

Son of John Groat and Caty, a Credit River Mississauga,
baptized by Rev. Peter Jones, live on New Credit Reserve.

Henry Groat

Probable son on Mike Sr. Dundas road Patroler

Henry Groat-Mike

Son of John Groat and Caty, a Credit River Mississauga, lived on New Credit
Reserve, children married into James Chrsyler-Sarah Addley family.

John Groat-Mike

Presumed son of Mike Sr., married Caty (Mississauga) died on New Credit Reserve.

Simon Groat

Presumed son of Mike Sr. Served in the Coloured Corps, moved to the Queen's
Bush, married Mary A. Lewis there in 1847, retired to Caradoc township.

Jemima Groat

Daughter of Mike Sr., wife of Ebenezer Guire, mother of Abigail Bradt.

Jemime Groat

Daughter of Michael of Nelson, as per his 1846 will.

Hannah Groat

Daughter of Michael of Nelson, sister of William of Guelph (1846 will.)

Hannah Groat Lillie

Daughter of William of Guelph and Elizabeth Adams, married to Thomas Lillie.
Ancestor of family historians Arlene Noble and Sharon Hewlett.

Margaret Groat

Tuscarora from NC, mother of Abram by William.

Margaret Groat

Daughter of Michael of Nelson as per 1846 will.

Margaret Groat-Mike

Daughter of John and Caty, born on the Credit among her mother's people, baptized
by Rev. Peter Jones, married Richard Lewis, removed from New Credit Reserve.

James Chrysler
Grandson of Michael of Nelson, parents unknown; inheritor of Mike Sr.'s land.
Thomas Chrysler
Possibly James Chrysler the inheritor; 1847 Guelph Line extension petitioner.
Adam Crysler
Captain Butler's Rangers, Blue-eyed Indian, brother of the Patriot-murdered
Balthus, uncle of John of Chrysler's Farm (1812 Battle site); owner of Tom
Blackman freed upon Adam's death.
Davis-Ghents
William Davis, NC Welsh, son of Thomas, plantation owner, loyalist, husband of
Hannah, father of Elizabeth (Ghent) and Mary (Gage) and Asahel, Sarah (John
Chisholm); founder Mount Albion Saltfleet, grandfather of Gilbert etc
Robert Davis, brother of William, probably died in captivity after the Battle of
Cowpens SC, husband of Jane, father of Robert Jr. John, Thomas
Gilbert Davis, 'subscriber' for the will of Michael of Nelson.

Thomas Ghent , son of Edward and, husband of Elizabeth Davis, settled Nelson
neighbour of Mike Sr., founder of Burlington fruit growing industry.
*William Ghent.,*son of Thomas settled the Queen's Bush , married Mary Fonger.
David Ghent, son of Thomas, next door neighbour of Michael of Nelson.
Gage-Davis
James Gage Jr., son of James Sr. and Mary Jones; nephew of Augustus Jones
husband of Mary Davis, father of Asahel and Mary (John Chrysler)
banker, creator of Wellington Square, partner of William Chisholm (founder of
Oakville), prominent Methodist.
Asahel Gage, son of James Jr. and Mary, husband of Nancy McCollum.
Jones
Augustus Jones, Welsh surveyor, landowner, Mohawk and Mississauga wives,
brother of Mary Gage, father of John, Peter, Polly etc.

Rev. Peter Jones, son of Augustus, grandson of Chief Wabanosay, brother of John
etc. half brother (Polly Brant) etc. husband of Eliza Fields, Methodist Minister,
Mississauga Chief, father of P.E Jones (Indian agent) etc.
Anglicans on the Grand
Rev. Abram Nelles, son of Robert Nelles – ally of Joseph Brant, brother of Robert Jr.
Rev. Robert Lugger, soldier, founder of school for slaves in Barbadoes, founder of
technical school Caradoc Reserve, friend of Clapham Sect.
Rev. Adam Elliot, husband of Eliza Howells, missionary to Coldwater Chippewa,
minister to Tuscarora, uncle of E. Pauline Johnson.
Howells
Henry C Howells, Welsh Quaker, American abolitionist, husband of Mary Best,
Harriet Joynter, Hannah Kells, father of 18 children, including Eliza (Elliot),
Emily (Johnson), Mary (Rogers) and Thomas. Friend and ally of Theodore Weld,
Gerrit Smith, Milo Townsend, William Garrison, William Beecher see below.
Eliza Howells, wife of Rev. Adam Elliot, mother of their children, died of TB.
Emily Howells, wife of Chief George Johnson (Mohawk), mother of five children,
including Eva' and Pauline.
Mary Howells, wife of Rev. V. Rogers, Kingston Anglican and abolitionist.
Thomas Howells, Brantford doctor, uncle of Pauline Johnson.
Baptists
Reverend James Sims, Queen Bush missionary and farmer, conducted the wedding
service for Simon Groat And Mary A. Lewis.
Reverend James Cusik, Tuscarora, founder of Six Nations/Kansas congregations.

Abolitionists

Beecher, Reverend Lyman father of Henry W., Harriet, William, Catharine and
      Head of the Lane Seminary, opposed to the Lane Rebels.

Beecher, Reverend Edward founder of the Presbyterian Church in Putnam, co-
      founder of the Ohio anti-slavery Society, friend of Howells.

Beecher, Reverend Henry Ward abolitionist, social Reformer and Congregationalist.

Beecher Stowe, Harriet Author of Uncle Tom's Cabin. Abolitionist.

Beecher, Reverend Charles Abolitionist, Congregationalist, m. Sarah L. Coffin

Beecher, Catherine Abolitionist, educator, founder of Hartford Female Seminary.

Brown, George/Peter/Gordon founders of the Globe newspaper, Presbyterians,
      founders of the Canadian Anti-Slavery Society.

Coffin, Levi co-founder of the Underground Railroad, "highland" Quaker, Free
      Produce movement leader, author of Reminiscences.

Coffin, Vestal older cousin of Levi, organizer of Quaker fugitive slave assistance in
      Guilford Co. North Carolina, follower of Benjamin Lundy, died young.

Gage, Mathilda abolitionist, suffragette, Native Rights Advocate, nominal Baptist.

Garrison, William "co founder" of the Underground Railroad, friend of Howells,
      friendly opponent of Weld's, co-founder of the anti-Slavery Society of
      America, publisher of the Liberator.

Hicks, Elias Quaker social reformer, abolitionist, fonder of the Hicksites.

Huber, Henry S. Kitchener Mennonite/Swenbourgian, abolitionist, good neighbour

Louguen, Rev. Jermain former slave, born Jarm Lougue, escaped to Canada via
      highland native trails, lived at Hamilton, returned to States, lived and led
      anti-slavery Activities in Syracuse New York, BME minister Nova Scotia.
      AME Zion Barbados.

Pastorius, Francis Daniel, Mennonite/Quaker, signee of the Germantown Quaker
      Petition Against Slavery 1688.

Sandilands, Thomas Guelph settler (1832) banker, planked-road financier, VP of
      the Anti-Slavery Society of Canada 1852, Reform Party member. Scot.
      Presbyterian.

Simcoe Lt. General John Graves, soldier, force behind the creation of Anti-Slavery
      legislation in Upper Canada in 1793.

Smith, David W. Surveyor General of Upper Canada, UC Legislative Assembly
      Compact Tory and supporter of the Anti-Slavery Act.

Smith , Gerrit Upper New York state abolitionist, ally of Howells and Weld, Liberal
      Party Presidential Candidate, Free Soil Congressman, financier of John
      Brown's raid on the Harper's Ferry armory, independent Christian.

Strachan Bishop John, rector of Toronto, Family Compact Tory, anti-democrat,
      fierce advocate for the abolition of slavery, mentor of Rev Elliot, and Rev.
      Rogers.

Tappan, Arthur/Lewis co-founders of the Anti-Slavery Society of America, and of
      the American Missionary Society, supporter of the Queen Bush mission,
      mentors and employers of Weld's, and Hiram Wilson, Congregationalist.

Townsend, Milo, Abolitionist, Social Reform, Brighton Pennsylvania Quaker, friend
      of Howells.

Weld, Theodore co-author of Slavery As It Is, friend of Howells, husband of
      Angelina Grimké, employee of Arthur and Lewis Tappan, speaker at the
      Ohio Anti-Slavery Society Convention in Putnam Ohio, Presbyterian,
      Lane Rebel

White, Chief Justice John author of Simcoe's Anti-slavery Act

Woolman, John 18th century Quaker preacher, slave manumission advocate,
      author of Some Considerations on the Keeping of Negroes

Preface

In November of 2011, I was phoned by Guelph musician and activist Wayne F. Smythe and told that a stone church important to local Underground Railroad heritage was being sold. He asked if I, a stone worker, would assess the state of the building, the British Methodist Episcopal (BME) church of Guelph. Wayne, I learned, had not only called me but had filed an offer to purchase the church via realtor Big John Leacock, and had also filed foundation papers for what is now called the Guelph Black Heritage Society (chaired by Marva Wisdom.) As a local historian, I was also asked by Wayne to research the building with an eye to creating a book.

It quickly became evident to all of us that closing the deal was going to be more complicated than expected, so I left the ad hoc steering committee wrestling with the issues surrounding the purchase and spent the next year and a half researching British Methodist Episcopalianism and its predecessor, the African ME Church, trying to figure out what the Underground Railroad actually was and wasn't, when it actually began and who did what before it existed; I studied slavery in North America, I went looking for Quakers, abolitionists, reformers and their connections to Upper Canada and Guelph and beyond.

I knew next to nothing about the Underground Railroad when all this began, but Wayne did not just want a book about a black church, he wanted books about emancipation itself, about the ongoing struggle to abolish slavery, both as it was practiced in the past and as it occurs today.

So I figured out when blacks, slave and free, first started coming to Guelph and the surrounding townships, in hopes of understanding where they came from and how they ended up here.

Being the author of Legends of the Morgeti, books on the Calabrian mafia clans of Guelph, which focus on large families caught up in historical events, I knew I had to get most of the genealogy right or fail at getting any of it right. In the mob series however, the stories are from archived newspapers and records, which didn't exist to the same degree for these new books. Finding the who, what, where, when, how and why of so large a subject as slavery and the emancipation movement, turned what was to be a single book into a series.

Wayne's only directives to me as a historian were to explore the legends of native involvement in the Underground Railroad, and to find and define the role of the AME/BME churches in helping fugitive slaves into Canada, and what help they provided the newly emancipated; I was also to give credit where credit was due, relative to the conflicting claims of other churches.

The resulting research proved I was still writing a crime series: American slavery is either a crime against humanity, or the many violations of US laws protecting the rights of slave owners - as first defined in the Fugitive Slave Act signed into law by George Washington in 1793 – were crimes. Hundreds and then thousands of 19th century reform advocates aided and abetted escapees, thus, viewed one way, abolitionists were the first, domestic terrorist enemies of the Republic. (Although, in Thirteen Colonies days, Patriots were seen as terrorists by loyalists before and during the Revolution, so, barring the psychotic, one man's terrorist is always another man's freedom fighter.)

As for the issue of giving credit where credit is due (relative to church involvement in anti-slavery activities) the easiest way of measuring that is the issue of law-keeping versus law-breaking. The conflict within churches wasn't so much a conflict between pro and anti-slavery factions as it was between those who obeyed the law and those who actively broke it. That conflict split every church and most congregations in the US except one: the African Methodist Episcopal* Church, founded in Philadelphia in 1815 by free blacks.

[*Episcopal means governance by Bishops.]

The A.M.E. aided and abetted fugitive slaves from its inception, united as it was in its efforts to emancipate both African-Americans and the world from slavery. At the invitation of white Upper Canadian Methodists in the late 1820's, the A.M.E. began founding churches in the colony to minister to the waves of former slaves flooding into Upper Canada; in 1840 they created the Canada Conference. The AME may not have been created until 22 years after the passing of the first Fugitive Slave Act, but it hit the ground running in 1815 and focused on Canada from 1827 on.

The Baptist Church, by way of comparison, suffered extreme schism among its adherents, members and whole congregations in America took difference stances both on slavery and on their willingness to support those who broke the law, while in Canada, schism arose between those willing to support American law breakers and those who opposed law breaking. Those schisms mattered because Baptist churches were otherwise independent and structured around neighbourhoods and communities and had no real hierarchy, no Bishops, and a simpler conference structure. There was no institutional unity on slavery or law breaking.

It took the Baptist communion decades to divide, heal, and reunite before they could function in an organized way, so that it wasn't until the passing of the second Fugitive Slave Act in 1850 that the Baptists really earned their credit, nearly 60 years after the first Fugitive Slave Act was passed. Exceptions however, were local and many on both sides of the border.

The Anglican Church, which had been replaced in America by the Episcopal Church, was the state church of Upper Canada, and stood apart from its American cousin. England itself had eliminated slavery in Great Britain in 1782, and in Upper Canada the Anglicans were pro-actively anti-slavery from the start, despite the existence of laws protecting slave-owning loyalists who had followed the British out of America. Even more importantly for the argument of this book, the Church of England was alone on the Grand River for over thirty years before the Methodists arrived in the mid 1820's. The Baptists didn't arrive until 1842, although they eventually emerged as the dominant church on the Six Nations of the Grand Reserve, largely because they had native preachers and democratic practices, while the Methodists were primarily associated with the Mississauga chief and missionary, the Reverend Peter Jones.

In Canada, abolitionists broke no British laws by helping former slaves, because in 1793 the Lieutenant Governor of the colony, John Graves Simcoe, an Anglican and former British anti-slavery parliamentarian, passed the first anti-slavery legislation in the British Empire outside of Great Britain. That legislation didn't end slavery (tied as the practice had been to the original deal between loyalists and the crown) but it did end the importation of new slaves, and it freed the children of slaves once they were 25, while institutionalizing an economic system beyond the framework of slave production.

That difference in Canadian and American law from 1793 on, was ultimately the reason that former slaves and their descendants built a church in Guelph in 1880. Those differences arose in loyalist times, and it is in those times and early colonial frontiers that this story begins.

The Loyalist Roots of Upper Canadian Abolition

Efforts to help fugitive slaves in the Loyalist period were undertaken by supporters of British law who had experienced the excesses of republican revolutionaries, and thus had no respect for the laws of the US or for American definitions of freedom.

In language, the 'excluded initiative' is the process by which humans seek words that define different states of being, such as conditions better than the ones in which they are living. Visions of possible futures and the actions required to bring those futures into being represent an excluded initiative: freedom is a powerful initiative when excluded.

People still argue that the Bible condones slavery, however, the words that gave African slaves power over their circumstances came largely from the Bible; so that once the phrases of captivity and exodus entered their inner mythologies, the cadences of scripture expressed the meaning of Moses, and they were on their way to the promised land, which, after 1793, appeared to be a fantasy realm called Canada.

It is certainly true that the colony later become known as a grudging receiver of escaped slaves, but by that time, years of contact with ever enlarging streams of newly freed sojourners had soured the relationship considerably. Which is why most pro-black activity in the province was focused on educating and training the newly emancipated in an effort to alleviate the growing tensions between established communities and dysfunctional hordes of escapees. Dysfunctional, because it must be understood that in any talk of emancipation, the idea of freedom and the practice of freedom are two different things. Free choice is a complex, not a simplex: once compulsion ends, some people just wind down like clocks, others fall into violence or alcoholism or crime, while still others survive and prosper. When that mix of choices is occurring within communities of free peoples (who understand both the limitations and possibilities of an otherwise highly structured class system) a volatile brew is mixed into every relationship that former slaves have. Wives and children especially, though not exclusively.

The role of evangelicals in salvaging the detritus of slavery that started to gather in every community in the colony/province - became one of Christianity's finest hours. 19th century Reform battled the forces of reaction on many fronts: slavery, workers rights, women's rights, education and native rights, making it the antithesis of the evangelical movements of the 21st century. There are 27 million slaves in the world in 2014, still of which evangelicals appear to be indifferent.

While the Anglicans, through Lt. Governor General John Graves Simcoe, unequivocally were responsible for bringing the anti-slavery legislation into existence, the Society of Friends, better known to most as the Quakers and less known to most as a child of the Church of England born in the mid 1600's, are the true creators of the entity known as the Underground Railroad, by which I mean the system of forwarding slaves into freedom using railway nomenclature as code for their activities, ie conductors and stations and termini.

The bed of that railroad however, was laid on native trails, on highland trails used almost exclusively by First Nations from the Appalachians to the Alleghenies to the Niagara escarpment, and then up the Grand River and north to the Queen's Bush settlement, where, by the late 1840's, 1500 former slaves were holed up about 20 miles north by north west of Guelph and all points in between.

The most important Quaker in this context I believe, was the Welsh-born American anti-slavery advocate and educator, Henry C. Howells, grandfather of the Mohawk poet, E. Pauline Johnson, daughter of Emily Howells and the Mohawk Chief George Johnson, translator for the Anglican church among the Tuscarora. (Pauline was also the niece of Eliza Howells, wife of the Reverend Adam Elliot, Anglican minister to the Grand River Tuscarora, niece of Mary Howells, wife of a prominent Kingston Anglican abolitionist, the Reverend Robert Vachon Rogers and niece of Doctor Thomas Howells, a Brantford physician.)

Mary, Emily, Eliza and Thomas were all born in England, but their father moved them and the rest of his larger family to America for the express purpose of fighting slavery, which is what he then did for the rest of his life.

The first strand of this volume therefor, will focus on Anglican and First Nations anti-slavers and on the individuals involved, with special attention to the role that might have been played on the American side of the border by Henry C. Howells, who was well known to American abolitionists of his day, if unknown to us now.

The second strand of Laying the Bed will follow the Groat family - a clan of mixed race Presbyterian loyalists - from the time of their arrival in the colony in 1794 traveling with a North Carolina plantation family who settled on the plateau above Stoney Creek, to their purchase of land from Joseph Brant in Nelson township (Burlington) in 1806, then into and out of the War of 1812 at the head of the lake, from whence they expanded through various marriages onto the Six Nations Reserve where they appear as Tuscarora Baptists; onto Mississauga lands as members of the Methodist congregation of the Reverend Peter Jones, as well as appearing in both the Queen's Bush settlement and in Caradoc township near and on the Thames River reserves and lastly, when one becomes the first free-born adult black in Guelph, all of which is woven into the contexts of Upper Canadian Loyalist history.

First Nations, Quakers and Slaves

The foundations of the American Quaker relationship with first nations were laid by William Penn. In 1681, Penn had been given large tracts of "crown" land in the Thirteen Colonies by King Charles II to satisfy a debt owed to Penn's father. The two future states of Delaware and Pennsylvania came out of those redeemed IOU's.

William Penn was a Quaker, although his father was a Baptist. Once the granted territory came into his hands, William Penn framed his government on what is known as *The Great Law*, the preamble of which declares: *That no person, now, or at any time hereafter... shall he or she at any time be compelled to frequent or Maintain anie (sic) religious worship, place, or Ministry whatever, Contrary to his, or her mind, but shall fully and freely enjoy his or her Christian Liberty in that respect, without any interruption or reflection. And if any person shall abuse or deride any other for his, or her, different persuasion and practice in matters of religion, such a person shall be looked upon as a Disturber of the peace, and be punished accordingly.*

The land of Penn's proprietorship was inhabited by Swedish and Dutch colonists from lands ceded to the British crown, and then parceled with Penn's. More importantly, his lands included territories occupied by sovereign peoples whose claim to them was much older than that of King Charles II of England, most notably the Lenape (Delaware), who had been subjugated by the Five Nations during the French Indian Wars. (The only people to defeat the Lenape militarily were the Five Nations, who then allowed the Lenape to retain control of their traditional territories.) In negotiating with the Lenape, Penn followed Five Nations friendship chain practices and in doing so developed what became known as Quaker Covenanting Chains, which he used in all his future dealings with First Nations.

The Delaware-Lenape, whose numbers had been diminished by the war against the Haudenosaunee and then by war's more dangerous aftermath, disease, had no need of all their old territories, so the deal with Penn allowed them to consolidate their tribe; and to finance their own survival.

The first anti-slavery activity in America, was also an initiative of the Society of Friends. In 1688, Francis Danile Pastorius, a Swiss Mennonite-turning Quaker met at a Friends meeting house in Germantown, Pennsylvania and with three members of the Society signed an emancipationist agreement now known as the *Germantown Quaker Petition Against Slavery*, committing them to stand against those who would *bring men hither, or to rob and sell them against their will.* [Davis]

Mennonites weren't abolitionists, although their large, 19th century settlements in Upper Canada became places where fugitive slaves could travel without fear of whites, from Lake Erie to Hespeler on the Speed River (a tributary of the Grand southwest of Guelph) to the Queen's Bush, places where simple acts of good neighbour graciousness weren't uncommon.

Brown-Kubisch [QBS p 41] notes that a Mennonite, Henry Stauffer Huber of Bridgeport (just north of Kitchener up the Grand) was well known for his abolitionist views and helped many blacks. According to a *Region of Waterloo* genealogy website Stauffer was born in Pennsylvania in 1818, served as Reeve of Berlin (Kitchener) in 1857, and became Warden of Waterloo County in the 1860's. The site however, lists his religion as New Jerusalem (a belief system started by Emmanuel Swedenborg) which reached Kitchener by 1833.

Huber began as a Mennonite and may have become a Swedenbourgian in 1851, when the County website states he was christened.

By the time of the Germantown agreement, the Quaker faith was less than half a century old, having been created following Oliver Cromwell's Civil War, when a man named George Fox began to believe that men and women could have a *direct experience of Christ without need of clergy.* The Society arose in response to the institutional religiosity of the Anglican Church and spread from Britain to Germany and Switzerland.

The American Society of Friends was itself full of slave owners until an 18th century preacher named John Woolman (Oct. 19, 1720 – Oct 7, 1772), spent his life convincing Quakers to embrace the Emancipation movement. In 1754, Woolman published *Some Considerations on the Keeping of Negroes,* and later abolitionists regard the book as the foundation of Quaker activism. By 1756 only 10% of Quakers still owned slaves; Woolman died before he succeeded in turning the Society completely against owning other human beings. By 1790, however, the Society of Friends unsuccessfully, but nonetheless significantly, petitioned the United States Congress to abolish slavery.

Woolman's colonial-era success in turning Quakers into abolitionists, later gave Quakers the moral authority to become the backbone of the Underground Railroad.

Woolman likewise helped establish a sound foundation for future Quaker relations with Native Americans, who he believed already had their own relationship to the Creator. He spoke both Mississauga and Haudenosaunee dialects.

The Anglican Johnsons

As noted, Quakerism began as a schism within the Anglican communion, and while their chief differences lay in the Society's abandonment of ritual, social privilege and worldliness within their worship and membership, both institutionally shared similar views when it came to the inhumanity of slavery.

Two of the earliest and – to this narrative – the most

important individuals to bridge the Anglican Quaker/Native gap were Sir William Johnson and his son John. William (1715-1774) who lived in the Mohawk Valley of upper New York state. Sir William served as agent for the British crown to the Five Nations. In 1756 he became Superintendent of Indian Affairs, during which time he also led an allied force of Five Nations and British troops against the French and their native allies, capturing Fort Niagara (on the American side of the Niagara River.)

After the French imperial presence in North America collapsed on the Plains of Abraham in 1759, King George II signed the Royal Proclamation in 1763, which declared native tribes to be sovereign nations and ordered its representatives to treat then as such); thus Sir William Johnson along with his Mohawk housekeeper, Molly Brant, (sister of Joseph Brant; and mother of his children, including John) together negotiated a series of treaties following the Seven Years' War, agreements that neutralized "the old French-Aboriginal alliance" by using the covenanting conventions established by Penn, to create treaties between sovereign nations in the cause of peace and in the spirit of native *friendship chains* that bound the crown to First Nations as allies, not overlords.

The nine tribes of French Catholic nations along the St. Lawrence River and the north shores of Lake Ontario were granted the security of their homes, the freedom to trade, and the right to pray the way they wanted.

Sir William Johnson's use of Quaker *covenant chains* allowed him to develop a reputation of being trustworthy: and his ability to deliver was the real reason for Haudenosaunee Loyalism in the Revolutionary War. (It should however be noted that the Seneca disliked Johnson for sending a war party against them during the Pontiac Rebellion in 1766 and the Oneida were outraged that Johnson became the largest landowner in British America. Both those tribes sided with the Americans against the British in part because of Johnson.)

In 1783, when Sir William's son, Sir John Johnson bought - rather than stole - land off the remnant Mississauga in order to settle the thousands of Loyalists fleeing America in the wake of the Revolutionary War, (including Joseph Brants' Confederacy of Tribes) Sir John followed the covenanting principles of the Quakers. The younger Johnson subsequently became the first head of the Indian Department of Upper Canada, and also oversaw the 1787 purchase of land from the Mississauga known as the Toronto Purchase (although that deal didn't close until 1805, after Johnson was gone and the deal was tainted by colonial land speculators - ending for good the spirit of the Royal Proclamation.)

The Mississauga First Nation had controlled the country north of lakes Ontario and Erie for nearly two hundred years before the British bought the lands from them. They were originally allies of the French and the northern Iroquoian peoples – namely the Huron, Petun, Neutral and the Erie, almost all of whom were decimated by the Five Nations during the English-French conflicts. By the end of the Revolutionary War, the Mississauga were a much reduced people who had sided with the British against the Americans, and had therefor been members of the Confederated Tribes headed by the Mohawk War Chief, Captain Joseph Brant. Considering the southern Iroquois had been their enemies for centuries, life in the new colony for the Mississauga was like being stuck between a rock and a hard place.

On October 25 1784, after the first Mississauga purchase and the Haldimand Proclamation that transferred half the purchased land to the Six Nations of the Grand, the Haudenosaunee clan mothers decided at Buffalo Creek (in Seneca territory) that the nations should divide, with half going to the Grand and the rest staying in what remained of their old New York territories.

The remnant Mississauga retained a portion of their lands at the mouth of the Credit River (lands later stolen by the Family Compact and another purchase that became known as the Toronto purchase.

For centuries the Iroquois (Haudenosaunee – the People of the Longhouse) had been a confederacy of Five Nations, the Mohawk, Oneida, Onondaga, Cayuga and Seneca; and it was only after the French-British Wars that the sixth nation, the

Tuscarora, made their way north from the swamps of North Carolina to join the confederacy (sponsored by the Seneca.)

Their story is one to which we will return in some detail,as they were the only tribe that had adopted black fugitive slaves from the swamps into their clan structure. Those former slave families can not only still be traced on Brant County census records, but three Groats and a man named Isaac Whitby are Tuscarora warriours named on an 1842 Grand River petition, who are later listed in 1852 census records in the category 'coloured-negroes'.

Long before the 1842 petition, and before the American Revolution, the traditional Mohawk territory was south of the St. Lawrence and east of Lake Ontario. Oneida turf lay south of Lake Ontario down to Lake Oneida in central New York state, (where they still have a reserve.) Next to the Oneida were the Onondaga, who lived on the south shore of Lake Ontario in the vicinity of Syracuse (they too still live on a reserve in their old turf), while the fifth tribe of the original confederacy, the Seneca, likewise, live on reserves in their traditional lands in the American Niagara Region. (Since the Tuscarora were adopted by the Seneca before the Revolutionary War, they also have reserves in Seneca territory, as well as among the Six Nations of the Grand.) As we will learn in more detail in *Exodus and Arrival*, Quakers worked extensively with Seneca in Upper New York State, running agricultural schools, and aiding and abetting fugitive slaves.

There was a census of the Grand River First Nations in 1785, which recorded the presence of 1,843 natives, including 448 Mohawk, 162 Oneida, 245 Onondaga, 381 Cayuga, 78 Seneca; 129 Tuscarora, and 400 individuals combined from the Delaware, Nanticoke, Tutelo, Creek and Cherokee. (The Delaware were of course Lenape, but also appear to have had Wendats (Wyandot) among them.)

The Delaware-Wyandot are really two peoples, having evolved in America under the name Wyandot in the post revolutionary war period. They eventually ended up in Oklahoma) but in Canada, the Wendat were known to the Jesuits of Ville Sainte Marie in the mid-1600's, first as the

Petun - the Tionontati, or the people of the Hills - who lived across Nottawasaga Bay from Huronia, and with whom the Hurons traded, and inter-married.

After the fall of the Huron and the Tionontati, the southern victors carried off Huron and Petun prisoners as slaves. According to the *Dictionary of Canadian Biography*, Chief John Norton, Joseph Brant's chosen successor, noted in his Journal* that Brant *was born at Cayuhoga (near Akron, Ohio) and was descended from Wyandot prisoners adopted by the Mohawks on both the father and the mother's side." William Allen, who had interviewed Joseph Brant's son Joseph, stated, perhaps on the son's authority, that Brant's father was an Onondaga chief.* V. 5 (1801-20)

* The Journal of Major John Norton, 1816 ed. Carl F. Klinck, 1908-1990.

In the century between the 1650's and the 1750's, the Brant family went from being slaves of the Iroquois to entering the highest levels of the matriarchy that governed the Haudenosaunee clan system, which is how Joseph Brant came to lead the Five Nations during the Revolutionary War.

Joseph Brant was also one of the largest slave owners in Upper Canada when he arrived with the rest of the Loyalists in the 1780's, although he freed the last of his slaves through his will after he died in 1807. Sophia Burthen Pooley, a child of slave parents stolen by one of her own relatives and sold to Brant, is one of the best known slaves of the Loyalist period.

Jane Mulkewich in *Sophia Pooley's Story*,* posted on the Dundas Valley Historical Society's website, notes that:
Joseph Brant purchased Sophia Pooley, and brought her to Canada in 1778. She states: "I guess I was the first colored girl brought into Canada", and "There were hardly any white people in Canada then - nothing here but Indians and wild beasts". Pooley lived with the Brant family at the head of Lake Ontario...

Joseph Brant never lived on the Grand River, he lived, as Pooley stated, at the head of the lake, where, in 1798, he was given nearly 3500 acres. It was out of that block that Michael Groat [hereafter identified as Mike Sr.] bought land off Brant just before the old chief died in 1807.

As for the presence of Cherokees on that 1785 census record, they spoke an ancient Iroquoian language, linked in the minds of modern linguists across a few thousand years of isolated development. The Cherokee, whose lands at the time of the arrival of the Europeans were in Georgia, the Carolinas and East Tennessee, seem like the diaspora tribe of diaspora tribes, with remnants everywhere, including Brant's chosen successor on the Grand River, Chief John Norton.

On their own lands, the Cherokee managed large plantations prior to European contact, growing corn, cotton, hemp, tobacco and wheat, using native slaves to work their lands.

By 1819, Cherokee territories in Georgia and Tennessee were governed by codes regulating the buying and selling of slaves, laws that forbade intermarriage, dictated punishments for runaways, and prohibited slaves from owning property, and by that time, black slaves were beginning to outnumber native ones.

By the time the new American government forced all the southern tribes to move to the Indian Territory in the west, it was the black slaves of the Cherokee who did the moving, and when they arrived, it was the slaves who created new plantations, and who then put thousands of acres into cultivation.

On Nov. 15 1842, slaves from surrounding plantations raided stores of weapons, ammunition, horses and mules and headed for Mexico, a free jurisdiction. The Cherokee Council immediately hired a militia to bring them back, which they did. At the start of the Civil War, there were more than 8,000 Africans enslaved in the Indian Territory, 14% of the Cherokee population.

The Creek of the 1785 census, on the other hand, were the Muskogee, descendants of the Mississippi Mound Builders of more ancient times.

The Nanticoke were from the Chesapeake Bay/ Delaware Bay area when Captain John Smith arrived in North America in the early 1600's, but they appear to have originally been from Labrador.

The Six Nations was thus, in essence, a refugee camp for remnant tribes, with the original Five Nations better off than others, including the Tuscarora. The Tutelo, before Asiatic cholera killed most of their remnant, had relatives in clans in reserves south of the border.

All the tribes on the Grand came and went between the two nations, using their old highland trails. It was those trails that escaping slaves also sought out, and that Quaker abolitionists eventually organized their anti-slavery networks around.

All the nations but the Tutelo still live within the remaining boundaries of the Grand River Reserve (the last of all known Tutelo died there on March 23 1898.)

In closing this overview we must once again return to the link between the natives, fugitive slaves and the Society of Friends.

In *Volume 58 of Canadian Quaker History*, published by the Canadian Friends Historical Association, is a paper – first delivered to the Annual Meeting, held at Sparta, Ontario, October 28, 1995 – entitled *Migrating Quakers, Fugitive Slaves and Indians: The Quaker Ties of New York and Upper Canada*. It was written by Christopher Densmore:

> *What is clear to me is that Quakers functioned as cultural mediators among the Iroquois. They were Euro-Americans, but clearly distinct from other Euro-Americans and perceived by the Iroquois as being well-intentioned toward the Indians and thus useful as a source of information about Euro-American behavior... they also taught by example that it was possible to dissent from the broader culture. Quakers provided an ethical basis for minority group survival....the Iroquois... could, like the Quakers, be selective in their choices...* [Densmore p. 6]

Densmore also observes that the Quakers were considered by American pro-slave forces to be in league with the British and the natives in a conspiracy against the economic interests of slavers:

> *The Quakers as allies of the British is the theme of a very curious piece of documentation that I encountered while working on this paper. The document is a print, first published during the War of 1812, and then reissued in New York during the Canada Rebellion. The title is "British Warfare in 1812, 1837-38." On the left side of the print is the depiction of a British soldier offering rum to an Indian in return for scalps; on the right side, a British officer*

encourages a slave to set fire to a building.

The print is made relevant to the Upper Canada Rebellion by the depiction in the background of the burning of the "Caroline." In the center of the print is the figure of a Quaker inciting a slave to arson by means of a document labeled "Liberty for Negroes." What this has to do with the Upper Canada Rebellion, other than a chance for a New York print maker to make money by recycling a twenty year old image and "twisting the British lion's tail" is beyond me. Why the Quaker?"

Densmore's rhetorical flourishes aside, it is obvious that the answer to his own question lies in the evidence he just provided of the link between Six Nations and Quakers on both sides of the border. As stated before, helping fugitive slaves escape into safety in British territory was regarded as terrorism by slavers, and they made that point in every way they could. As for the scale of that early link between *The Society of Friends* and fugitive slaves, Densmore concluded his article with this:

We know a little bit about Quakers in New York and Upper Canada, and a little bit about Quakers and abolition, and a little bit about Quakers and Indians, but we do not fully understand all of the connections or the implications of those connections. There is much work to be done. [Densmore 7]

One of the aims of *Laying the Bed* is to add what can be added to the work of Densmore and company. That said, there is still some credit left over for the Baptists that needs to be mentioned before meeting the Groats.

Baptists and the Tuscarora Groats

On the website for the Grand River Branch of the United Empire Loyalists is an account, headlined *"Remembering African-American Canadian Settlement In Brantford"** [from the files of Angela E.M. May 1999, Vol.11 No.1,] that state in part:

According to local oral history, Tuscarora Baptist Natives guided the refugees up the Grand River from Buffalo and Niagara Falls. [May p 6]

To understand the importance of that statement, it needs to be placed against a second fact: in the *Early Days in Brantford*, JJ Hawkins notes: *"Mohawks were twenty years (1783-1803) settled upon their land along the Grand River when the first few white traders came amongst them. Mohawk Village was the chief seat, and being near the main highway from east to west, gave the first start to the village of Brant's Ford, surveyed in 1830. The surveyed lots were then sold to English Irish and Scotch, native Canadians, United Empire Loyalists and Americans. There was also a large inflow of escaped slaves from the United States who fraternized with the Indians, and the village became a very turbulent and disorderly place. Whites petitioned the government to send the blacks to the Queen's Bush.* (Hawkins p 97)

There is a document to which we will return in more detail, from 1842, which is a petition of Tuscarora Baptists to the new Lieutenant Governor, Charles Bagot, requesting help in a conflict the petitioners were having with Anglican Tuscarora, who were upset at them for leaving the Church of England (a petition to which there is also a response from the Reverend Adam Elliott, husband of Eliza Howells.)

Among those Tuscarora were the Groat family, connected to both Guelph and the Loyalist community of Nelson Township (now Burlington.) Three of the Baptist Tuscarora 'warriours', are Groats, and the fourth, is a Groat relation; all are identified in the 1852 census of Tuscarora Township as coloured-negroes.

Guelph township, in which the city was founded, was in fact originally a crown land reserve specifically set aside to benefit the Six Nations through monies raised from the sale of properties here, monies then held in trust for the tribes. The western boundary of Guelph Township bordered the eastern edge of the original Six Nations Reserve, which stretched all the way from the mouth of the Grand River at Lake Erie north to what is now the town of Arthur in upper Wellington County.

I first came across the name Groat on the old Guelph Museum webpage *Black Families in Guelph* (no longer online); a few paragraphs about a free black named William Groat who was born in Saltfleet Township/Stoney Creek in 1820, and who moved to Wellington County from Nelson Township in 1842.

I went on to delve more deeply into his life and posted an article to the blog I had created to help organize the stories I was working into what was then called *Blood in the Mortar* (now the title of book three in this series.) The article, *William*

Groat: the Coloured Man from Marden was a stand-alone chapter since he wasn't a member of the Guelph B.M.E and so wasn't connected to the rest of that narrative.

William Groat has, in this book, become William of Guelph, since there are three other William Groats in this story, two of whom are named in the 1842 Tuscarora petition and one of whom served on the 1813 Dundas road patrol manned by the loyalist families of Nelson township, tasked with guarding the road from the mouth of Burlington Bay to Burlington Heights.

The Groat family, as this book will show, is one of the most important free black families in Upper Canadian history and through their connection to the Tuscarora, are the single best placed family to be regarded as responsible for helping to turn Brantford into the wellspring that gave rise to the first waves of the black, Queen's Bush settlers.

The Loyalist frontier from Toronto (York) to Niagara became home to other respected free blacks around whom later churches like the Baptists and Methodists built their memberships, free blacks who must also be regarded - if not individual by individual – then as a group, as being among the creators of the abolitionist movement in loyalist Upper Canada prior to the creation of the Underground Railroad. (And in the cause of giving credit where credit is due, it should also be noted that the Nelson township Groats were Presbyterians.)

Mixed-blood, and born free above Stoney Creek in 1820, William Groat of Guelph grew up at the head of the Lake surrounded by natives and loyalists, free blacks and newer, fugitive slave arrivals; when he moved to Guelph he married a white Scots Irish woman who had just come south from the Queen's Bush. That may all have been coincidental of course, and he may never have helped an escaped slave in his life, but then again, he may well have aided and abetted many.

Meet the Groats

The longer family tree in Appendix 1 is a modified version of one created by Andrew Jtimlek, with information from Eric Jensen's *Haudenosaunee Project* etc.

1 Mike Sr. Michael GROTE African GROAT b.NC(?)d.UC
    (1794 free negro petition/Nelson township assessments)
    + unknown wife
.... 2 William GROAT-Tuscarora Negro 1783-1852,1842 petition
.................+ 1st 'marriage' Margaret Tuscarora N.C.
...............3 Abram GROAT -Tuscarora/Negro 1814-1904, 1842 petition
     + Sarah Ann Williams Tuscarora b. Lewiston NY
      died 1868, dau of John Williams, sister of Jacob
.............+ 2nd marriage Wm Groat = Amelia (Emily) SMITH
    1789–1871 (mother? Molly Turner; m. Mr . Smith*)
     *Haudenosaunee Project1819 – 1852 census
.... 3 William -Tuscarora- GROAT 1822-1852 census,1842 petitn.
.... +Mary w -Tuscarora-1832 – 1852 census
.... 3 Sarah -Tuscarora- GROAT 1832 – 1852 census
.... 3 John -Tuscarora- GROTE GROAT 1833 – 1852 census
.... 3 Hannah -Tuscarora- GROAT 1835 - 1852   census
.... 2 Jemiah b. (c) 1784 UC + Ebenezer Guire   1777 US
.... 2 Simon Groat 1793-1880? b. US died Caradoc, On
    + Mary Ann Lewis (m. 1847)
.... 3 William 19 1871   parents?
.... 3 Hugh   10 1871   parents ?
.... 2 Michael GROAT 1795-1846 (Nelson, b US m. unknown)
.... 3 William (1820-1901) born Saltfleet, lived Nelson,
    Guelph, Marden m Elizabeth Adams Guelph 1846
.... 3 Peter
.... 3 Jemime
.... 3 Margaret
.... 3 Hannah
  2 Margaret GROAT b. 1797 US + Abram TOP b 1792 US
    3 Abram TOPP 1819 Quaker + Jemima, lived Norwich twsp
    3 Hannah TOPP 1821 + Rev Lindsey Anderson, Ottersville "
.... 2 Peter GROAT   1813 Dundas Rd patrol
    'Pete Groat' 1830 Nelson assessment
.... 2 John GROAT Mike 1801
    +Catherine Mississauga. b. Credit River
    3 Peter + Sophie Bellevue
    3 Margaret + Richard Lewis
    3 Henry
    3 William

Linguistic Apologia

The words negro, mulatto and coloured appear in this work, almost solely where they are used by others. When I was a boy some time ago, the members of Reverend Martin Luther King's movement proudly defined themselves as negro, likewise when I was a boy my father took a felt marker and went through a collection of children's stories called *Trails and Tales*, that included narratives about little Black Sambo, and into which, my radically minded father blackened out the word black. Black is now the only word we're allowed to use for 'negroes' or 'coloureds' beyond African American/ African Canadian et al.

Language use changes with time, especially after a word creates a perceived path of destruction. Mulatto was an old word for mixed race, either black/white or black/native, so I try not to use it, except in the context of sources such as the following, which speaks to the essence of what life for the Groat family would have been like under American law (and in some company in early Upper Canada.)

And for clearing all manner of doubts which hereafter may happen to arise upon the construction of this act, or any other act, who shall be accounted a mulatto, be it enacted and declared, and it is hereby enacted and declared, That the child of an Indigenous and the child, grand child, or great grand child, of a negro shall be deemed, accounted, held and taken to be a mulatto.- Henigs Statutes, Virginia 1705.

While that kind of precision was never used in Canada, under those definitions, the Groat family were mulattoes through their Tuscarora blood and their black and white family lines. It is unclear however, whether Mike Sr. the founder of the family in Canada was of mixed blood or not. What he unequivocally was however, was free, since the first record of him in the colony is as a signee of the 1794 *Petition of Free Negroes.*

The Petition of Free Negroes

The Petition was submitted to Lieutenant Governor Simcoe on June 29th 1794, so it was an early document in our colonial history, but it was denied by the Legislative Council, presumably because Simcoe was trying to develop a House of Lords out of his council of appointed legislators; he needed their unity to keep democratic sympathies in check: land-granted communities of free negroes were not part of the unanimous deal that had sealed the fate of slavery. Here in full is the petition signed by Mike Sr. and others.

That there are a number of Negroes in this part of the Country many of whom have been Soldiers during the late war between Great Britain and America, and others who were born free with a few who have come into Canada since the peace, - Your Petitioners are desirous of settling adjacent to each other that they may be enabled to give assistance (in work) to those amongst them who may most want it.

Your Petitioners therfore [sic] humbly Pray that their situation may be taken into consideration, and if your Excellency should see fit to allow them a Tract of Country to settle on, separate from the white Settlers, your Petitioners hope their behaviour will be such as to shew, that Negroes are capable of being industrious, and in loyalty to the Crown they are not deficient.

Jack Baker, Jack Becker, John Cesar, John Dimon, Tom Frey, John Gerof, Peter Green, Michael Grote, [Mike Sr.] John Jackson, Adam Lewis, Peter Ling, Richard Pierpoint, Pompadour, John Smith, Saison Sepyed, Simon Speck, Robert Spranklin, Thomas Walker and Jack Wurmwood.[1]

1. Petition of Free Negroes, June 29, 1794, 68, Upper Canada Land Petitions, RG 1, L 3, vol. 196, F Bundle Miscellaneous, LAC microfilm C-2022, AO.

We will return to the rest of the signees as peers of Mike Sr. later in the book. Only two of the men appear in other books, Pompadour and Richard Pierpoint - the most famous free black in Canadian history -who, in the 1820's, settled in what became Fergus ten miles north of Guelph up the old native trail from the head of the Lake.

First however, we will examine the response of the Anglican hierarchy to the existence of slavery among the Loyalists and consider what they did about it in 1793.

Anti-Slavery in Upper Canada

Arriving in Upper Canada in the summer of 1792, Lt. Governor Simcoe was soon made fully aware that the horrors of slavery were not unknown in his new Province. While he was preparing his anti-slavery act, one event triggered his completing it, the stealing of a black girl named Chloe Cooley and an unnamed man who was taken across the American border in front of witnesses. W.R. Riddell in the *Journal of Negro History, Volume 4, 1919* describes how the abduction was received by Simcoe.

At the Council Chamber, Navy Hall, in the County of Lincoln, Wednesday, March 21st, 1793... Peter Martin (a negro in the service of Col. Butler) attended the Board for the purpose of informing them of a violent outrage committed by one ...Frooman) and, an Inhabitant of this Province, residing near Queens Town, or the West Landing, on the person of Chloe Cooley a Negro girl in his service, by binding her, and violently and forcibly transporting her across the River, and delivering her against her will to certain persons unknown; to prove the truth of his Allegation he produced Wm. Grisley (or Crisley).

"William Grisley... says: that ... he was at work at Mr. Froomans near Queens Town, who in conversation told him, he was going to sell his Negro Wench to some persons in the States, that in the evening he saw the said Negro girl, tied with a rope, that afterwards a Boat was brought, and the said Frooman with his Brother and one Vanevery, forced the said Negro Girl into it, ... then taken and delivered to a man upon the Bank of the River...

"Resolved.—That it is necessary to take immediate steps to prevent the continuance of such violent breaches of the Public Peace, and for that purpose, that His Majesty's Attorney-General, be forthwith directed to prosecute the said Fromond. "Adjourned."

Riddell then points out that the Attorney General John White, *knew that the brutal master was well within his rights in acting as he did. He had the same right to bind, export, and sell his slave as to bind, export, and sell his cow... Nothing came of the direction to prosecute and nothing could be done.*

Riddell notes that two months later, at: *the Second Session of the First Parliament which met at Newark, May 31, 1793, a bill was introduced and unanimously passed the House of Assembly...*

royal assent was given July 9, 1793, and the bill became law.

The Act itself noted that it was unjust that a people who enjoy freedom by law should encourage the introduction of slaves, and that it was highly expedient to abolish slavery in the Province so far as it could be done gradually without violating private property; and proceeded to repeal the Imperial Statute of 1790 so far as it related to Upper Canada, and to enact that from and after the passing of the Act, No Negro or other person who shall come or be brought into this Province ... shall be subject to the condition of a slave or to" bounden involuntary service for life.

...an important proviso... continued the slavery of every "negro or other person subjected to such service" who has been lawfully brought into the Province. It then enacted that every child born after the passing of the act, of a Negro mother or other woman subjected to such service should become absolutely free on attaining the age of twenty-five, the master in the meantime to provide "proper nourishment and cloathing" for the child, but to be entitled to put him to work, all issue of such children to be free whenever born. It further declared any voluntary contract of service or indenture should not be binding longer than nine years.
(pp 375-385)

The man to whom a good portion of the credit should go for Simcoe's *An Act to Prevent the further Introduction of Slaves and to Limit the Term of Contracts for Servitude within this Province*, was John White, of Hick's Hall, Middlesex England (1761).

According to the *Dictionary of Canadian Biography*, White became a lawyer in 1785, moved to Jamaica the year after that but by 1791 had given up and was back in Wales with his family, thinking of becoming a clergyman, when someone

recommended him as a suitable attorney general of Upper Canada to William Osgoode, who had been selected as chief justice of the new colony... White was appointed on 31 Dec. 1791.

He and the surveyor general, David William Smith*, led the support of government-sponsored legislation in the assembly, including the 1793 bill which provided for the eventual abolition of slavery in the province. Volume IV (1771-1800)

*David W. Smith, the man who assisted White in shaping the Act, was born in 1764 in Salisbury England, had been posted to Fort Detroit with the 5th Foot in 1790, and had been with the regiment since he was fifteen. He became Simcoe's surveyor general, and resigned from the army in 1794. He articled under White but never did court work.

David W. Smith was also member of the Upper Canadian House of Assembly and was a man without much regard for class equality, a fact that is important to remember: some individuals thought slavery was a sin but that social inequality was perfectly acceptable. (A la the mudsill theory.)

"The more broken heads and bloody noses there is, the more election-like," as he wrote... He found the first assembly to have "violent levelling Principles," although all but 3 of its 16 members were either active loyalists or British immigrants... He was convinced that there was a "country party" with republican sympathies and that a "court party" of gentry and officials was necessary to manage the assembly. Dictionary of Canadian Biography V. 7, David W Smith

A Family Compact conservative who despised democracy, Smith, as a high Anglican, agreed with John White and Simcoe on slavery and the class system, and between the three of them, they worked to create the legislation that sounded the death knell of slave economics in Upper Canada, while also working on bills that preserved the prerogatives of the rich.

The 1793 anti-slavery legislation wasn't a perfect bill, and it would take the British Emancipation Act of 1833 to end slavery on British soil, but it was better than George Washington's Fugitive Slave Act that turned his republic into a slave prison in 1793. Simcoe's legislation set the stage for seven decades of emancipationist activities in Upper Canada/Ontario.

Anglican Abolitionists on the Grand

More than any other man, perhaps, the person who did the most to abolish slavery in the British Empire was William Wilberforce, a Parliamentarian, evangelical Anglican and a dogged believer in the equality of humanity. He didn't create the British abolitionist movement, and is more second generation than first, but it was William Wilberforce who shepherded the Slave Trade Act of 1807 into law, making it illegal to sail slave ships under the British flag, and while that act produced real results, it did not end slave owning by Englishmen outside of Britain, and so Wilberforce continued to fight for its abolition within the Empire for the next twenty-six years, dying three days after the passing of the Emancipation Act of 1833.

William Wilberforce never came to this province, but there are two Upper Canadian Anglicans associated with the native reserves of the Grand River who went to England and met with Wilberforce and his associates in the so-called Clapham Sect, the first was Joseph Brant's chosen successor, Chief John Norton, and the second was the second Anglican missionary to the Six Nations, the Reverend Robert Lugger.

Chief John Norton

Norton's trip to England took place while Brant was still alive. The reason for him being sent, was because the tribes were in constant conflict near the end of Brant's life: within their own ranks and within the colony, over the issue of forest management and land ownership. Brant believed that the Six Nations owned the land as a sovereign people, but also believed that individual members of the nation owned the lands on which they settled, which meant they also owned the trees on their lands, and could therefor benefit from operating them as woodlots. However, he also believed that even if someone sold their property, the lands themselves remained part of Six Nation's territory. Other native leaders (more traditional and less European) believed that the community owned the sovereign lands and thus shared all the resources, which none of them had a right to sell without common consent, as dictated by ancient practice and custom.

British authorities like Simcoe and his heirs in the military regime that ran the colony, believed that the Six Nations of the Grand River lived on crown land held in trust for the tribes in perpetuity, which was a complete reinterpretation of the Haldimand Proclamation that created the Territory in 1783 (also a story to which we will return.)

Forest management was an important issue because at the beginning of the colony the land was primeval forest, full of giant trees of every kind, from pine to oak, spruce to maple, beech, walnut etc. It was a treasure trove of wealth. After Simcoe left in the late 1790's, the military regime that ran the colony thereafter, was as anti-democratic as ever, but also less concerned with native rights, increasingly allying itself with the speculators and wannabes of the local landed classes. C.F. Klink notes about Norton in the *Dictionary of Canadian Biography,* that *Brant finally decided to go over the heads of Upper Canadian*

> *officials and to appeal to the Privy Council of Britain. With considerable secrecy, he sent Norton to plead the case in London. Norton was, in fact, eager to go because he wished to enlist in the British army for service in the war which had been declared against France... His hopes for enlistment failed, and his mission to the government brought only disappointment when... some councils of the Six Nations...denied Norton's authority because he was disreputable and unworthy.*

Since Norton underwent a conversion experience while in England, the description by his enemies of his being unworthy may have had a basis in a fact of which he himself must have agreed, except he would have thought himself more redeemable than they did.

Norton was the son of a Scots woman and a Cherokee father, as detailed by Klink:

> *Norton's trip from 1804 to 1806, nevertheless, was a personal triumph... His closest friends were members of the Society of Friends: the scientist William Allen and the Philadelphia-born brewer Robert Barclay. Through Barclay, Norton became associated on friendly terms with the members of the famous "Clapham sect,"* (of which William Wilberforce was the leading light.)

Through Clapham, Norton got involved with the British and Foreign Bible Society, who funded Norton's translation of the gospel of John into Mohawk.

After Joseph Brant slipped toward death at the head of the Lake, Norton's pursuit of native land claims in England ended. His return was financed by the Bible Society. The arrival at the Reserve of a new John Norton, saw a man on fire for the God of England's reform movement, which is to say that the causes of education, emancipation and rights had become his to proclaim.

What Chief John Norton found when he returned to succeed Brant, was the Family Compact taking hold of members of the Council of Chiefs: *Those antagonistic to Norton saw his idealism as hypocrisy, his claims for Indian ownership of land as greed, his loyalty to Britain as treachery, and his whole attitude as a threat to privilege. Humanitarian projects had to be postponed. Personal attacks upon him increased and he wished to retire.*

Despairing of his hopes for the Six Nations, Norton nonetheless had, after his trip to England, both the wherewithal and the connections to travel extensively on the continent, which he did starting April 9 1809, leaving the Grand River for Ohio, Kentucky and Tennessee in search of the native members of his father's family, intent on examining *"the situation of our brethren the Cherokees."*

Norton was back by June of 1810, and found the place depressing. Just as he was about to leave again, the War of 1812 altered everything: he was elevated by Major General Robert Hale Sheaffe to the Rank of Captain of the Confederate Indians" – *the same rank that Joseph Brant had held during the American revolution. His reputation was made at the Battle of Queenston Heights, so that by 1815, the conflict over, he was able to travel again to England, this time as a war hero.*

Before the second trip to England, Norton had married a Lenape woman named Catherine in an Anglican service at Niagara. She was younger than he was by several years.

After his return from Britain to Upper Canada, Norton's support for Brant's position was upheld by the new Governor General, Sir Charles Prevost at Quebec City, and thus the Upper Canadian department of Indians was ordered to leave Norton and the Grand River alone. The principles of the Haldimand Proclamation were thus restored for the time being.

While in England, John Norton had spent more time with his friends among the Clapham 'Saints', so that when he returned his hopes had not only been restored, but they had matured.

From 1816-1824 Norton remained on the banks of the

Grand, publishing his Mohawk translation of the Gospel of Matthew. His life was seemingly a quiet one until a sexual misconduct incident involving his wife caused him to fight and win a duel, in which he killed the man in question. He offered to stand trial without contest so that he wouldn't bring shame on his wife by forcing her to tell her story on the stand; he was convicted of manslaughter, fined and allowed to leave Upper Canada. Catherine begged his forgiveness but he never saw her again. Before going however, he signed his 1812 war pension over to her.

According to Klink in the *Canadian Dictionary of Biography,*

> The Colonial Advocate of 9 March 1826 reported that a friend of Norton had received at least one letter from him, written from Laredo (then in Mexico) "in November last." Norton had then "expected to come home." There is no evidence to show that he ever returned to the Grand River. As late as 4 Sept. 1851, a nephew and reputed heir-at-law stated to a lawyer that he was prepared "to prove [Norton's death] in the month of October 1831." No proof has been found.

Although written not longer after the end of the War of 1812, Norton's journals remained unpublished for more than 150 years, when the Champlain Society finally brought them out under the title *The Journal of Major John Norton, 1816,* ed. C. F. Klink and J. J. Talman (Toronto, 1970)

In Christopher Densmore's work on Quaker abolitionists there is mention of John Norton, although the context is the War of 1812, not anti-slavery activities:

> Quakers from New York and Philadelphia Yearly Meetings worked with the Senecas in New York State from the 1790s onward. An intriguing result of this Quaker effort came in June 1812. Major John Norton, at a council held at Grand River, was attempting to enlist Iroquois support for the coming war between the United States and Great Britain. During this council, two of the "most respectable" of the Seneca chiefs approached Norton and stated their intentions to stay out of the coming conflict.

> "Seeing therefore, that no good can be derived from War, we think we should only seek the surest means of averting its attendant Evils: -- We are of the opinion that we should follow the example of some of

*their people [the Quakers], who never bear arms in war, & deprecate
the principles of hostility."*

It was in the post-war quiet of Norton's life on the reserve
between 1816 and 1824 when his focus was on education
among the Six Nations: which is when I believe Chief John
Norton may have instituted abolitionist activities among the
tribes.

There is no evidence of Norton doing anything connected to
abolition, there is only his connection to William Wilberforce
and the Clapham Sect on which to speculate a probable role in
aiding and abetting fugitive slaves from America. So while it
can't be proven, Chief John Norton is the almost certain
founding father of anti-slavery activities on the Grand.

The Reverend Robert Lugger

There is another article, also in Volume 7 of the *Dictionary of
Canadian Biography,* about an Anglican clergyman and
educator, Robert Lugger, *whose knowledge of the Iroquois came
from extensive reading and from conversations with William
Wilberforce, the abolitionist, who had informed him of the
educational work at Grand River of John Norton. Like Norton and
like the Moravians, who worked among the Delawares at New
Fairfield (on the Thames River above Chatham), Lugger
planned to combine conventional religious instruction with
training in the mechanical arts.*

(Chief Norton's wife, it will be remembered, was a Lenape-
Delaware, possibly with Wendat bloodlines.)

Robert Lugger, the son of a gentleman, had been stationed
in Barbados as solider during and after the Napoleonic wars,
and by 1817 *had become a teacher. Backed by the Church
Missionary
Society, he organized what he called a National Negro School on
the island in 1818 and endeavoured, through the use of the
innovative Bell system of monitorial instruction, to deal with the
circumstances of a slave society. The experience convinced him that
"education alone will never do, unless the ground be broken up and
the good seed sown at the same time." His subsequent missionary
career in Upper Canada would be fully committed to a merger of*

the tutorial and the spiritual.

Reverend Lugger began his missionary career in Upper Canada in 1827, just before the Underground Railroad came into its own, arriving on Six Nations' territory after Norton had vanished from the Grand, so while it is possible that the two men exchanged letters, there is no evidence that they knew one another, and no evidence that Lugger was involved in abolitionist activities while working with the Six Nations, though once again, his work in Barbados; his commitment to personal and spiritual emancipation through education and faith, and his friendship with Wilberforce and the Clapham Sect, suggest that he almost certainly helped fugitive slaves into Brantford.

In fact, given the reality that from the beginning the Tuscarora Christians would have attended the Anglican Church because it was the state church and therefor the only church on the Reserve, and given the fact that the 1842 Tuscarora petition is from newly minted Baptists (who had formerly been Methodists and originally had been Anglicans) Lugger's conversations with William Wilberforce about the education of blacks among the emancipated seems almost certain to have something to do with the Groats since they and theirs were the only mixed-race, black-natives in the Tuscarora equation. Lugger however, may have inherited the church after some of the flock had escaped Anglican formalism for the Methodist revivalism of Rev. Peter Jones from the mid 1830's on, thus it cannot solely be the baptists among the Tuscarora responsible from blacks in Brantford.

The Quaker-Anglican abolitionist best placed to have aided and abetted fugitive slaves out of America and towards the Grand after the 1830's however, was Henry C. Howells, grandfather of the Mohawk poet, E. Pauline Johnson.

Henry C. Howells: the Quaker Link
to the Tuscarora of the Grand

Emily Johnson, mother of the poet, was the daughter of a Welsh Quaker named Henry Charles Howells (1784-1857?) Howells began his working life as a tinsmith, but turned himself into a well-heeled teacher in Bristol, England, around the time that Wilberforce managed to ban slave ships from flying the British flag. Emily was born in Bristol.

In annotated notes created for a re-publication of E. Pauline Johnson's autobiography *The Moccasin Maker,* it is notes that, in 1805, Henry C. Howells had to leave the Society after he married Mary Best, an Anglican. She gave birth to 13 children, and died in 1828 when Emily was four. The year after Mary's death, Howells remarried, this time to a Quaker, Harriet Joynter, and was allowed to rejoin the Friends. [Brown Ruoff p 3]

In 1832, Howells gathered up his family and sailed for America, with the express purpose of becoming involved in the Underground Railroad. [Gray p. 6]

(In the convention records of the 1843 London Anti-Slavery Convention at which Howells was a speaker - and the representative of the 'coloured population of Pittsburgh', Pennsylvania - he told those assembled that he had *been an abolitionist for years before I left my native country.)*

They landed in Manhattan and then went to Worthington, Ohio (now part of Columbus) where his eldest daughter, Mary Best Rogers, lived with her husband, the Reverend Robert Vachon Rogers, an Englishman who had become rector of St. Phillips Episcopal that same year. *Henry took considerable risk in aiding and abetting runaway slaves"... at one time having twenty of them in his attic. He would use a cart piled with old furniture and get his son Thomas*, dressed as a labourer, to move them across Columbus. He hid them in armoires, chests and bureaus. He would tell the story in later years of mobs composed of hundreds intent on tar and feathering him.* (Gray 6-7)

[*Dr Thomas Howells later moved to Brantford, but whether he was active there is unknown to me, if nothing else, he would have a been a good neighbour to fugitive slaves. His children grew up with E Pauline Johnson and her siblings.]

Reverend Rogers was one of two representatives from the

Columbus area who attended the 1835 Ohio Anti-slavery convention in Putnam, Ohio, which Howells also attended, having moved from Worthinton across the river to Zanesville where he had helped found the Muskingum County Anti-Slavery Society on June 24 1833. Zanesville was pro-slavery.

According to Putnam's heritage website* *Putnam is one of the oldest settlements in the state of Ohio, established around 1800, and annexed into the adjacent city of Zanesville in 1872.*

According to the online heritage designation for the Stone House in Putnam Ohio, which was run by William Beecher, is this statement on that critical 1835 anti-slavery convention:

Anti-slavery New Englanders settled Putnam while pro-slavery Virginians and Kentuckians settled Zanesville. The Emancipation Society of Putnam formed in June 1831... In March 1835, noted abolitionist speaker Theodore D. Weld* came to Zanesville to lecture but was turned away by pro-slavery sympathizers.

When the Stone Academy in Putnam provided a room, the lecture was disrupted by a mob and Weld took refuge in the home of church Elder A.A. Guthrie. After seeking the Sheriff's and County Prosecutor's protection, the Muskingum County Emancipation Society invited the Abolitionist Society of Ohio to hold its convention in Putnam in April 1835. Again, a pro-slavery mob disrupted the proceedings.

*Theodore Dwight Weld (1803-1895), one of the most important but now largely unsung anti-slavery activists of his day, is a man universally described in encyclopedias as *one of the leading architects of the American Abolitionist movement during its formative years from 1830-1844. Weld played a role as writer, editor, speaker, and organizer. He is best known for his co-authorship of the authoritative compendium, American Slavery As It Is: Testimony of a Thousand Witnesses, published in 1839.*

Weld was born in Connecticut, the son and grandson of Congregational ministers. When he was 28, the abolitionists and social reformers Lewis and Arthur Tappan, hired him as the general agent of the Society for Promoting Manual Labor in Literary Institutions.

The Tappans were also founders of the American Missionary Society, whose work extended into helping African Americans in Upper Canada, including the Queens Bush Settlement.

Weld had become an abolitionist at Western Reserve College. In 1833, he became a student of the Presbyterian Lane Theological Society where he became the leader of the "Lane Rebels", in essence, a free speech club focused on slavery and ways to help local, free blacks.

Lyman Beecher (father of Harriet Beecher Stowe) ran *Lane* and shut down the rebels on behalf of the Board because of the incendiary talk of *immediate emancipation*, an action that led to the Seminary losing 80% of its students, most of whom transferred to the seminary at Oberlin, except Weld, who moved to New Jersey to head the training program for the new *Anti-Slavery Society of America* founded by the Tappans and William Garrison. (One of the Tappans was also an attendee and speaker at the 1843 London convention with Howells.)

Some of Stowe's *Uncle Tom's Cabin* (1852) is based on *Slavery as it Is* (1839) a book written and researched by Weld and his wife Angelina Grimké, and her sister Sarah, all of whom were friends with Reverend William Beecher, the brother of Harriet, who ran the Presbyterian Church in Putnam. Harriet's elder brother Edward, younger brothers Henry Ward and Charles, and sister Catherine were all abolitionists.)

At the 1835 convention Rogers was elected to the agenda committee, and Howells to a committee tasked with writing a letter to congress.

Howells was also one of the signees of the final declaration, which includes the following: *This is Slavery – slavery as it exists today, sheltered under the wings of our national eagle, republican law its protector, republican equality its advocate, republican morality its patron, freemen its bodyguard, the church its city of refuge, and the sanctuary of God and the very horns of the altar its inviolable asylum. Slavery being sin we maintain that it is the duty of all who perpetrate it immediately to cease; in other words that immediate emancipation is the sacred right of the slaves and the imperative duty of their masters.* It was after that, that: *Pro-slavery forces...threatened the homes and property of... H.C. Howell etc.*

Henry Howells came close to being tarred and feathered by his neighbours in 1835; it was a story he told for the rest of his life. But he had come to America to fight slavery, and in doing so he had become a friend and ally of many of the movement's leaders. His hero however, from 1835 on, was Theodore Weld.

Immediate Emancipation remained Weld's demand from the establishment of the Lane Rebels under Lyman Beecher's unhappy eye until the Emancipation Proclamation of 1862.

William and Harriet brother, Henry Ward Beecher (1813-1887,) later became a Congregationalist minister after having been a Presbyterian minister in Indiana from 1837-1847. He was known as the Great Orator and later fiercely opposed the 1854 Kansas-Nebraska Act that opened up the new territories to slavery.

Henry Ward Beecher supported a political alternative to armed insurrection, via the Free Soil Party (1848-1852) The Party's greatest strength was in New York State, their argument being that *"free men on free soil comprised a morally and economically superior system to slavery."*

Mark Twain's memory of Beecher, included this description of the preacher's pulpiteering, *"sawing his arms in the air, howling sarcasms this way and that, discharging rockets of poetry and exploding mines of eloquence, halting now and then to stamp his foot three times to emphasize a point."* (Applegate 372)

These were the kinds of people that Henry C. Howells had as friends, people who steered fugitives to the Queen's Bush.

As for Weld: *The concern over the sin of slavery had been growing in western New York, and it was to reach new heights in the 1830s... By 1834 the nascent American Anti-Slavery Society in New York City realized that upstate New York was ripe for the dissemination of its "immediate abolition" doctrine; soon the national society would have some 2,000 branches (of which 200 were in New York) with 200,000 members.*

Weld was urged to return to New York, which he did in 1836 to further the cause in western New York. (ie in the Rochester-Niagara region.) Meantime, a number of church organizations had actively proclaimed slavery as a sin, and these included Congregational and several church organizations...

Weld...remained active in the American Anti-Slavery Society until the 1839-1840 national convention in which Garrison packed the house with his followers and wrested control of the Society. Weld ... resigned ... to form the new American and Foreign Anti-

Slavery Society in its place.

Theodore Weld was not always greeted with acclaim on his speaking engagements, for he soon became known as "the most mobbed man in America" as those who opposed abolition attacked him and attempted to break up public meetings which were in favor of abolition. [Crooked Lake Review; Fall 2005 John H. Martin]

On May 18 1838, the week after Weld married, the Philadelphia Hall was burnt to the ground after he spoke there.

E. Pauline Johnson probably never met her grandfather, but she wrote about him in nothing but negative terms, accusing him of being cruel. It may be that her sense of his cruelty had partially arisen from his unwillingness to defend her mother from Emily's stepmother's malice toward the children of his first marriage, but her stories of daily confrontations with Zanesville's slavers may also have had something to do with it, since it can't have been easy on the children or his wife facing such a barrage of hatred.

Peace at home and the safety of his family may be why they left Ohio for slave-free Pennsylvania by 1837, when he was listed in a city directory as living in Pittsburgh (Allegheny Co.)

Howells was also a correspondent with one of America's foremost reformers: Milo Townsend, of Brighton, Pennsylvania, a Quaker and a man much admired by abolitionist Gerrit Smith of Oswego, New York. (More on Smith shortly.) Smith identifies Howells as a friend in an 1846 letter to Townsend. Two of Howells' 97 letters to Milo were published in *Milo Adams Townsend and Social Movements of the Nineteenth Century.* Townsend (1817-1877.)

Brighton sits where the Beaver River met the Ohio River, and it was there that Milo and his family would meet escaping slaves at the mouth of the river and hide them on islands, in caves and in cellars, before forwarding them to safety down river.

At the time of the letters, Howells lived in Allegheny about 30 miles from Brighton, (which must he how and when Henry's 1843 London convention connections to Pittsburgh's 'coloured' community were created.)

Howells returned to Bristol, England [Ruoff] to clear up his first wife's estate and where he presumably spoke to abolitionists. How long he stayed isn't known, but he attended both the 1839 anti-slavery convention in Putnam and the June 1839 marriage of his daughter Eliza to Reverend Adam Elliot, the new Anglican missionary to the Tuscarora of the Grand River. The wedding was presumably held in Allegheny.

Rev. Elliot had arrived in York (Toronto) in 1828 from Picton, (near the Bay of Quinte) with the intent of becoming an Anglican minister, to which end he had petitioned Archdeacon John Strachan for help. Strachan took a liking to him.

Adam became the Reverend Elliot in 1832 and spent the next five years as a missionary to the Chippewa of Lakes Huron and Simcoe, who had been settled by the government at Coldwater River Narrows in Severn Township.

The Reserve sat on the original portage between Lake Simcoe and the Coldwater River route to Georgian Bay. The trail was cleared by the tribe into a farming road (now part of Highway 12 northwest of Orillia.)

Adam Elliot had met Eliza Howells at her sister Mary Rogers new home in Kingston, Upper Canada, where Rev. Rogers had relocated a few years after leaving Ohio, having been driven off for his own abolitionist activities.

After serving the Chippewa, Reverend Elliot was sent to the Tuscarora, following the retirement of Reverend Lugger in 1835. I have yet to link Elliot's name with abolitionist activities, but he was friendly with Quakers, is mentioned in the Canadian Quaker History Journal as having contacts with the Uxbridge Friends in the 1830's, and was mentored by Strachan.

It is hard to imagine that Elliot and Howells would not have discussed the subject of slavery in great detail, if only around the time of the wedding, if that is when they first met. They could also have done far more than just talk about abolition and Christian activism, they could have coordinated their efforts

It should also be noted that all this flurry of activity in the early 1830's was linked to an event in Quaker circles known as *The Great Separation* that occurred in 1827-28, a schism created by a man named Elias Hicks who is discussed in greater detail in *Exodus and Arrival*, where I trace the origins of *Separation* over issues as diverse as enforcement of the marriage strictures that ejected Howells from the Friends when he married his Anglican wife, to disagreements over abolitionist stances and the divinity of Christ.

In essence however, it was only after 1833, when the Hicksites finally completed organizing new Yearly Meetings of their own, that the Underground Railroad became an entity defined by its use of railway talk. It was thereafter only Hicksite Friends became the only Quakers willing to break the Fugitive Slave Act of 1793, and thus the only Quakers to whom researchers need turn their attentions after the 1830's.

Given how little has been written about the role of Canadian Quakers in the UGRR, the fact that they are more easily traceable by whether they were followers of Elias Hicks or not, should focus the field of study from here on in.

The Yearly Meeting that matters most to this narrative was the Genesee Yearly Meeting founded in 1833, because it was that Meeting that was responsible for slave crossings at either end of the Niagara River (ie., from Buffalo in the west and Lewiston, New York in the east.) Bertie township, near Fort Erie, Ontario became known as a Quaker township: unsurprisingly it has a Hicksite burial ground. The road to the village of Indiana in Haldimand Co on the Grand, began in Bertie as an native trail on the Canadian side of *The Crossing*. The now defunct village, founded in 1830, prided itself as an termini of the Underground Railroad.

1833 marks the beginning of unparalleled activity, for two reasons, one was a now fully unified Hicksite community; and the other was the passing of the British Emancipation Act that turned Canada into a haven for fugitives.

As stated, 1833, the year of the creation of Genesee Yearly Meeting was also the year Howells helped found Muskingum's Anti-Slavery Society, and the year of the Lane Rebels.

That aside, aside, 1839, the year that Eliza Howells married Reverend Elliot, was also the year that Theodore Weld's book, *Slavery As It Is: Testimony of a Thousand Witnesses* was published. The compilation had been created by Weld, his wife, Angelina Grimké, and her sister Sarah, and it was the culmination of his work since Lane and at Putnam in 1835. Howells would not have missed that book launch for the world.

Pauline's sister Eva, stated that their mother left Cincinnati for the Six Nations forever *in 1845*. It was not however, Emily's first trip to the Grand, since she had come and gone from the Tuscarora reserve since 1840, the year after Eliza's marriage, when Emily was sixteen, the year she'd first laid eyes on Elliot's translator, George Johnson and he, on her. [Ruoff 4]

The move from Pittsburgh to Cincinnati had occurred in 1842, after Henry's second wife, Harriet had died in Allegheny, and he had married Hannah Kell, the servant who had accompanied the family from England ten years before, and with whom he then also began to have children. The 1850 census of Ohio lists him as living in Hamilton township, out of which Cincinnati was then growing. It was the same year that enforcement of the original Fugitive Slave Act was re-enacted.

The township sits across the river from the slave state of Kentucky, so there can be no doubt that Henry Howells became even more active in the movement there.

Levi Coffin, the master organizer and the semi-official founder (along with Garrison) of the Underground Railroad, had moved to Cincinnati in 1847 to operate a warehouse selling goods produced by free labor. The Free Produce Movement had been created by Quakers in the 1790's as an alternative to buying slave grown produce. A Free Produce Association was created in 1838. Garrison, in the pages of *The Liberator* proclaimed it as ineffectual. Coffin's venture however, did make a profit.

As both a Quaker and an abolitionist, Howells must have known Levi Coffin in Cincinnati in the late 1840's-1850's. There is, so far, however, no evidence I've seen that suggests that Coffin and Howells ever did anything together. Howells is not mentioned in Coffin's *Reminiscences*.

Coffin, and his cousins Vestal and Lucretia Coffin Mott will be discussed more fully in *Exodus and Arrival*.

Howells appears only once in all of the volumes of *The*

Letters of William Lloyd Garrison, in a letter from 1846 that refers to 'my worthy friend' HC Howells, who is identified in footnotes as a Bristol, England educator listed in City Directories from 1812 to 1849.

[It is probable that Howells kept his boarding school while living in America, thus accounting for his continued presence in the English Directories.]

The last that is known of Howells comes from Chapter 17 of the Milo Townsend book: *In 1854 Henry C. Howells was a member of the Raritan Bay Union,* founded by Rebecca Spring and her husband. A school there was under the direction of Theodore D. Weld. (Howells was a teacher.) see Appendix 4*

*The Raritan Bay Union was an offshoot of the North American *Phalanx*, a communal society developed on the principals of Charles Fourier. Fourier was a social thinker akin to the founder of the British cooperative movement, Robert Owen of Lanark. Raritan Bay Union was on land surveyed by Thoreau]

Abolitionists Angelina... and Sarah Grimké were teachers in the school which was run by Angelina's husband... Several other noted reformers came to teach and lecture at the school. The Welds' school operated until about 1861, but it isn't known how long the Union itself endured. [Green]

At the time of his March 26, 1857, letter to Milo, Howells was ill and believed he would soon die. However, the only available reference to his death, if the same Howells is referred to, appears in Gerrit Smith's April 13, 1862, letter to Milo a little more than five years later: Smith wrote, *Dear Father Howells!*

I knew him well and to know him well was to love him greatly. I regret to learn of the straitened circumstances of his family and of the state of health of his widow. [Chapter 17]

Gerrit Smith (1797 -1874) was undoubtedly also a friend of the Reverend Robert V. Rogers, son-in-law of Howells (more on their probable relationship in a moment.) Smith was born in Utica, Oneida County, New York, the son of a partner of John Jacob Astor, and therefor a member of one of the richest families in America. Gerrit's father was at one time the largest landowner in the republic. Smith inherited the lands and his father's estate in Peterboro, New York, where he later tried and failed to establish a viable free black community (it failed mostly because the Adirondacks have poor soil.)

He began life as a Presbyterian, but since he thought that

divisions between believers were sins, he left that denomination in 1843, and financed the building of the Church of Peterboro, open to all Christians, where he both preached and practice his own liberal theology.

Gerrrit Smith

Back in 1840, Smith's wife's sister married James G. Birney, the first Candidate for President of the Liberal Party, which was the party of the radical abolitionist movement. Gerrit Smith was chosen as the Party's candidate for for the same office in 1848 1856, and 1860. He served 18 months in Congress as a representative of the Free Soil Party from 1853–54.

In Smith's first address to Congress, he gave voice to his causes by stating that: *all men have an equal right to the soil... that wars are brutal and unnecessary... that slavery could be sanctioned by no constitution, state or federal... that free trade is essential to human brotherhood... that women should have full political rights...*

At the end of the first session, Smith resigned his seat, having lost the fight against the Kansas-Nebraska Act, which allowed territorial governments to decide if they would become slave states or not. That defeat led him to become a direct action abolitionist.

In 1859, Smith became one of the Secret Six, the men who financed John Brown's raid at Harper's Ferry, West Virginia. His role was outed by the Chicago Tribune. Brown had partly organized the raid in Chatham, Ontario.

Senator Jefferson Davies, the future President of the Confederacy of slave states, wanted Smith tried and hung with Brown. Smith had a breakdown, later writing *That affair excited and shocked me, and a few weeks after I was taken to a lunatic asylum. From that day to this I have had but a hazy view of dear John Brown's great work. Indeed, some of my impressions of it have, as others have told me, been quite erroneous and even wild.*

Gerrit Smith escaped being hung. The hanging of John Brown however, was one of the last shoes to fall before the Civil War was triggered in 1860. We will examine that event in relation to Chatham, Ontario in a later book.

Even after the Civil War, Smith's integrity was such that he became an advocate for allowing Davies to remain free on bond before the secessionist President's trial, arguing in a pamphlet called *Gerrit Smith and the Bailing of Jefferson Davies*,

that I have ever held that a sufficient reason why we should not punish the conquered South is that the North was quite as responsible as the South for the chief cause of the War. The North did quite as much as the South to uphold slavery : - and let me also say that she did it more wickedly because more calculatingly. Slavery was the evil inheritance of the South - but the wicked choice, the adopted policy, of the North. The unfortunate South felt that she must take slavery for better or for worse, for gain or for loss. But the mercenary North coolly reckoned the political, commercial and ecclesiastical profits of slavery, and held to it.

Gerrit Smith died in 1874.

Kingston, the home of Mary and Reverend Robert V. Rogers, sits at the lower end of Lake Ontario where it becomes the waters of the St. Lawrence River. The citadel still guards the city. It is a place with its own fugitive slave narratives, many of which included arriving on ships from Syracuse and Rochester (turf of the great black emancipationist Frederick Douglass.) The online webpage *Stones: Black History in Kingston, Ontario* shows a downtown map with fifteen sites connected to emancipated slaves.

There was a local chapter of the *Anti-Slavery Society of Canada* in Kingston. In *Terror to Evil-Doers: Prisons and Punishments in Nineteenth-Century Ontario*, it is noted that Mary's husband, the Reverend Rogers, became the chaplain at the Kingston penitentiary *after he studied at Cambridge and served as a traveling missionary in the United States "until his strong anti-*

slavery sentiments made his ministry very difficult." [Oliver p 68]

Arriving in Canada, Rogers worked at first in Midland, where he probably met Reverend Elliot among the Chippewa, and then took over St. George's Anglican in Kingston. While there he became a leading voice for the rehabilitation, rather than the simple incarceration of prisoners. His enthusiasm eventually soured, but that had more to do with a lack of opportunity for prisoners once they were released than it did with his beliefs, since he remained convinced that prisons should be moral schools rather than security measures.

In *Hard Time, Reforming the Penitentiary in Nineteenth-Century Canada*, it is noted that: *before 1850 there was a widespread*

> *view in Upper Canada that black convicts made up a disproportionate part of the penitentiary population.*
>
> *Kingston's Protestant chaplain, R. V. Rogers, argued in 1841 that the premise was deeply flawed: "Let our neighbourhood to nearly three million slaves be considered, that the coloured population of Canada is largely composed of runaway slaves, and a reason is at hand for the large number of coloured Convicts, without seeking for one, which white malignity has ever at hand, in the alleged idleness and viciousness of that race." Rogers advanced a more nuanced explanation for the perceived criminality and ignorance of black convicts than his colleagues in the penitentiary. "The previous education of slaves should be considered," he wrote, "or rather the absence of education. —Living as they do on the majority of plantations, in a state of the grossest ignorance and vice, can it be wondered at that some on reaching this land of liberty should commit crimes which render punishment necessary?"* [McCoy p 121]

In *Light of Nature and the Law of God: Antislavery in Ontario, 1833-1877* the Kingston Anti-Slavery Society (ASC) is stated to have been founded by the black abolitionist and Congregational Minister Samuel Ringgold Ward, who we will meet in later volumes. The Society doesn't seem to have lasted long, although *Rev. R.V. Rogers, the incumbent at St. James Anglican Church served on the ASC committee in 1852. (Stouffer 124)*

Reverend Rogers remained an active abolitionist in the larger Canadian organization even though the local committee faltered. As a member of that society, he would have known Thomas Sandilands of Guelph, also a Vice President in 1852.

In *Ontario's African-Canadian Heritage: Collected Writings by Fred Landon*, the editors noted that *The Argus*, published at Kingston, was quoted by *The Liberator*...of May 20, 1851, as saying *"That ... inhabitants of Canada can sit still and look upon this struggle going on in the neighbouring republic is utterly impossible... Every town and city along the line which boasts of a dozen Christians should have its branch anti-slavery society forming so many harbours of refuge where the weary and hunted fugitives may find protection from the human bloodhounds who pursue them."* (p237)

What is especially telling, is that Fred Landon also makes note of the fact that Jerry McHenry, (William Henry) a famous slave who was broken out of jail in Syracuse, New York on October 1 1851 with help from Gerrit Smith, died in Kingston in 1853. (Smith got McHenry out of Oswego in his cart.) That Jerry ended up in Kingston, suggests that Rogers helped.

In *The Underground Railroad, Slavery to Freedom, Wilburt Siebert* notes that: *So far as known Lake Ontario had only a few comparatively insignificant routes: at the upper end of the lake were two, one joining Rochester and St. Catherines... at the lower end of the lake, Oswego, Port Ontario and Cape Vincent seem to have been connected by lines with Kingston.*

While Siebert knew a great deal about the Underground Railroad, he doesn't seem to have known about the role of the Tuscarora of the Grand, and apparently knew little about what went on in Syracuse or in Frederick Douglass' Rochester.

The fact, however, that the eastern American lake ports sent their fugitives on to Kingston, cements the certainty that the Reverend RV Rogers was the key player there.

As for the legacy of Henry C. Howells, most of what is known about him before this book has come from Pauline Johnson, whose diatribes against her grandfather's treatment of her mother, are in part disputed by Charlotte Gray, who quotes the poet's sister Eva (Evelyn) as saying that Pauline was always developing *a story to suit herself.*

As noted, Pauline accused Howells of being cruel and abusive, which may have partly been based of the poets' belief that she thought her grandfather was a racist hypocrite for opposing her mother's marriage to George Johnson. However, Johnson's own mother had also objected to the marriage because she herself had a white mother and feared that not only would the couple face discrimination from Mohawks, but the marriage could have political consequences within the tribe since George might become a chief and a member of the Six Nation's Council and thus, with mixed blood on his mother's side; his children might not be Mohawk enough for the Haudenosaunee matriarchs. However, the birth of the first child brought George's mother around.

It is not clear how Howells responded in the long run. However, he had raised all his children to pity the conditions in which both blacks and natives were placed by whites. And he had objected to the marriage because he feared that Emily would be ostracized by Brantford whites, a fear rooted in his own treatment by the Friends after marrying Emily's mother.

Emily had come to the Grand to look after Adam and Eliza's children, but Eliza and the children died of TB in 1849, so Emily went to live in Kingston. Rogers however, refused to marry Emily and George, presumably in deference to Henry's refusal to bless the marriage. They were finally married across the Inner Harbour of Kingston in Barriefield. [Keller 17].

Undoubtedly, Howells was a complex man, but what concerns us here, is that in the very of heart of the Six Nations Reserve, at the Anglican mission to the Tuscaroras, the most clearly anti-slavery church in the colony and tribe in the Haudenosaunee confederacy, there were two women who had been raised by the man William Garrison called *our worthy friend*; and the man Smith defined as *Dear Father Howells!...to know him well was to love him greatly.*

Having come of age inside the American abolitionist movement, Howells' daughters on the Grand River may or may not have assisted their father's friends and allies to the same degree as their sister Mary's husband, but both women were connected to the Tuscarora and both husbands were key to the Tuscarora Anglicans, men linked to the traditions of Lugger and Norton, and through them, to both William Wilberforce

A Young Henry C. Howells

and to the Clapham Sect.

It is probably not just coincidence. One thing is known however, and that is that Pauline's sister, though called Eva, wasn't named Eva, but Helen; she was given the nick-name Eva because that was the name of the little girl who befriended Uncle Tom in Harriet Beecher Stowe's book, a novel that was published around the time of Eva's birth, a novel that Emily Howells must have loved. [Keller 17]

Methodists in the Mix

The historian quoted most often by Christopher Densmore in his 1995 paper *Migrating Quakers, Fugitive Slaves and Indians: The Quaker Ties of New York and Upper Canada*, is Arthur Garrat Dorland, the man who organized and published the core materials of Canadian Quaker history in 1920.

Dorland was born just west of Guelph in the village of Bloomfield in Waterloo Co. He studied at the Society's school, Pickering College, and his papers form the basis of the Society's national archives and are kept at Pickering. His ancestors had been Bay of Quinte Friends who had arrived at Adolphustown with the Loyalists. (As pacifists, Quakers weren't regarded as Loyalists.)

In his *History of the Society of Friends in Canada* Dorland makes the following observations, *The early history of Methodism and of Quakerism in Canada exhibit many interesting parallelisms. Both sects secured a footing in Upper Canada about the same time in the Niagara and Adolphustown district... both lack official standing...both spread from the United States... both sects place*

special emphasis on the personal character of religion,...
Methodists talked about "the Witness of the Spirit" in which there
was much in common with the Quaker doctrine of "The Inner
Light"... Our conclusion is... that of all the forces outside the Society
of Friends which have influenced the religious thought of Canadian
Quakerism, the most important has probably been evangelical
Methodism. (pp 132-133)

Thoughts Upon Slavery

Early in the 18th century, John Wesley and the other
members of the Oxford Holy Club were all Anglicans, but they
were searching for a more immediate experience of the divine
than high or low Anglicanism provided them. Their methodical
approach to Bible study and analysis of the history of the
spiritual revival that was sweeping England, so characterized
them that they were referred to by other students as
methodists. After being ordained an Anglican minister in 1734,
John and his brother Charles (author of many of the hymns in
the Wesleyan canon) sailed to Savannah, Georgia at the behest
of that colony's governor, to minister to the new parish.

On the way over they traveled with some Moravians, yet an
other German peace sect (some of which, as earlier noted, later
settled on the Thames River with the Delaware-Lenape, and
whose educational work inspired the Anglican minister of the
Six Nations Reserve, Robert Lugger.) Wesley was deeply
impressed by the example of the Moravians during a storm in
which the ship's mast was smashed and all the passengers
panicked, except the Moravians who sang hymns and prayed,
the only calm in the storm.

Wesley's experience was also overshadowed by his
involvement with a woman on board who, once on land, claimed
that he had promised to marry her; after hearing his story, the
Moravian minister he had traveled with counseled Wesley not
to marry, and eventually the beleaguered minister had to make
his escape and arrived back in England depressed, but deeply
inspired by the Moravians.

On May 24 1738, he underwent a religious experience at a
Moravian meeting on Aldersgate Street, London, after which,
though he remained an Anglican the rest of his life, the

movement he and his brother and the other founders of Methodism began, became the most rapidly expanding denomination in Britain, sending out what became known as hedge row preachers to walk and minister to commoners on the newly built roads created by commercial interests across England designed the break the hold of London and Glasgow on trade.

Methodism emigrated to North America, the carry on of British adherents from all corners of the realm to the vaster, wilder colonies and territories free of hedge rows required horse-mounted circuit riders. The denomination became the largest in the Thirteen colonies; post-Revolutionary War America and British North America

After the Revolution, the legal problem for the English Wesleyans were their property claims within the newly minted United States, but using a system of trustees and national conferences, the Methodist movement resolved its political schism and prospered, remaining in communion with, but distinct from, the British Wesleyans, who have no bishops.

The Canadian Methodist movement was largely created by American missionaries sent into the new colony, after the Revolution. British immigration after the loyalist period led to the establishment of Wesleyan congregations, which then led to a union of the two groups into the Wesleyan Methodists; and finally, later formed one of the three denominations - Methodist, Presbyterian and Congregationalist - that became the United Church of Canada in 1924. All three of those denominations played significant roles in the 19th anti-slavery movement in both America and Canada. Schisms over the issue of violating the Fugitive Slave laws divided all three churches in America, and caused problems for congregations in Canada.

Significantly for *Laying the Bed*, the Guelph Conference of the Methodist church was so important to the development of the denomination in Upper Canada, that it was given the task of establishing and maintaining churches in every county in south southwest central Ontario, excluding Peel and York, but including congregations on the Six Nations and New Credit reserves.

For the Methodists, there was no doubt of where John Wesley stood on the matter of slavery, since in 1784, the year after America was created, Wesley penned *Thoughts Upon Slavery.*

I include a synopsis of *Thoughts...* in part because they have a singular presence in Christian doctrine, but when combined with Methodism's emergence from Anglicanism, both in Wesley's own life; and in the lives of abolitionists on the Six Nations of the Grand River Reserve. *Thoughts Upon Slavery* shed light on the mindset of adherents and established the Wesleyan Methodist case for early credit in helping fugitive slaves away from American borders. I believe the Guelph Conference is how the Queen's Bush absorbed 1500 fugitives.

The *Thoughts* were first published in 1784, the year after Upper Canada was formed. Wesley himself died in 1791, two years before America became a slave prison and Upper Canada a semi-haven.

[On the website *Documenting the South* there is a summary of the *Thoughts* by Christopher Hill, reprinted in Philadelphia "with notes, and told by Joseph Cruikshank, 1784."]

Summary

Wesley's pamphlet *Thoughts upon Slavery* opens with a definition of slavery. His first note of condemnation appears when he shows that slavery first originated in "barbarous" times and died out with the rise of Christianity in Europe. He proposes that it was only the discovery of America and the need for large amounts of inexpensive labor that brought it back. Wesley then moves on to refute the notion that slavery rescues Africans from the harshest of conditions, quoting from many authorities attesting to the great fertility of Western Africa. He also points out that African nations are highly organized and cultured, using examples from several major tribes and nations to prove his point. Given this evidence, Wesley cannot support the notion that slavery represents an improvement to the Africans. Wesley's third point discusses how African slaves are procured and brought to America... he recounts numerous instances of fraud and violence... describes the middle passage in some detail... describes the inhumane treatment of slaves in the West Indies and other slave states ... providing ...modes of punishment and the laws that allow punishments to be meted out without limit.

After revealing the conditions of the slaves, Wesley then questions whether the system is defensible,on *the principles of even heathen honesty?* Human law, in his estimation, is powerless to confer right without consideration of mercy and justice. Wesley denies that slavery is necessary to support the colonial economies, pointing out that no benefit is worth any injustice made to receive it. The penultimate section of the tract is an appeal urging those involved in the slave trade to quit the trade; Wesley uses appeals ranging from fear of God's judgment to pity for the Africans. Finally, Wesley relates unpleasant Dutch and French experiences with slaves. These specific instances and stories further illustrate Wesley's point that the institution is at its core dehumanizing and barbarous.

With Wesley's *Thoughts Upon Slavery* as their shield, there can be no doubt that Methodists - though riven by schism in America over the issue of whether to break laws against aiding and abetting escaped slaves - were otherwise left without room for equivocation about the wrongness of the practice, however many American Methodists still tried to rationalize the enslavement of others.

During the 1830's, however, Canadian Wesleyan Methodists, in the cause of denominational unity with their American brethren in slave states, stopped using their influential publication *The Guardian* as a voice for the abolition movement and fell silent on the subject, however much work they may have done with former slaves escaped into Canada. And once again, the Canadian conference of the African Methodist Episcopal Church, was the exception to that rule, a subject to which we will return in a later volume.

Detail of a portrait of John Wesley

by John Harley

Augustus Jones and the Mississauga Methodists

Augustus Jones (1757-1836), a Loyalist of Welsh descent, who had been a New York City surveyor before the Revolution, became assistant to the deputy surveyor of the Niagara district in 1788. Augustus was responsible for most of the early surveying of many of the townships in the Niagara region, and was also the man who surveyed the Grand River Reserve, the Dundas Road, and Yonge Street, for Lt. Governor Simcoe.

Jones Sr. also surveyed the shore of Lake Ontario from Toronto to the Trent River (Peterborough). He is as well, the Jones of the Jones Baseline, a still extant road in places, but one that began as a survey line from the head of Lake Ontario at Nelson township on the edge of Burlington Bay, to run north-westerly at an angle of 45 degrees, until it crosses what Jones and his Mississauga guides thought was the Thames River, but which was in fact, the Conestogo, itself a branch of the Grand. (The survey ended where the town of Arthur now sits.)

The Jones Baseline is the fixed point within the original Mississauga Purchase from which all the townships on either side of it were surveyed; Nelson, Flamborough, Puslinch, Guelph, Nichol, Eramosa, Garafraxa, Pilkington and Peel (now Mapleton).

The survey of the boundary of the Six Nation's Reserve was made in 1791, and extended six miles on either side of the Grand River from Lake Erie to Arthur and the Baseline.

Augustus Jones was given ten square miles of land on both sides of the Grand in payment for the survey. In fact, by the time he was done being paid for all his work, he was one of the largest landholders in the colony. His family originally owned property in Saltfleet township (Stoney Creek), where William Groat of Guelph was later born.

Augustus gave up surveying in the early 1800's, and took up farming on the family's 300 acres there, and thus would have been well known to the likewise Welsh descended, Davis Ghents with whom the Groats are associated.

In 1806, Mike Sr. bought his land in Nelson from Brant, through Augustus Jones, and lived in the vicinity of the Davis Ghents the rest of his life, and may in fact be buried in their family plot.

Augustus Jones had a sister, Mary, the widow of James Gage Sr. Her son, James Gage Jr., owned the farm on which the battle of Stoney Creek was fought in 1813. Gage married Mary Davis, a daughter of William's. He was was one of the most important Methodists at the head of the Lake.

The Gages of Wellington Square and Oakville

The community originally known as Port Nelson became known as Wellington Square in the 1820's after James Gage invested in the township and began developing business ventures. James Gage (Jr.) was born on *June 25th, 1774 at Greenbush N.Y. ...married Mary Davis in 1796. There (sic) sons name was Asahel Gage, born in Stoney Creek, Upper Canada, Sept.28, 1798. died July 1, 1861... he had a daughter named Mary Ann Gage born in Hamilton Ont. Nov. 16,1824 and married John Chrysler, Dec.19, 1844 in Hamilton. Jon Chrysler.* (We will come back to the Chrysler-Gages.)

According to his entry in the *Dictionary of Canadian Biography,* James Gage was a Methodist, and moved to Upper Canada and Saltfleet township in 1790. As already stated, his mother Mary, was the sister of Augustus Jones, making James a first cousin of Chief Reverend Peter Jones of the Mississauga. Gage married Mary and their home became a centre of Methodist activity in the colony.

In 1810, Gage bought the land that became the core of Wellington Square from Catherine Brant and Augustus Jones, the executors of Chief Joseph Brant's will. William Case, an itinerant Methodist preacher and a great ally of Reverend Peter Jones, owned a large lot in Nelson township in 1818.

Gage did not actually live in Wellington Square himself, according to Burlington historian and columnist Helen Langford (*Gazette* Nov 7 1978), he remained in Stoney Creek. He did however, build the early mercantile infrastructure of the Nelson community starting in 1815, which is to say after the war of 1812, and before the Guelph Line was surveyed and the township size was doubled.

Gage sold land to his workers, providing them with building

materials and flour. Wellington Square, according to Langford *did not exist until 1820-1830*. Gage himself moved from Stoney Creek to Hamilton in 1835 and started a bank. He is the Gage of that city's Gage Street.

His wife's sister, Sarah Davis, was married to John Chisholm, the customs collector, who was also the militia captain of the Dundas road patrol during the War of 1812. The Groats served in Chisholm's company. Both James Gage and William Chisholm (brother of John) are important to Oakville history.

In 1827 Oakville was founded by Colonel William Chisholm, after he purchased 1000 acres of Crown land at the mouth of the Sixteen Mile Creek. Chisholm's great dream of building a privately owned harbour for Upper Canada was quickly realized in 1834, when Oakville was declared a Port of Entry into Canada....

William Chisholm established Oakville's first shipyard on the south bank of Sixteen Mile Creek at the north end of Navy Street....

For fifty years, wind-driven fleets carried freight from Oakville...

Oakville reached the height of its shipping trade in the 1850s. It became an official Canadian Port of Entry, collecting duties on imports from the United States, with William Chisholm acting as customs agent. The coming of the railroad is 1855 meant that wheat and timber could be shipped to the larger harbours at Toronto and Hamilton. The harbour fell into disrepair, and was sold to the Town of Oakville in 1874 for $250. [Mathews]

James Gage became involved in the development of Oakville in 1841 at the mouth of the 16 Mile Creek, where he developed a grain shipment business around Lake Ontario with a man named Benjamin Hagaman from Oswego, New York. There is no evidence that Hagaman was an abolitionist, however, there are 11 *National Register of Historic Place* underground railroad sites in Oswego County according to the tourist website Visit Oswego County. An *Underground Railroad Interpretative Centre* was opened there on Dec. 1 2012. As examined earlier, Gerrit Smith, the anti-slavery associate and friend of Henry C. Howells lived in Oswego.

The National Historical Park Service website * notes that Network routes were formed from the South through Ithaca, Cayuga Lake, Auburn, and Oswego. Selected ships that came and*

*went from that port would have carried fugitive slaves across the
lake to freedom.*

Three Oakville ship captains are known to have played
significant roles in the Underground Railroad and one man in
particular, a free negro named James Wesley Hill worked out of
Oswego. Their stories will be told in a later book.

The Sixteen Mile Creek leads north from Oakville and onto
the Niagara Escarpment heights of Nassagaweya township,
due east of Puslinch township (south Guelph). More than one
fugitive made their way from the creek to the Queen's Bush.

In *Oakville and the Sixteen*, Hazel C. Matthews, speaks
about JW Hill settling on the 9th line of Trafalgar township,
where his daughter lived until her death in 1946, Mathews also
notes: *The Johnsons, Wallace's, William Holland, Benedict
Duncan and Lloyd Brown remained in the locality, but others, who
had been aided by Hill joined the Negro Community at Dresden,
near Chatham, where lived the Reverend Josiah Henson. The
"Uncle Tom" of Harriet Beecher Stowe's ... novel.*

The Oakville Johnson family later married into the family of
the Reverend Junius B. Roberts, the man who oversaw the
building of the Guelph BME in the 1880's, Robert's grandson
Ira Johnson, was the object of the wrath of the Hamilton KKK
in the 1930's, a story told in detail in *Blood in the Mortar.*
There was also a family of black Johnsons living near Guelph
on what is known as the Guelph Line in Nassagaweya
township and to whom we will also return. The first Canadian-
born Bishop of the African Methodist Episcopal Church, Albert
Johnson, was born in Oakville and was in attendance at the
1880 cornerstone setting ceremony and thus is likewise to be
returned to...

With Gage undoubtedly having been influenced by John
Wesley's *Thoughts Upon Slavery*, and considering the fact that
he grew up with free blacks, and was married into the Davis
family with its strong links to the Groats, there are grounds to
believe that James Gage's ships were part of the Oswego to
Oakville Underground Railroad route.

According to the *Dictionary of Canadian Biography*, the
Reverend John Saltkill Carroll, (the man who baptized William

Groat's family in Guelph in 1867) regarded Gage as having been *"famous for his hospitality, and for his liberal contributions to Methodist institutions."*

The fact that the Groats had a long history in both Saltfleet and Nelson with the Gage family even before the founding of Wellington Square or Oakville, is not proof of a shared interest in abolitionist activities, but then, neither is that proof that they had no shared interest.

The Reverend Peter Jones

Augustus Jones had two wives, both native, Sarah, whose father Henry Tekarihogen, was a hereditary chief of the Mohawk and the man who had supported the leadership of Joseph Brant since a critical time in Brant's early career. Jones was one of two executors of Brant's will. Augustus Jones and his Mohawk wife became Methodist Episcopalians in 1801.

The other wife of Augustus Jones was also named Sarah, and was the daughter of the Mississauga chief, Wabanosay, the man who had guided Jones during the creation of the Baseline and other early colonial surveys. Jones married Sarah Henry/ Tuhbenahaneequay in a native ceremony in the mid- 1790's.

Her first son with Augustus was Theyandanegea – (Brant's name) but he was also known as John Jones and later named as his father's heir. Her second son with Augustus, born in 1801, was Kahkewaquonaby, the Reverend Peter Jones.

Jones Sr. made every effort to see that the two boys were taken care of, especially after Augustus became a Methodist the year that Peter was born, which was also the year he married his Mohawk wife in a Christian service, and abandoned polygamy by giving up Tuhbenahaneequay.

The Mississauga, unlike the Mohawk, were a tribe on the verge of collapse, especially after the War of 1812 and the subsequent famine of 1816, which led Augustus Jones to bring his children to live with him in Saltfleet with his other family.

In *The Autobiography of Rev. Alvin Torry: first Missionary missionary to the Six Nations...* Torry notes that Peter Jones was living with his father's Mohawk friends and family when the missionary first met Peter at a camp meeting run by

Reverend William Case on Methodist Mountain. (Jones was baptized on the Mountain (Ancaster) at the age of 21 (1822). (Torry arrived from the States in 1820.)

Peter's Mohawk sister Polly later married Jacob Brant and in the 1852 census of Brant County they were next-door neighbours of Isaac Whitby, (half brother of Abram Groat.)

Rev. Torry goes on: *Toward the close of this year, I felt an impression of mind that I must visit the Six Nations of Indians, whose Reservation lay to the west of my circuit....I was accustomed to cross the Grand River within a few miles of the Mohawk tribe, and frequently met with groups of them here and there, and not unfrequently saw them lying drunk around huckster's shops, kept by white people for the purpose of getting the Indians drunk, and then robbing them of all that was of use to them. But it had never occurred to me that the Gospel of Christ could be the power of God to the salvation of Indians.* [p. 46]

Traditionalist native leaders and Christian ministers had many points of disagreement, but a common concern was the danger of alcohol to the tribes. The 19th Century Reform movement held temperance to be crucial to the survival of not just whites and natives, but former slaves.

In speaking of Peter Jones, Torry notes: *Not long after his conversion, he began to talk of trying to hunt up his mother, and of persuading her, and the tribe to which she belonged, to come up to Grand River, and share with the Mohawks in the blessings of the gospel... No one cared for these poor Indians, nor would any one give them shelter from the weather, unless to get their money, or their furs from them. When these were gone, they were turned into the open air...*

This constant exposure to the in-clemency of the seasons, together with their habitual use of the "firewater," caused a rapid diminution of numbers, and when I became acquainted with them, they were comparatively few in numbers. (p. 96)

Peter had been appointed an exhorter for the Church in 1825, which is when he moved with his Mississauga believers to lands on the Grand River Reserve owned by Chief Thomas Davis, a Mohawk War Chief. Thomas Davis was a cousin of Joseph Brant's (and no relation of the loyalist William Davis.)

The settlement was known as Davisville, and was five miles

north of Brantford below a large bend in the Grand River. It lasted two years, and was the first community of Mohawk and Mississauga to ever live in peace, since the two tribes had been enemies since before the arrival of Europeans.

The Wesleyan Methodist mission on the old Mohawk War Chief's land sat within a primeval oak forest on the banks of the Grand. In the summer of 2004, the Grand River Conservation Authority published findings of an archaeological survey of the Davisville site that were reported in the Grand Action/Grand Strategy newsletter the following September, in which Gary Warrick noted that: *In 1787, about 500 Mississauga lived at the*

western end of Lake Ontario. But measles, smallpox, tuberculosis and alcohol abuse had reduced the population to 200 by 1819...

Warrick then notes that Rev. Alvin Torry administered the Davisville Mohawk missionary field and was the agent by which Jones and his Mississauga Methodists were invited to settle. Some accepted... *and moved in early 1824. In the spring of 1825 about 35 Mississauga arrived and by the summer, 45 more joined them... as many as 100-150 may have lived there between the summer of 1825 and the spring of 1826... the Mississauga lived in tents or wigwams within earshot of the Methodist Mission house... a few Mississauga remained at Davisville as late as January 10 1827.*

Members of Mike Sr. family may have been among that congregation, in particular John and Caty Mike.

According to a document in C.M. Johnston's *Valley of the Six Nations,* in a chapter called *Christianity in the Longhouse,* on Wednesday March 5 1828, the Reverend Peter Jones

went to Brantford and saw Mr. Lugger, the Church (Anglican) Missionary. A number of the Mohawk Methodists were assembled to have an audience with him...the object of their coming was to inquire whether he would allow them the privilege of holding their meetings in the Mohawk Church, provided they granted him similar liberty to preach at the Salt Spring. Mr. L. replied that he had no objection to their attending his church whenever there was Divine Service (communion), but that he would not suffer them to preach, and consequently in danger of spreading erroneous doctrines, and causing enthusiasm, and wild fire,&c.... after much discussion on both sides, they parted with this resolution, that each should keep to their own ranks and not interfere with the other party. I advised the Methodist Indians to be careful not to speak evil of the Church of England, but go peaceable on in the way they thought right, and rejoice if the Church of England minister did any good amongst the Indians. They appeared to approve of my advice, and we parted. pg 258

Peter Jones' personal transformation seems to have been so impressive to his mother's people that most members of the remnant of the Mississauga tribe – including her - converted to Methodism when he and his Davisville followers returned to the mouth of the Credit (Etobicoke) after 1829. The Groat-Mikes appear to have remained on the reserve, perhaps because of Tuscarora cousins.

On the Credit, the Reverend Peter Jones became the spokesman for the Christian Mississauga, and he was elected a chief. Jones had already been adopted by the Mohawk, in whose language he was also fluent.

Bishop Strachan, the Family Compact's spokesman in Toronto, offered to pay Peter and his brother John more money that the Methodists paid them if they became Anglican preachers but they both said no. Reverend Torry continued as mentor to Jones and continued his battle with "hucksters".

In his autobiography, Reverend Torry does not write about anti-slavery activities except when speaking about a Reverend Schuyler Hoes from New York State, *a strong opposer of American slavery... he boldly denounced it as a great sin, striving with his brethren, to show them the enormous guilt of slave-holders; but some of his quondam* (former) *conservative brethren, looking upon him as a dangerous innovator and disturber of the peace of Zion, and being in authority over him, dealt so severely with him as to cause him to leave the Church and join the Wesleyans.*

(Methodist versus 'Wesleyan' had to do with American v. British congregational origins, Methodists being American.)

Subsequently, some of these men have, by their actions, acknowledged him their superior in judging the signs of the times, and now tacitly, as an atonement for their want of penetration, they follow in the path marked out by him, and, in their zeal, carry their measures to such extremes as were never advocated by him. (p 229)

Who the converted are that he is referring to is not stated, but Torry's views on slavery are clear.

In *Paddling Her Own Canoe: The Times and Texts of E. Pauline Johnson (Tekahionwake)*, Veronica Jane Strong-Boag and Carole Gerson, note: *In their struggle to be heard and to make larger sense of their struggle, Indigenous peoples also maintained links across the British empire and the English speaking world. Britain's anti-slavery community provided an important reference point for those like the Anglo-Ojibwa-Kahkewaguonaby... Reverend Peter Jones (1802-56), who traced the struggle of colonized peoples in Asia, Africa, Australia, New Zealand, California. (p 28)*

The struggle that Peter Jones was caught up in for the rest of his life was to get the Indian Department to take Mississauga land claims seriously. The Six Nations have a distinct place in Canadian history as an sovereign nation given lands the Crown bought for them. The fact that the land was bought from the Mississauga proves right of ownership: the tract was split into the Gore District and the Six Nations Reserve; the so-called Toronto Purchase was further evidence of recognized sovereign ownership. It was only after the death of Sir John Johnson in 1805 that the spirit of The Royal Proclamation of 1763 died. Along with that, so also died the use of Quaker covenanting principles and native friendship chains, leading to the expropriation of Mississauga territory.

Peter Jones went to England and won Queen Victoria's approval of the tribe's claim to the mouth of the Credit River,; an approval ignored by colonial officials.

In 1847, Jones finally led the tribe away from the fight and accepted land near the Haudenosaunee, where they were given a reserve now called Mississauga of the New Credit. Peter Jones died in Brantford in 1856.

There can be no wonder that the Reverend Jones, *the Anglo-Ojibwa-Kahkewaguonaby,* became fascinated with the slave trade and the histories of disenfranchised peoples around the world.

> *Speak, speak for the nation which smiles in its hardship,*
> *usurped of its plenty, crushed, dogged and debased.*
> *For the spirit of freedom swells high with emotion,*
> *and wild torrents murmur, 'we will not be slaves.'*
> - E. Pauline Johnson

There is, however, no evidence that Rev. Jones played any role in the Underground Railroad. He did have connections to the Clapham Sect through their work with natives via the *Aborigine Protection Society*, the successor to the *British Anti-Slavery Society created* by the 'Sect' after the abolition of slavery and the death of Wilberforce in 1833. Nonetheless, there is no doubt that Jones supported blacks and mixed-race marriages since he baptized Peter and Margaret Groat Mike in 1833.

Eliza Fields, the English woman who married Reverend Jones in New York in September of 1833 (a few months after the passing of the Emancipation Act.) noted during the four days before her husband-to-be arrived in New York, that she

> *found racial prejudices openly expressed and opinions voiced that the Indians constituted a substandard inferior race. Many felt that blacks and Indians could not be changed by either education or by an improved environment. It made her feel ill.* (Smith, DB p 141)

Her feelings of unease grew the more widely it became known that she was in New York awaiting the arrival of Jones.

> *Many Upper Canadian newspapers joined in the chorus of disapproval, although the Niagara Gleaner stated: the Indians and even the Negroes are looked upon and treated as human in all the dominions of Britain.* (ibid)

Eliza was no shrinking violet, and had, according to Smith in *Sacred Feathers*, begun her own spiritual journey at Chapel Hill, Surrey, a decade earlier, under the guidance of Rowland Hill, *who preached a social Christianity, and* who *supported a number of reform groups, including the Anti-Slavery Society...* (ibid)

At the same time, one of the most important allies of the Reverend Peter Jones, was the Reverend Egerton Ryerson, a career-long friend, and the man from whose house Jones returned the night before he died in Brantford in 1856.

In 1833, the Ryersons, father and two sons, all supported and oversaw the transformation of the Canadian Methodist Episcopal Church into a member of the British-based Wesleyan Methodist Conference.

The British immigrant wing of the church in Upper Canada was anti-slavery and pro-family compact (or at least supported the authority of the colonial government - which amounted to the same thing to the former Methodist Episcopalians with American roots, who were in favour of democratic reform.)

Their struggles to keep the Church whole was an echo of the split between William Garrison and Theodore Weld: Weld (and presumably Henry C. Howells) believed, like Ryerson, in the necessity of avoiding division among churches, while Ephraim Evans, a British Wesleyan Methodist tory and charter member/ Secretary of the newly formed *Anti-Slavery Society of Upper Canada* (created on January 4 1837) had used the denominational paper *The Guardian* to denounce slavery, and those who supported and allowed it.

[The other founders of that first society were Egerton's brother John, and Tiger Dunlop's brother, Robert Graham Dunlop, an Anglican from Goderich.]

Unfortunately for Evans, in the wake of the failed rebellion of 1837, the denomination was concluding negotiations for conference parity with American Wesleyan Methodists, and thus Ephraim's anti-slavery writings were causing problems for negotiators, even while his anti-democratic writings were upsetting the Canadian reformers within the denomination.

Evans lost to Ryerson when the Conference superintendent in Upper Canada supported the reformers by agreeing to the reappointment of Ryerson as editor of *The Guardian*, which restored the focus on democratic and educational reform, but silenced the attacks on slavery.

The Reverend Peter Jones undoubtedly shared his wife's views on the sin of slavery but Jones and his mother's people had problems enough of their own, ones that kept him and them busy the rest of their lives. His 1833 baptism of the Groat Mikes, however, proved he had no issue with a mixed-race black man marrying Mississauga women or bringing their children into the communion.

Egerton Ryerson, went on the become one of those powerhouse oddities of early Victorian colonial administration, since he thereafter served as the all but self-appointed minister of education, grappling with concerns about religious and public school systems then being explored for the newly re-united Provinces of upper and lower Canada. His 1850 *Common School Act* created public education in Ontario.

However, because he supported a majority rights position to local schooling, local parents had considerable leeway in running schools: many blacks regarded Ryerson - and some still regard him - as supporting racism, because in communities where racists were the majority, black children went to segregated schools because the majority of parents wanted that.

Arguably, Ryerson could have instituted desegregation, since he was personally powerful enough to have done so. But he had taken his stand on the principle of localism, so between that stance and his being the one who silenced the denomination's voice just as the newly created Anti-Slavery of Upper Canada had clambered into prominence on the Guardian platform, the Wesleyan Methodists lost favour with Upper Canadian black activists. Ryerson believed that education and democracy could be achieved by focusing on those two goals together, and that enlightenment and empowerment would then create the social momentum to allow the creation of a future without slavery.

At the same time however, by the post-Rebellion period, the African Methodist Episcopal church was ready to fill the Wesleyan void. And Ryerson knew it.

As for the legacy of Reverend Peter and Eliza's Jones, their son, Peter E. Jones grew up to advocate for voting rights for First Nations and women. Later in this book, Peter E. appears in his role as Indian agent in the late 1870's, attempting to mitigate efforts by the Mississauga band council to have the Groat-Mikes (two of whom had been baptized by his father back in 1833) removed from the reserve for not being Indian enough, because their father 'was a black man", although, in a letters to Jones, one of John Groat Mike's sons, Henry, refers to his father as a 'mulatto.'

As much as Dorland thinks Methodism and Quakerism had a lot in common, Reverend Alvin Torry refers to Hicksites as *Hickorys* in a discussion on a theological dispute over the value of the Old Testament with a former Methodist turned Quaker who had come to believe that belief required only the New Testament. Torry was as partisan about Methodist doctrine as Lugger was about Anglican, and no friend of the Friends.

Syracuse, New York and the Six Nations

For all the Quakers and other denominational Christians so far mentioned as being involved with the Underground Railroad and natives, there is one American, Matilda Joslyn Gage (1826 - 1898), whose activities and connections to the Haudenosaunee were essentially non-religious, although *her name ... (was) retained on the roll of membership of the Fayetteville Baptist church the past thirty-five years. She never lost faith in the old fundamental truths of religion, and while not adopting in full the theories of any of the new schools of thought, she claimed to be an investigator on those fields, especially of psychology and theosophy.*

On the New York history webpage called Matilda Joslyn Gage, Forgotten Feminist, her concern with churches may best be summed up by herself: *As Miss Grew has truly said, it is not religion that has opposed woman suffrage, because true religion believes in undoing the heavy burdens and letting the oppressed go free. But from the church and from theology this reform has met opposition at every step.* [Wagner]

According to the website created in her honour, she was born Matilda Joslyn in March of 1826 in Cicero, Onondaga County, NY, the daughter of Dr. Hezekiah Joslyn and Helen Leslie, daughter of Sir George Leslie, a Scot from Aberdeen.

Matilda was raised wealthier than anyone else in what was then still a pioneer community. She also grew up in a safe house for fugitive slaves. In an online Your Dictionary biography of Gage, it is noted that *Her parents... were both supporters of liberal social reforms and took an active role in the education of their only child... As she grew older, however, her parents decided she needed a more formal education and enrolled her in the Clinton New York Liberal Institute.*

She elsewhere noted that: *my father ...taught me to think for myself, and not to accept the word of any man, or society, or human being, but to fully examine for myself.* [Warner, web]

When she was 18 she married Henry H. Gage (who does not seem to have been related to the loyalist Gages although they too were from upper New York.) Matilda and Henry settled at Syracuse and later moved to Fayetteville N.Y. H.H Gage was a merchant: *General Dry Goods, Hats, Caps, Boots, Shoes, Clothing and Groceries. Matilda Gage furthered her studies of Greek and taught herself Hebrew. She also began to devote her energies to various social causes...*

[Memories of Fayetteville website]

In *Native Americans Today, A Biographical Dictionary* the authors noted that: In 1850, Gage stated publicly that *she would accept a six-month prison term and a $2,000 fine because she opposed a new fugitive-slave law, which made a criminal of anyone who assisted slaves toward freedom. "Until liberty is attained—the broadest, the deepest, the highest liberty for all—not one set alone, one clique alone, but for men and women, black and white, Irish, Germans, Americans, and Negroes, there can be no permanent peace"*

Matilda Gage also worked with Elizabeth Cady Stanton, of Seneca Falls, New York who was a "member of the triumvirate" along with Susan B. Anthony of the "suffrage leadership" in America during their day.

Stanton's second cousin, Peter Shenandoah Smith, was the brother of Gerrit Smith, the abolitionist who wrote to Milo Townsend in 1846, identifying Henry Howells, E. Pauline Johnsons' abolitionist grandfather as "a friend."

Chief Shennandoah of the Oneida was a family friend of the Stanton-Smiths, and Stanton's nearest neighbour in Seneca Falls, Captain Oren Tyler, had been adopted by the Oneida.

In the *Encyclopedia of American Indian History* edited by Bruce Johansen and Barry Pritzker, the authors asked: *How did the suffragists know about Haudenosaunee? While they lived in very different cultural, economic, spiritual and political worlds during the the early 1800's, Euro-American settlers in central and western New York were, at most, one person away from direct familiarity with people of the Six Nations...*

In 1852, at the *Third National Women's Rights Convention* in Syracuse, Matilda, *at the age of 26, was the youngest speaker at the event, her words were so well-received that they were later published and circulated to gain support for the cause. Gage's talk focused on the numerous accomplishments of women throughout history and the need for women to escape the legal and economic shackles placed on them by society. She drew a parallel between the limited rights of women in America and the institution of slavery, stating that both forms of oppression stemmed from the same patriarchal attitudes.* [Johnson/Pritzker]

Matilda Gage also wrote about the role of Haudenosaunee women in the power structure of the Iroquoian Confederacy, while also taking on those trying to act as if that Confederacy was not composed of sovereign nations, nations with whom America had treaty rights. The Haudenosaunee, *who kept their their ancient practice of adopting individuals of other nations... adopted Matilda Josyln Gage, who "received the name of Ka-ron-ien-ha-wi, or 'Sky Carrier', or She who holds the sky." from the Wolf Clan.* [Johnson/Pritzker]

[Note: Matilda Gage's daughter Maud, married Frank L, Baum, and their daughter, Dorothy, was the inspiration for Dorthy Gale in Baum's Oz books. Which puts Dorothy freeing enslaved Flying Monkey's into a different light.]

Gage was working on a book about the Iroquois when she died in 1898. In 1888, at the *International Council of Women,* Gage had spoken about her introduction to the abolitionist movement . . . *I think I was born with a hatred of oppression... in my father's house, I was trained in the anti-slavery ranks, ... Well I remember the wonder with which, when a young girl, I looked upon Abby Kelly, when she spoke of the wrongs of black women and black men. Then I remember...in my city of Syracuse ...a large and enthusiastic anti-slavery convention was held ... attended by thousands of people who all joined in singing William Lloyd Garrison's song, I'm an Abolitionist and Glory in the Name, and as they rang out that glorious defiance against wrong, it thrilled my very heart, and I feel it echoing to this day.* [Johnson/Pritzker]

(Abby Kelley and her husband Stephen Symonds Foster also worked with Theodore Weld and his wife Angelina Grimké and also with Milo Townsend, all friends of E. Pauline Johnson's grandfather, Henry C. Howells.)

As part of that same eastern New York anti-slavery world as Gerrit Smith, Matilda Gage's connection to Canada was through a man baptized on Methodist Mountain around the time Reverend Peter Jones was salvaging the remnant of the Mississauga. That man, Jarm Logue aka Jermain Wesley Loguen, has the distinction of having published one of the only first hand accounts of escaping slavery using native highland trails, a story to which we'll return shortly.

In May 1880, in an article in her newspaper, *The National Citizen and Ballot Box*, (vol 5. no.1) Matilda Gage wrote:

> *One of the proudest acts of my life; one that I look back upon with most satisfaction is that when Rev. Mr. Loguen [Syracuse conductor of the Underground Railroad] ... went to the village of my residence to ascertain the names of those upon whom run-away slaves might depend for aid and comfort on the way to Canada... Myself and one gentleman of Fayetteville, were the only two persons who dared thus publicly defy 'the law' of the land, and for humanity's sake rendered ourselves liable to fine and imprisonment in the county jail, for the crime of feeding the hungry, giving shelter to the oppressed, and helping the black slaves on to freedom.*

Reverend Jermain Wesley Loguen began life as Jarm, a child of rape (his mother having been a slave impregnated by her master 'David Logue'.) In *The Rev. J. W. Loguen, as a Slave and as a Freeman. A Narrative of Real Life* Loguen tells the story of his life through the lens of the A.M.E Church.

The editor of Loguen's book notes in the preface: *We have proposed to write the Biography of Rev. JERMAIN WESLEY LOGUEN, and we have given its features in the following pages accurately. We took the features from him and filled up the picture. We began with his parents, infancy, childhood, and traced him from the Southern prison through the wilderness, and Canada, and back to the United States again, to fight the enemy all through the anti-slavery war to the end of the Jerry Rescue--giving the particulars of that Rescue, with the names of persons engaged in it, on one side and on the other.*

The latter half of the life of Mr. Loguen stands out before the world. The other half is buried in the cimmerian night of slavery.

Syracuse, N. Y. Publisher J. G. K. Truair & Co., Stereotypers and Printers 1859

What immediately stands out in the above is the connection to the McHenry rescue, tying him to Rev. Rogers in Kingston.

In 1835, when Jarm Logue first escaped from the plantation on which he was born, he crossed into Kentucky and through a portion of Ohio into Indiana with another man, where they received the help of a colored man named Mr. Overrals, *who advised them not to conceal the fact that they were slaves, if it was necessary to speak of it at all, unless to those known to be enemies--for the reason that the people among whom they would travel, as a general thing, were more willing to befriend slaves than colored freemen. With such counsel, he sent them to a Quaker settlement, about forty miles from Indianapolis.*

The Quakers received them with characteristic hospitality, and advised them to be careful and not bear to the east--that they had best go directly north, or north-west--for that emigrants from the slave States had settled into southern and eastern Indiana; that a large wilderness, occupied only by Indians and roving hunters, separated them from settlers from the northern and eastern States-- that those northern settlers were unlike the white men of the south and east--that they had been brought up in freedom, and knew nothing of slavery--that though they had an unaccountable prejudice against color, they would regard them with curious interest if they were slaves and would help them on to Canada. They also advised them that they were safer in this wilderness, among hunters and Indians, than with any other people short of those northern settlers, and advised them to go directly through the wilderness to them... (p324)

Supplied with *provisions and comforts* they headed through the wilderness to Canada, unafraid of winter, and convinced that they endured cold better than whites, but they also did as they had been advised and took the wilderness route:

The natives were a proud and stalwart tribe, dressed in their own costume, often ornamented with wampum and feathers, and generally armed with knives, or bows and arrows or rifles. Coming suddenly on them, as they did sometimes, the fugitives were startled by their ominous umph and imposing savageness. But after traveling among them and experiencing their harmlessness, they were quite disarmed of apprehension on their account.

Occasionally, too, they met white hunters in the woods, less reliable than the savages. These hunters told them to look out for wild boars, panthers, bears and wolves, especially the former monster beast, which they hunted with caution and peril. Not without cause, they feared to start up these terrible animals. They often saw their tracks, but if they came near the boars, they knew it not.

As a general thing, they were received kindly, by night and day, and fed freely on the wild meats and indescribable dishes prepared for Indian palates. (p327)

The two men nearly died in a snow storm, but survived the night as did their horses, discovering themselves near a native cabin and clearing, *It so happened that one of the natives talked bad English well enough to be understood by them, and acted the part of an interpreter. When the Indians found they had been lost in the woods, and in the storm all night, they (especially the women) expressed great surprise and sympathy ... (p330)*

The editor goes on to note how Loguen in later life remembered *"the good of life," or "natural good," of these Indians, and contrasted it with the religion of the whites.* [Truair pp 327-331]

He was cheated out of his horse by a Quaker when Jarm needed money. The cheat was another thing that he never forgot: the fact that the outside look and beliefs of a man did not always match their inner lives or actions, Quakers included.

Horseless, and now distrustful, the two fugitives headed deeper into winter, miles from settlements, getting further from Detroit, rather than closer, lost following the north star to nowhere. Eventually the two spoke to a mountain man who sent them back south east... eventually they staggered into Detroit, all but frozen and starving.

The trip stayed with Loguen the rest of his life; shaping him almost as much as his childhood: the trek also severed him from his old life as sharply as the freedom he discovered by crossing the Detroit River and standing on land not governed by American law.

When Jarm Logue first arrived in Hamilton after his travail from Tennessee to Detroit he found work, made money, share-cropped and profited, took a partner; lost money and moved to St. Catharines, bought land with his remaining cash, but then went back to Rochester in 1837 at the age of 24, where he worked at the Rochester Hotel, did well and prospered, before finally stopping to figure out what he really wanted to do. He went back to St. Catharines and sold his property, then crossed back into the US to attend the Oneida Institute, which is when he met William Sills, the great chronicler of the Underground

Railroad, who taught at the Institute. Jarm told Sills of his intent to work with fugitives and for the improvement of blacks.

After graduating from the institute he went to Utica and began to teach, and then, in 1841, moved to Syracuse, which is when he met Matilda Gage. Most of the town's abolitionists belonged to the Presbyterian church. (Methodist and Congregationalist anti-slavers soon joined forces after Loguen's arrival, and Gage, a nominal Baptist, worked with them as well.)

In a letter to Frederick Douglass, dated Syracuse, N. Y., May 8th, 1856, Loguen describes ... and contrasts Hamilton as it now is, with what it was: *"On the western termination of Lake Ontario is the village of Hamilton. It is a large, enterprising place, amid scenery, placid, beautiful and sublime. It is in a delightful valley, which runs east and west.*

On the north is a beautiful lake, and on the south a perpendicular mountain towers up some two or three hundred feet, and hangs its brow over the village. Here are quite a number of our people, doing well so far as I could learn--able and willing not only to help the fugitive, but to join with able and willing white men around them to furnish him an asylum. How changed in twenty years! My dear friend, indulge me here a moment. Hamilton is a sacred and memorable spot to me; and I cannot slightly pass it. I could not stand upon its soil without a flood of sad and sweet and gushing memories. It seems to me, and ever will seem to me, a paternal home. I shall never visit it without the feelings which a child feels on returning after weary years to his father's house... they taught me letters the winter of my arrival, and I graduated a Bible reader at Ancaster, close by the succeeding summer...(p 338)

Milton Sernett notes in *North Star Country,* that Syracuse became known as "the great central depot" of the underground railroad in New York State, the "Canada of the North." Loguen was known as the "Underground Railroad King." Up to 1500 fugitive slaves passed through his home on their way to freedom.

In *One Hundred Years of the African Methodist Episcopal Zion Church; or, The Centennial of African Methodism*: James Walker Hood (1831-1918) states that *In the year 1872 he* (Lougen) *was*

granted a local preacher's license, and on the 18th of May, 1873, was
ordained to the order of a deacon in the British Methodist Episcopal
Church and in the first Bermuda Annual Conference by Bishop W.
Nazrey. He continued to follow teaching school, visiting his charges
on Sundays and once during the week days. As no clergyman in
Bermuda at that time was allowed to exercise all the functions of
his office without permission from the governor and council, who
had first to approve of credentials and qualifications, he was
approved and licensed January 24, 1876.

... July, 1877... he was transferred to the Nova Scotia Conference
and assigned to the church at Liverpool, where he remained for two
years
His next charge was at St. John's, N. B.
... in April, 1880, he came to America and visited the African
Methodist Episcopal Zion Conference in the city of New Haven,
Conn., where... he decided to make application for membership.
(p319) (New York: A.M.E. Zion Book Concern, 1895.)

The Reverend J.W. Loguen passes out of the purview of
this book with his departure from the B.M.E.

What he brought to African Americans from the time he
established himself in Syracuse was a connection to the
Methodists of Hamilton/St. Catharines and the head of the
Lake, connections that eventually led him into the British
Methodist Episcopal Church in both Bermuda and the
Maritimes before he finally returned to America for good.

Loguen's links to Matilda Gage and her links to the
Haudenosaunee, all speak to the fullness of his abolitionist
activities from the 1840's until the Civil War, but it was his
experiences on the highland trails - his understanding of the
need for information and guidance along those ways - that
mark out Loguen's place in the narrative of those who took the
freedom trails and turned them into the bed of the
Underground Railroad.

The Loyal Groats of Upper Canada

It was the Guelph Museum website entry on their Black History in Guelph and Wellington page that brought the Groat clan to my attention: so I'll begin where they ended: *William Groat died on August 27 1900 at the House of Industry* (now the Wellington County Museum) *where he spent his last three years.*

The House of Industry would have made Dickens wince. It was an embodiment of that form of Christianity best described as grudging; to this day its surly aspect still haunts what is now the Museum. It is the story of the bleakest of bleak houses. The plaque for the former poor house reads, in part: *The Wellington County House of Industry and Refuge was built in 1876-1877 as the shelter of last resort for the homeless and destitute in Wellington County. Its original inhabitants traded their domestic or agricultural labour for spartan living accommodations. In later years it became a home for the elderly and infirm.*

According to Fergus historian Pat Mestern: *Truth be known, once a person was signed into the Poor House, especially during the period c1877 through c1925, they were often out-of-sight, out-of-mind. Having no relatives.... keen on claiming the body, their remains were interred in the Home's burial ground. Dr. Abraham Groves wrote that on many occasions he, the Keeper, grave digger and minister were often the only people in attendance at many of these burials.*

...at one time it was widely publicized that there were nearly two hundred... in the plot. ... uncaring officials have allowed the road to expand into the old burial ground's territory until there's only a small portion remaining today, planted with Scotch Pines.

The county archives were put into the attic of that building after the 'poor house' finally closed; the museum and gallery took over the rest; now the archives are laid out behind the *House of Industry* in new buildings where the remnants of the past are tended, and where the doors open by blocking a photon beam, making it possible for shades of former inmates to get the hell out of there I suppose.

In the records examined for me by Archivist Karen Wagner, William Groat could not have been a victim of the road expansion, since his body was removed in 1925 by a grand daughter, Mrs. C Farley* and placed in the Lillie burial plot in the Belsyde Cemetery.

The House of Industry, where William Groat died

courtesy Wellington County Museum and Archives

Mrs. Farley was the daughter of Hannah - William's eldest - and Thomas Lillie. According to Wagner and the record book, William was the only individual ever reclaimed by a family (although that's not what an exhibit in the Museum claims.)

The information in the Wellington County Archive's Groat family file comes from Arlene Noble a descendant of Hannah Lillie. In an email exchange, Arlene made it clear to me that her belief in the family's Canadian origins as Davis-Ghent servants or slaves is rooted, among other records, in the following note: *I*

> *corresponded with Charlie Davis who still lives on the property and he told me that family tradition says that coloured people are buried in unmarked graves on the farm. No records exist for the early years. It could well be the grave site for Michael and his wife...*

Assuming that the township census for 1842 is correct, Michael of Nelson was born in the US in 1795, possibly among the Tuscarora at Lewistown; or at Fort Niagara (the border between the two countries was not established until after the Jay Treaty was signed in 1796.)

The Davis-Ghent-Phillips Clan

Under the assumption that most loyalist slaves cannot be known except by the movements of their masters, then according to United Empire Loyalist (UEL) historian John A. Aikman's version of the Davis-Phillips-Ghent family, William Davis was born on December 23, 1741 in Baltimore, Maryland. His father, Thomas Davis (1708-1748) was married to Mary Wright, both were born in Wales. Thomas and Mary had seven children, all of whom were born in Maryland, the last as late as 1744. (see family tree, end of chapter.)

The Burlington, Ontario historian Helen Langford notes in a March 21 1978 Gazette that: *William's father Thomas, died when William was seven leaving him a legacy of descendancy from the Welsh King David of Cadawallader.*

Leaving aside the possible royal connections to a long dead king, according to another UEL source, William's father Thomas was born in Wales in 1712 and died in 1748 in Baltimore; and was the brother of a Solomon Davis, [Paul L. Bingle] [Solomon has an interesting story of his own beyond the scope of this book.]

In *William Alexander Davis and Thomas Ghent*, Aikman notes: *As a young man, William went to Virginia (Yorktown) where he met and married (1771) Hannah Phillips.* (Hannah was the daughter of David Phillips and Hannah Chase - who had married David in Barbados on January 7, 1737.)

According to Bingle, William and Hannah Davis settled along *Forresters Creek, in the newly created **Orange County, North Carolina where his older brother, Robert had 385 acres.*

On the website, *Native Heritage Project*, there is a June 24, 2012 post stating: Tuscarora Historical location... *villages were located along the Neuse and Roanoke Rivers. Estimated population precontact – 25,000; By 1700 that population was... roughly 5,000.*

It is evident that the Davis family plantations in North Carolina on Forresters Creek were near historic Tuscarora turf.

(*Forresters Creek is an old, no longer used name for a minor tributary of the Neuse River that flows southeast from the Piedmonts into Pamlico Bay.)

[**The term Orange County is modern usage, and is based on former boundaries and earlier county lines: Edgecombe was one such early county that occupied some of the same land as later Orange County.]

On the same webpage is the following information about the

African-American population of that colony just before the Davis-Ghents left America for Upper Canada: *1790 NC Census Data Total 393,751. Free white persons 288,204. other free persons 4,975 (including Indians) Slaves 100,572...* Thus for less than every four free whites there was one slave in North Carolina.

In another *Native Heritage Project* post entitled *A Report on Research of Lumbee Origins* by Robert K. Thomas there is this reference to a small tribe known as the Haliwa as being

part of the Pan-Indian"pot" in the Granville-Edgecombe area in the 1750s. After 1802, I think at least some of the remnants of the Tuscaroras in Bertie County* moved into the Richardson area....

The presence of Tuscarora homelands and Davis plantations on a tributary of the Neuse during the early/mid-1700's creates a high probability as the place of origins for the Groats.

[*The wikipedia entry for Bertie notes: *In 1741 parts of Bertie Co. became Edgecombe Co. & Northampton Co.*,which means that the Tuscarora in Richardson, South Carolina came from Edgecombe NC, a point of interest relative to the wife of Abram Groat's second wife, Sarah Williams.]

William and Robert Davis Family Tree

1. Thomas DAVIS (b. Abt 1708;d.1748-Baltimore Co. MD)
   + Mary WRIGHT (b. Abt 1715)
   2. Robert DAVIS (2) (b. Abt 1730; d. Abt 1781)
      +Jane ROBINS (b. Abt 1739; d. Aug 1794-Ancaster)
         3. Robert Jr DAVIS (2) (b.1762; d.20 Oct 1825)
         3.   John UEL DAVIS (2) (b.1759; d.23 May 1827-Norfolk)
         3.   Thomas UEL DAVIS (2 (b. NC 4 May 1765- 1822 UC)
   2. William UEL DAVIS (1) (b.23 Dec 1741; d.1834 Nelson
      + Hannah PHILLIPS (b.1745; m.'71; d. Mar '93 UC
      3 Elizabeth DAVIS b: 29 OCT 1772 d: 21 JUN 1841
         + Thomas GHENT b: 1770 d: 15 MAY 1824
         4 Mary GHENT b: 19 OCT 1794
            + Thomas BARNES b: AFT 1790
         4 William GHENT b: 23 OCT 1796 d. Ap. 15 1848
            Glen Allen/ Queens Bush
            + Mary FONGER b: 1803 m 1818
         4 Sarah GHENT b: 1 AUG 1798 d. 22 AUG 1841
            + James DAVIS b: 28 MAY 1798 d. 24 APR 1864
      3. Asahel DAVIS (1) (b.24 May 1774 d. 24 Mar 1850)
         + Ann MORDEN (b. Abt 1775; m. 2 Jun 1796)

4 Gilbert (executor of the will of Michael of Nelson)
3. William Jr DAVIS (1) (b.12 May 1776)
   + Mary LONG (b. Abt 1780)
3. Jonathan DAVIS (1) (b.25 Jan 1783;d.1857)
   + Jane LONG (b.1788)
3. Kezia DAVIS (1) (b.27 Apr 1785-NC)
   + John Jr CLINE (b.5 Jun 1783-Hagerstown,MD;
3. Mary Jane Davis
        + James Gage Jr. June 25th, 1774 Greenbush N.Y.
        4 Asahel Gage Sept 28 1798- July 1 1861
        + Nancy McCollum 1801-1847
        5 Mary Ann Nov 16 1824 1-1919
        +John Chrysler 1816-1895
3 Sarah Davis + John Chisholm

Grote-Groat Origins

While no evidence exists of where the Grote-Groat name was
first used by Mike Sr. and then his children (beyond the 1794
petition) the last name itself has three origins. The earliest
would have been among the German Palatines who arrived in
Upper New York State in 1710, settling in the Hudson River
Valley, the Mohawk River Valley, and finally the Schoharie
Valley.*

The above-mentioned Palatine immigrants had been
cannon-fodder refugees from religious wars in Germany.
Having been displaced from their homes they managed to get
themselves to Britain to seek help from the newly installed
Hanover monarch, George the First, the German prince who
had just succeeded Queen Ann (the last of the Stuarts) as
monarch of England. The English however, were having a hard
enough time adjusting to a German-speaking King and court,
and had no patience for a
horde of impoverished Germans religiously allied to the
Huguenot/Presbyterians of France and England, and so the
King redirected the Palatines to the Thirteen Colonies.

[*The valley played a critical role in the Revolutionary War, and from which
came the Loyalist Chryslers, the so-called Blue-eyed Indians who served
with the Butler's Rangers.) The Chrysler connection is of interest since
Michael of Nelson willed Mike's Sr.'s farm to his own grandson, James
Chrysler.]

About 300 of those Germans ended up in North Carolina. It is presumably among that group that the first Grote/Groats of any colour could have arrived in that colony a few decades before the Welsh Presbyterian Davis-Ghents. (When William Davis arrived in Saltfleet township, Upper Canada, he founded an Auld Scots Kirk. Michael of Nelson was listed as a Presbyterian in the 1842 census.)

Without being able to say for certain that Mike Sr., signee of the 1794 free negro petition, was descended from slaves owned by German Huguenots, the reality is that the Palatine settlers tended not to own slaves, though blacks were not being the only slaves in the colonies, so the Grote/Groats may have themselves become indentured; then enslaved and then married blacks.

Ramapough DeGroats

A second possibility for the origins of the Groat name, is one that can be found in an anthropological study involving what began to be identified in the 1970's as 'tri-racial isolates', clans of mixed-race blacks, whites and natives.

In 1974, Rutgers University Press published *The Ramapo Mountain People* by David Steven Cohen, which deals with a tri-racial group of people who lived in the Ramapough Mountains, mountains which are defined as: *A loose geographic designation covering the area where the four counties of Orange and Rockland, N.Y. and Passaic and Bergen, N.J. meet.*

Cohen also notes that the people he studied: *then known as "the Jackson Whites" were descended according to legend from Hessian deserters, escaped slaves, Tuscarora Indians migrating from North Carolina to New York, and a group of Revolutionary War prostitutes known as "Jackson"s Whites" and "Jackson"s Blacks" after the man who allegedly solicited the ... women.*

Cohen however, argued that *the surnames Van Dunk, De Groat, and De Freese were Dutch names, not German as would have been the case with Hessian soldiers...*

Suggestively for us, he mentions a report entitled *"A Branch of the Ramapough DeGroat family of upstate New York, Ontario, Wisconsin and Minnesota...* However, he never discusses James DeGroat, the man traced, so there is no proof they were our

Groats, although Steve Williams of the Six Nations of the Grand and Leroy Doslon an elder of Canadian Delaware-Munsee both wrote letters in 1995 supporting the Ramapough claims. [p3] (Again, Abram Groat's second wife was a Williams and he, she (and Simon) lived near the Munsee in Caradoc.)

Cohen also compiled genealogies of the most common surnames...and proved that they were descended from free black landowners who were culturally Dutch... *These families were a small part of what Cohen called the "Afro-Dutch" population in New York and New Jersey, the most famous among whom was the abolitionist and feminist leader Sojourner Truth...*

Their claim was that they were descended from "pure-blooded Indians of the Iroquois and Algonquin [sic] nations," for the first time suggesting that they might have Lenape or Delaware ancestry, the indigenous Indians of Pennsylvania, New Jersey, and southern New York State... the community was also known to have spoken English and Jersey Dutch in the past."

The story of tri-racial isolates involves over 200 clan groups, and form narratives parallel to the Groat-Mike stories.

The alluded-to migration of the Tuscarora out of North Carolina on their way to being adopted as the sixth tribe of the Haudenosaunee, began in the Great Dismal Swamp of North Carolina where the tribe's survivors fled following the so-called Tuscarora Wars in the early 1700's. Slaves hiding out in the Swamp are known to have been adopted into the tribe.

After leaving the Great Dismal Swamp together, the mixed Tuscarora went north and eventually arrived in the Niagara region in the late colonial period; they settled near Lewiston, New York, near the Niagara River Whirlpool. After the defeat of the British, 129 of the Tuscarora crossed into Upper Canada and settled at the Grand River: their numbers, as noted, were recorded in the 1785 census of the Grand River Reserve.

The non-Six Nations of that census included some Lenape-Delaware, some of whom later settled Moraviantown on the Thames River. William of Tuscarora, according to the 1852 census of Tuscarora township, was born on the Grand River in 1783, which means that he almost certainly had a native mother, since there weren't any white women in the colony

before it was one, least of all on land about to be ⁻ or just ⁻
bought from the Mississauga and given to the Six Nations.
Thus, it is also conceivable that Mike Sr.'s "wife' was a Lenape⁻
Delaware, or his Groat origins were Dutch from the
Ramapough mountains, and that he met the Davis⁻Ghents in
Saltfleet township. The truth may or may not be found in the
family tree of the Ramapough James Degroat, and why both
Steve Williams and Leroy Dolson supported the claim of the
Ramapough for recognition as a tribe. It is possible that the
Groats and DeGroats are not related.

Scots Groats

The third and final European group that could have
supplied the last name Groat to the family were the Scots. A
groat is the Scots' word for the British four cent silver coin
known as the fuppence, which was the price of the ferry from
the northernmost point of mainland Britain ⁻ Lands End at
John O'Groats ⁻ to the Orkney Islands. The ferry was originally
run by a Dutchman named Johannes DeGroat, so there again
is the Dutch connection. However there are scores of Scots
Groats immigrants to the 13 colonies in the earliest years of the
British administrations, some of whom were Scots⁻Irish.

A Groat/Fuppence from the time of Edward II

The Scots Irish also have the dubious honour of being the
source of the largest number of white slaves in North America.

In a an online* document called *Irish Slavery in America* the
writer notes *First serious enslaved African conspiracy in Colonial
America, Sept. 13. 1663 Servant betrayed plot of White servants and
enslaved Africans in Gloucester County, Va. ... given that it's 1663,*

these white servants were probably Irish slaves captured and sold during the heyday of the Irish slave trade (1649-1657) under Cromwell. The Cromwellian (i.e., Puritan) government in Ireland gave the slave monopolies to good Puritan merchants who then sold them on to other good Puritan merchants in the Caribbean, Virginia, and New England. (The Royalists/Anglicans got nearly nothing out of the Irish slave trade.)

While the document seems to begrudge the Puritans for not having given a cut of the white slave trade to Royalist/Anglicans, Cromwell's military-mercantile protectorate played an important role in establishing mixed-race slavery in the early years of the Thirteen Colonies.

Since many of the enslaved Scots-Irish would have found themselves living among African and native slaves owned by the Puritans (whose British power lasted for about forty years starting in the 1640's) clans of mixed-race families would have emerged over the century and a half before the Revolution.) There is no evidence that the ancestors of Mike Sr. were former white slaves, but it might once again account for the name Groat (African slaves had no last names in America, while Scot's Irish ones did.)

In the 1852 census of Canada West (Ontario), there are Irish-born 'coloured-negroes' who show up in mixed families in places like Nelson township and elsewhere throughout the province, so it is conceivable that some might have been former Puritan slaves or British, and freed after 1833.

In the days of the Revolutionary War and before, many white slaves began their lives in the colonies as indentured servants who were never freed once their contracts were completed, a common occurrence in early America. (Not all holders of servitude contracts were slavers: William Davis' father, Thomas, had worked off his passage to the colony by becoming an indentured servant, but once his contract was fulfilled he and his wife were free to start their own plantation.) The Palatine Huguenots had likewise been indentured servants, and were known as Redemptioners, having arrived in North America by indenturing themselves to sea captains to pay back (redeem) the cost of the ocean crossings, but once in the colonies, the bond would be auctioned or sold by the Captain to those on land needing workers or house servants et al. Many ended up slaves.)

It was the Scots-Irish, however who arrived in North Carolina as slaves in the largest numbers. In *Henry McCulloch, Esq. - A Man of Mystery Uncovered*, on a webpage entitled *The Royal Colony of North Carolina*, is this history:...*the introduction of the Scots-Irish in North Carolina is concisely stated by the Rev. J. Rumple, D.D., in the Home Magazine of March 1881, as follows:*

"In June 1736, Henry McCulloch, from the province of Ulster, Ireland, secured a grant from George II of 64,000 acres in the present county of Duplin, and introduced into it between three and four thousand emigrants from his native county. These were the Scots-Irish descendants of the Scots settlers who James I had induced to move to Ireland and occupy the immense domains that escheated to the Crown after the conspiracy of the Earls of Tyrconnel and Tyrone in 1604.

Rumple goes on the widen his history:

About the same time (1730-1740) the Scots began to occupy the lower Cape Fear River region, and after the fatal battle of Culloden Moor, in 1746, great numbers of Highlanders implicated in the rebellion of Prince Charlie emigrated to America, and occupied the counties of Bladen, Cumberland, Robeson, Moore, Richmond, Harnett, and parts of Chatham and Anson. Thus it happened that the Scots obtained the ascendency in the region of the upper Cape Fear, and have retained it till this day.

The French Huguenots and English... migrated from Virginia along with Scottish Highlanders... came from the upper Cape Fear region, also with African-Americans...and settled on the west side of the river on Goshen Swamp, Goshen was south of the Great Dismal Swamp) deep inland in north central North Carolina.

And ...later...Presbyterians ...established the Goshen congregation in 1736... called the Grove... it was the first Presbyterian church in the state and is still active today. Once again, we have a source for Scots last names and Presbyterian beliefs.

There were Dutch and German Grote/Groat families in Upper Canada, but it was from the Scots-Welsh Presbyterians that William of Guelph traces his religious ancestry.

The Welsh Tract Loyalists in North Carolina

So how do the Davis-Ghent-Phillips family fit into the above picture, and therefor, how might Mike Sr. have come to live among them in Saltfleet and Nelson township?

John A. Aikman notes that William Davis of Forresters Creek: *soon became a wealthy plantation owner with a large tract of land, a beautiful home, large distilleries and breweries and many black slaves.*

Alongside the Davis' plantation was the Gant (Ghent) family, also of Welsh descent; they became friends as well as neighbours.

In a rootsweb.ancestry web-article on the subject of the *Welsh in North Carolina*, it is noted that: *The Welsh settlements in the Carolinas were settled from the Welsh Tract in Pennsylvania, (later New Castle County, Delaware) in the early eighteenth century.*

The Welsh who migrated to the Carolinas were Calvinists; those going to North Carolina were Presbyterians from Pencader...as early as 1725...

Pencader is where Maryland meets Virginia at Pennsylvania's southeast corner, it is also a place where the Welsh married into the tribes of the so-called five Civilized Nations (which is not a reference to the Iroquois but to the Cherokee, Choctaw, Muskogee, Chickasaw and Seminole.)

There was a Rachel Davis in Loudoun County, Virginia who is not necessarily related, but her story provides parallels to the Davis-Ghents, since her family *came from Pembrokeshire, Wales where they founded Cilfowyr Baptist Chapel in the beautiful parish of Manordeifi. The entire Davis family, together with another family named Phillips, left Wales on a small ship out of Cardigan Bay. They first landed in Pennsylvania, where they helped found the Church in the Great Valley at Tredyffrin Township in Chester County, on the original Welsh tract.*

While it remains difficult to find traces of William's father, Thomas Davis in Baltimore County before the birth of his son, there is a 1748 will called *DAVIS, THOMAS, Back River, Baltimore Co.* from the same year that UEL sources say William's father Thomas died.)

To sons Robert, William, & Daniel Davis, equ. div., after the mtge. is paid, part of Norwich, 200a on Back River Neck. To wife & extrx., Mary Davis, for life, my dw.(deeds and wills) *plntn,*(plantation)

Dukes Discovery 80a,(acres) *& on her d.,*(death) *to son Thomas Davis. The residue of my p.e.*(personal estate) *to be equ.div. among my 5 sons & my dau. Witn: Christopher Duke, Sarah Duke, John Garner, Walter Dallas. 28 July 1748, sworn to by Sarah Dukes, Dallas, & Garner.*

If the Maryland Davis-Phillips were part of the nearby Pennsylvania Davis-Phillips families of Hazel Davis Clark, then the fact that the former married *into the Cherokee tribe and into other tribes of the 5-civilized tribes* at least brings back to mind the 1785 census* of the Six Nations of the Grand River mentioned earlier, in which there were 129 Tuscarora, and 400 individuals combined from the Delaware, Nanticoke, Tutelo, Creek and Cherokee tribes.) [*Kelsay]

There is no evidence that any individual among the smaller tribes in that census were mixed African-First Nations, not even among the Tuscarora, which is not to say that there weren't any, since it is almost certain that some were. There is later evidence that the Tuscarora of the Grand did have black members as noted in Science Volume 17 (1891):

Mr. J.C. Hamilton M.A., L.L.B., of Toronto, who has devoted much time to the study of "Africans in Canada" is the written authority for the statement that on one of the reserves in Ontario considerable intermixture with the negro had taken place. This opinion is confirmed by Odjidjatekha, an intelligent Mohawk of Brantford, who states that the Tuscarora reserve near that city is the one in question. [p. 85]

There is no evidence of Davis-Ghent marital links to native families or negroes in that time period, but that is not to say that such relationships didn't exist.

Since the UEL clan did not leave North Carolina until 1792-93, nearly ten years after the end of the Revolutionary War, it is instructive to continue considering their experiences in America since they arrived just before Mike Sr. signed the 1794 petition, so, having no evidence to say he wasn't with them, we may as well continue looking at them to understand how and when and why they came, since he may well have come with them.

The Battle of Cowpens

In *Twelve Families: An American Experience,* William F. O'Dell notes: *A great granddaughter* [Nancy Ghent Triller] *of Edward Ghent's stated that General Cornwallis made his headquarters at Edward Gant's plantation during the Battle of Guilford Courthouse [NC, March15, 1781] and that this plantation and that of William Davis were devastated during this conflict.* [O'Dell p. 19]

[Edward Gant was the father of Thomas Ghent who married Elizabeth, daughter of William Davis'. (See family tree at end of the chapter.) The name Gant was changed to Ghent upon reaching Upper Canada.]

The Battle at the Guilford Court House took place on March 15 1781. Before then, the British general, Cornwallis, had burnt his own supply lines in an effort to become mobile enough to catch the rebels prior to the battle at Guilford; he failed to engage them and so retreated to Hillsboro, (ie to Orange County, North Carolina) to rest and revitalize his troops. (Which is when Cornwallis stayed at the Davis-Gants.)

In a genealogy thread it is noted: *Wanda, p. 89: has a writeup on Regulators, him (Gant) being loyal to the Crown & called Loyalists or Tories...*[beastybob/1/data/1481]

The Regulators were much like Upper Canadian Reformers during the 1837 rebellion in Upper Canada, they wanted to regulate the excesses of the Tory compact, not raise arms against the crown. Thus, the pre-Revolutionary War Regulator conflict, was a collision between the older plantation society and lawyers and hustlers intent on dislodging them from the resources they controlled. William Davis, descended from indentured parents who had gained their family a vested interest in plantation society, may have had Regulator sympathies, because by Revolutionary times, as Aikman notes:

When the troubles turned into War in 1775, William (Davis) remained out of the actual fighting although he was a loyal supporter of the King.

UEL historian Paul Tingle tells a different story. He notes that William and Robert both served, and sends readers to the *Muster Roll of Captain Jacob JAMES' Troop of Hussars of the British Legion Commanded by Lieutenant Colonel TARLETON from 25th October to 24th December 1781-Fosters Meadow*

In that record, it is noted that William and Robert Davis were both taken prisoner on January 17 1881. A quick search of the Revolutionary War for that date leads us to volumes of encyclopedic information on *The Battle of Cowpens*, South Carolina.

James' troop is also discussed in a book called *Tories: Fighting For the King in America's First Civil War* in which the author notes that: *when the British evacuated the city (Philadelphia)... Either the entire unit — or former members of it — were first attached to the British Legion (also known as Tarleton Rangers) and the Queen's Rangers.* (Simcoe's regiment.)

The Rangers were commanded by Lieutenant Colonel Tarleton from 25th October to 24th December 1781.

At the Battle of Cowpens, on January 17 1781, Tarleton's mounted troops, including *most of Captain James' men, were mowed down. Tarleton himself fled the battlefield and got away with no more than 250 men.*

On the webpage *Taken from Muster Rolls of Loyalists in the Southern Campaign of the Revolutionary War, *...* the site lists 11 members of Captain James' troop - including William and Robert Davis - as men taken alive. It is not clear how long they were prisoners, but thirteen months after the battle they are still on a list that was finalized on February 23 1782. [* Murtie, June Clark]

Bingle's genealogy chart of the Thomas Davis-Mary Wright family notes: *Robert DAVIS . b. Abt 1730; d. Abt 1781.* Given the uncertainty of the death date and Robert's name on the prisoner list, it is probable that he died as a prisoner, or soon after, either of wounds, disease etc.

That same year, Thomas Ghent's father Edward Gant *was killed by a fall from his horse,* his second fall in two years. *This apparently had nothing to do with the Revolutionary war...* (Bingle)

The chart also places Edward (born Edgecombe N.C. in 1744 and died on May 28 1782) as the son of John Gant and Ann Phillips. Ann was a daughter of David Phillips, which is the also the name of Hannah's father, which could make Thomas Gant and Elizabeth Davis first cousins through their mothers (or there was an earlier David Phillips.) What is interesting to note, is that the Gants did not arrive wealthy, in fact, they also arrived as indentured servants like the Davises.

> *John Gant, arrived in Maryland from Wales in 1737... spent two years working on a tobacco plantation to pay for part of their passage. Then John Gant purchased land in North Carolina and established his own plantation.*

> *When the family moved to Orange County, North Carolina, they became close friends with their neighbour William Davis and his family. John Gant died the year after his son Edward, father of Thomas Gant.* [Maya-Harris...0001/UHP-0181.html]

Edward Gant's plantation consisted of *100 acres on the waters of Little Alamance & Haw River ... later in Alamance Co. [NC]. - 1780 Chatham District tax list by Wm. Rainey - 300 acres, 2 horses &8 cattle.* [beastybob/1/data/1481] (ie Burlington NC)

Clearly the family's wealth was relative to the poverty around them. What wealth they had, however, was arguably earned through the work of their slaves.

At the same time, since many of the early plantation owners were not rich, they would have worked as the overseers of their own projects, and working with people always has a way of humanizing them, assuming the owners were humane to begin with. Which may be why the Davis-Ghents and the Groats continued to live interconnected lives in both Saltfleet and Nelson townships. If the clan had mixed native-African-Welsh blood, it could presumably be proven through genetic testing of descendants.

After the Battle of Cowpens, when William and Robert Davis both became prisoners of war, General Cornwallis (according to the *Bladen Journal's* Stephen Weaver) *turned his army away from Guilford ... 1,400 hungry, ill-equipped, worn-out soldiers who faced a long, dangerous march back to... South Carolina.*

According to John A. Aikman (who has Cornwallis at the Gant and Davis plantations): *The British left and soon after the "Rebels" swept in and completely destroyed the (Davis-Gant) plantations.*

Whether Mike Groat Sr. was with the family at that point, or whether other member or members of his family was or were, the Davis-Gants, according to both of the above Loyalist historians, gathered up what they could and fled to David Phillip's home in Yorktown, Virginia.

On March 14, 1781, Major General Marquis de Lafayette arrived in Yorktown. The 23 year-old leader of 1200 poorly supplied troops had been sent by General Greene to capture Benedict Arnold (who, by coincidence, had become commander of the loyalist forces in Virginia after the death of a Major General William Phillips on May 13.) Phillips, born in 1731,

was descended from an ancient line of Welsh warriors dating back to the period of the Roman conquests of England & Wales.

As he lay gravely ill... British forces in Petersburg were being shelled by the Marquis de Lafayette's cannons positioned in the heights north of the river, today known as Colonial Heights, Virginia. His final words — uttered after a shell struck the home and killed an African-American servant named Molly — are reputed to have been Won't that boy let me die in peace? He and Molly were said to have been buried together...

[surnames.phillips/9391/mb.ashx]

There is no evidence of a family relation between Major General Phillips and the Davis-Phillips, however, that doesn't mean no relation exists, only that it hasn't been found by me. What is almost certainly true, is that the death of Major General Phillips, would have come as a considerable blow to the loyalist Welsh in North Carolina. Things were starting to go seriously sour, William and Robert were still prisoners of war and Edward Gant had fallen off his horse for the first time.

In Aikman's tale, after the destruction of their plantations, the Davis family fled to the *Phillips' home in Yorktown, Virginia...*

John Graves Simcoe (Queen's Rangers) was entertained and cared for by the Phillips and Davis families.)

The loss of Robert and the imprisonment of William may have been another reason why Simcoe became a good friend to the Davis-Ghent-Phillips clan while they were huddled with Cornwallis near Yorktown. Lafayette's army kept guard on them until George Washington sent troops to hem them in for good. Aikman's statement that Simcoe *...was entertained and cared for by the Phillips and Davis families* was probably not the best choice of words for the reality of the growing trauma being experienced by the mixed households - including the servants and slaves – holed up for the last stand of Yorktown.

It is possible that Simcoe had met Robert and William Davis through Captain Jacob James, the commanding officer of the Hussars, since James had been with the Queen's Rangers in 1778. According to an online document in the loyalist collection at the University of New Brunswick (The *Queen's Rangers* had *been created in 1776 and on 15 Oct 1777, command of the regiment was given to Major John Graves Simcoe...on 25 May 1778 he was promoted to the Provincial rank of Lieutenant Colonel.)*

Cornwallis surrendered his army on Oct 19 1781. The war was over for the Davis-Gant-Phillips. If there were any Grote/Groats with them, the war was over for them too.

The Surrender of Cornwallis at Yorktown   Godefroy, François, 1743?-1819

If Mike Sr. was fighting with the Six Nations via the Tuscarora or Delaware-Munsee, he could have been working from Fort Niagara, British headquarters on the south bank of the River before it enters Lake Ontario's southwestern head. So if William of Tuscarora was born on the Grand River in 1783-84, the Revolutionary War was officially over. Mike Sr. and his 'wife' may have been in the Niagara region since 1781 because she was native, possibly Mississauga who 'owned' the area. Mike never petitioned for land to claim a soldier's share. The land he got, he got through Augustus Jones and Chief Brant, which might have been acceptable for his service with the tribes. There is no evidence of what he paid for the property, but somehow or other, he was connected to or reconnected with the Davises.

After the Fall of Yorktown

According to Aikman: *After the surrender, the Davis family, along with Hannah's ill parents, the Phillips, returned to Orange County, North Carolina and tried to re-establish the plantation. They endured a cruel barrage of abuse from the victorious rebels and the harsh taxes. When the elder Phillips died in 1791 the Davis family decided to seek opportunity and remain under British rule in Canada. Simcoe had been made Lt. Governor of the new Province of Upper Canada.* (Aikman)

Author Adrienne Shadd adds these details: *they loaded up a covered wagon with carpets, a grandfather clock, and other fine pieces of furniture, and began the eight-hundred mile journey with twenty horses, their eight children, and "several faithful slaves." Everyone, and many things, including slaves began the 800 mile journey...* The names of the slaves are of course not provided, but Groats could have been among them, even Guires.

The route they took is not given, but the Davis-Gant party had one wagon and twenty horses, so they presumably came by roads when they could, and on trails when they couldn't.

Aikman notes that: *Hannah rode on horseback all the way, sitting proudly on a hunting saddle trimmed with blue velvet, ornamented with a pair of brass powder horns. At one point the horses became stuck in the mire, and seven out of twenty were lost.*

The Hamilton UEL webpage on Davis notes that: *The party finally reached the mouth of the Genesee River (now Rochester area) and realized they could not go any further by land.*

The Genesee River was, at that point, just being recognized as the centre of the Seneca Nation through the Treaty of Canandaigua (Nov, 11 1794).

The Genesee, arising as it does in the Allegheny mountains, later served as part of the Underground Railroad (Howells lived there) but in those first days of the 1793 Fugitive Slave Act, the Davis-Gant-Phillips household would have traveled out of the mountains and down the eastern edge of the limestone river canyons which eventually plunged over High Falls (now in downtown Rochester) before reaching the river flats of the delta on the south shore of Lake Ontario.) They could go no further on land with the cart because the river canyon, falls and flood plains were a barrier to their party moving west by land and presumably winter was coming.

In *Burlington, the Garden of Canada* Martha Craig notes: *Arriving at Rochester during the fall they remained there till the next spring... ie* they wintered in Seneca territory.

Aikman furthers the plot: *Thomas Ghent (husband of Elizabeth Davis) and Asahel Davis (oldest son of William Davis) set off on horseback to Newark (Niagara-on-the-Lake) in search of John Graves Simcoe. They were received and Simcoe sent a government gunboat, the Bear, to bring the entire party to Newark.*

If Mike Sr. had come with the Davis-Ghents in 1793, it may not have been his first time north of the Niagara River, since William Groat of Tuscarora was born on the Grand River around the time of the Mississauga land purchase, Even if Mike only came to Upper Canada in 1793 it explains how he came to be one of the free negro petitioners of 1794.

While he may not have been a slave, Mike Sr. could have been freed by the Davises at any time; or he could have been freed as soon as he entered the colony, by virtue of Simcoe's slave importation ban. Whoever the faithful slaves were - who came to Canada with the remnant of the Davis-Gant-Phillips clan - they too were probably a remnant.

As for how Simcoe became commander of the new colony, in the *Muster Books and Pay lists for the Queen's Rangers* held in the library at the University of New Brunswick, the online backgrounder notes that: *The Queen's Rangers was taken with the British Establishment on 25 December 1782, and at the end of the war the Regiment was disbanded in Saint John, New Brunswick (then Nova Scotia...) In 1802, the Queens Rangers as a unit was disbanded, only to be revived and reorganized as the militia of York County* (a militia that included the Dundas Road patrolers) *in the War of 1812-1814 and in the Rebellion of 1837.*

After spending a brief period in England after the loss of the Thirteen Colonies, Simcoe was made Lt. Governor of Upper Canada reporting to Sr. Frederick Haldimand, the Governor General, who was stationed at the citadel of Quebec City, overseeing what remained of British North America.

The Davis-Ghents had wanted to settle with other 'Orange County' North Carolina Loyalists, including Thomas, the son of William Davis' deceased brother, Robert: the first of the larger Davis family to come to Upper Canada (1790.) Thomas Davis, his brother John and mother Jane settled first in Wentworth County and then moved on to the north shore of Lake Erie at Long Point in Norfolk County. Two of William Davis' three surviving brothers *are supposed to have emigrated to the Maritime Provinces after the American Revolution.*

Due Bills Presented

Davis took the Due Bills given him by Cornwallis for the supply costs and damages sustained to the plantation, and presented them to Simcoe, who forwarded the documents to London with a note supporting a "Crown Grant" for Davis, Claims for Loyalist losses had stopped being processed in 1790, which is why London turned down the request for land. At that point, as Aikman notes: *Hannah, William's wife, Ghent's mother-in-law, died and was buried at Chippewa.* (Chippewa is a village near Niagara Falls.) Things weren't going much better in the new colony for William Davis than they had gone in the old one.

Bingle notes that with Simcoe's support, William Davis again made a land request: *In the following year, 1794, he petitioned again and ultimately obtained 2,300 acres in Barton and Saltfleet Townships. The sons and daughters of William, including Elizabeth now a Ghent, received 200 acres each. This may have been part of the 2,300 acres above. Thomas Ghent obtained an additional grant of 300 acres adjacent to the Davis property... Of all his Saltfleet and Trafalgar properties his most famous was Harmony Hall, a colonial mansion built at Mt Albion, Hamilton (L34 C6, near where Mud St intersects with Lincoln Alexander Parkway.)*

(It was undoubtedly at that point that the newcomers, including the Groats, met Augustus Jones, the surveyor, who owned 1,200 acres in Saltfleet.)

In John A. Aikman's chapters on Thomas Ghent and William Davis, Aikman paints a portrait of the life that the Groats of Saltfleet township would have lived before they moved to Nelson township.

> The area of land we are talking about is Glendale Golf Club ... the top of the escarpment at Mount Albion (Hamilton/Stoney Creek). Mount Albion owes its existence to William Davis and his family. "Harmony Hall" the Davis' new plantation in the north, included a tannery, distillery, an orchard, a herd of Ayrshire cattle and a saw and grist mill on the Albion Creek. Davis had the Auld Scotch Kirk built... while his mill served as a local hub of commerce and services for the rural countryside.

According to Adrienne Shade in *The Journey from Tollgate to Parkway: African Canadians in Hamilton*, for the first winter

> two log structures were built on the land, one was inhabited by these enslaved individuals....."Harmony Hill" was soon built to replace the...original log cabin. It was a more palatial residence with colonial pillars and a second floor ballroom... the possibility that African slaves were the builders... [Shadd 32]

Since it seems unlikely the Davis family would have been allowed to import slaves into the colony after 1793, free blacks were more likely involved in the construction of Harmony Hill.

Aikman adds: *In 1806 Thomas Ghent (bought) 205.5 acres of land from Joseph Brant. The land was very good for growing fruit trees. The families had brought fruit seeds from North Carolina... They became part of the group of founders of the fruit growing industry in Burlington.* (1806 is also the year Mike Sr. bought land.)

In *The Garden of Canada, Burlington, Oakville and District*, Martha Craig notes of the Davis-Ghents and their first forays into Nelson township : *They had lived in Saltfleet long enough to raise apples from seed. The young trees they dug up...(and they) brought them in a canoe across the bay, carried them through the forest, and cleared the land on the new homestead, where they were planted. Those trees grew and prospered...*

> *Mr. Ghent chose an elevated position to avoid the tamarac swamp,*

which occupied the land where Burlington Station now is. They had all the difficulties, dangers and trials of new settlers, but these they grappled with and overcame.

According to Aikman: *Around this time Asahel Davis... also purchased property in Brant's Block ...in "Freeman".*

Freeman

The area became known as Freeman only after Joshua Freeman built a house on the corner in 1818. He was an Englishman whose father immigrated from Yorkshire to Nova Scotia in 1756. Joshua came to Upper Canada in 1816; he was a farmer on Plain's Road but his two eldest sons, Edwin and Wesley, ran the general store and post office, as well as owned the Hamilton-Nelson Road Company which operated and maintained the toll road from the Guelph Line to the Valley Inn at the west end of Burlington Bay (ie Burlington Heights). The year Freeman built his cabin,1818, was the year the Guelph Line opened and the settlement of East Flamborough and Eramosa townships began.

Joshua Freeman married Elizabeth Black, the eldest child of Reverend William Black. According to *The Historical record of the posterity of William Black*, the Reverend was a white Baptist and his circuit included Eramosa. The Wellington County Museum has his baptismal record book, but otherwise nothing but the above family posterity record remains of Black. Freeman was also a Baptist. There was, however, no Baptist church in Burlington before 1850. The Freeman cemetery now sits just south of the QEW highway.

Burlington was originally known as Port Nelson, because of the small port formed on the lake side of the sandbar that shields the mouth of the Bay. The sandbar was created by silt from the mouth of Lamabinicon Creek. Burlington historians claim that *lamabinicon* is a Mississauga word, but the only place the word occurs on the internet is in Burlington. However, since the French were allies of the Mississauga, and since they controlled the north shore of Lake Ontario before the Six Nations, then a creek named La Mabinicon begins to resemble The Trout Head Creek, via the French word *la* and the Anishnabe word *mabinicon*.

Eventually the waterway became known as Rambo Creek, after a Loyalist family* of that name; now it is simply called Indian Creek. Its mouth was where Augustus Jones' began his survey of the Baseline that still bears his name.

*Rambo Creek is named after a man of Swedish descent, Elias Rambo/Rambough son-in-law of a Butler's Ranger who originally lived in Marbletown, Ulster Co., New York, and who died in 1809 in Nelson (which was then half the size of the later township created in 1818 when the Guelph Line became a trail north into southern Wellington County.)

If, as Charlie Davis told Arlene Noble, there are 'coloured people' buried in the Davis plot at Freeman or on the Davis farm itself, the most likely people are the Groats and/or Guires.

The Black Peers of Mike Sr.

The Petition of Free Negroes, submitted to Lieutenant Governor Simcoe on June 29th 1794, contains the following names: *Jack Baker, Jack Becker, John Cesar, John Dimon, Tom Frey, John Gerof, Peter Green*, Michael Grote, *John Jackson, Adam Lewis, Peter Ling, Richard Pierpoint, Pompadour, John Smith, Saison Sepyed, Simon Speck, Robert Spranklin, Thomas Walker* and *Jack Wurmwood*.

Considering that these names are the only list of free blacks in Upper Canada available from the earliest days of the colony, and the fact that the men are seeking land together in a single settlement area, it suggests that they all knew one another, or at least knew of one another through one another. How the petition came into being doesn't seem to be known.

The fact is however, the petition was refused, which led to the dispersal of the group, if group is even the right word for whatever relationship they had before the submission of the petition.

Most of the names on the list are difficult to trace, including all the men listed before Grote. Saison Sepyed is as mysterious as his name, even Google can't make sense of the name beyond links to the petition names, which would have been hand written, and thus might be read differently by different transcribers. There are also no traces of Peter Ling although there is a Joseph Lings in the 1842, Barton twp census records.

Next to nothing has been written about any of the men on the list with the exception of Pompadour and Richard Pierpoint - Captain Dick - about whom much has been written, including the recent *A Stolen Life*, by David and Peter Meyler which details Pierpoint's African origins, slavery, loyalism and death in Wellington County in what would later become Fergus. Considerable research has already been done on Pierpoint, so we'll skip his story. His time in Wellington will be examined in *Exodus and Arrival.* There is an exhibit on him at the Museum.

Pompadour was a servant of the Colonial Administrator, Peter Russell, and we will return to him later in the chapter.

Some of those who signed the 1794 petition had been *soldiers during the late war between Great Britain and America, and others ... were born free with a few who have come into Canada since the peace...* Four men men were Rangers: Pierpoint, Baker Cesar and Simon Speck. Lewis was a free black from New Jersey, the rest may have been like Mike Sr., either new arrivals *since the peace*, or men who had been born free or freed because they entered the colony *since the peace* and after the 1793 ban on slave importation, ie, among the first black escapees in Upper Canada to have outrun the American Fugitive Slave act of that same year.

Butler's Rangers was a British Revolutionary War unit

raised in New York by Colonel John Butler; it had a company of a hundred men. There were rumours of there being between two and over a dozen slaves in the unit fighting for the promise of freedom made to them by the British. Some historians dismiss the idea of there having been blacks in the regiment at all. The evidence, however, suggests otherwise. Mike Sr. probably did not serve with the Rangers, since he seems to have made no other land claim after 1794, while several of the others did. Mike Sr. was however, the only one to buy land from Joseph Brant, perhaps the only black to do so, a curiousity in itself.

The Butler's Rangers were led by Pennsylvania Captain William Caldwell, and they fought with Joseph Brant and his tribal confederacy, ranging from western New York and Pennsylvania to Virginia, Ohio, and Michigan, wintering at the the Niagara River mouth at the southwest end of Lake Ontario.

In a website* posting entitled *Days of the Flockey* by Jeff O'Connor, there is an article that notes:

> On August 13, 1777, the American Revolution's long and brutal path toward independence came to the grain-rich Schohary district of Albany County, New York.
>
> It had been a summer of great tumult on the New York frontier. Two British armies were invading... from Canada, through the Champlain and Mohawk waterways. A third army was poised to march up the Hudson... Severance of New England from the central and southern colonies was the ultimate goal...
>
> A growing corps of loyalists in Albany and Tryon counties stirred to action. Adam Crysler of Vrooman's Land in the Schohary Valley recruited some 70 men and most of the Schohary Indians to join Burgoyne. Other crown supporters in surrounding settlements raised more than 200 and waited to join those at Schohary...
>
> The loyalists had retreated to Crysler's farm in the upper part of Vrooman's Land, which was near a low, flat flood plain referred to by the native Germans as "Die Flache." A stand was made and Harper's mounted column was ambushed. Despite the loss of a lieutenant and several wounded, the Light Horse charged and drove McDonnell's and Crysler's forces ...out of the valley.
>
> The loyalists were scattered, but hardly beaten. They would return to Schohary many times to destroy the precious grain crop and try

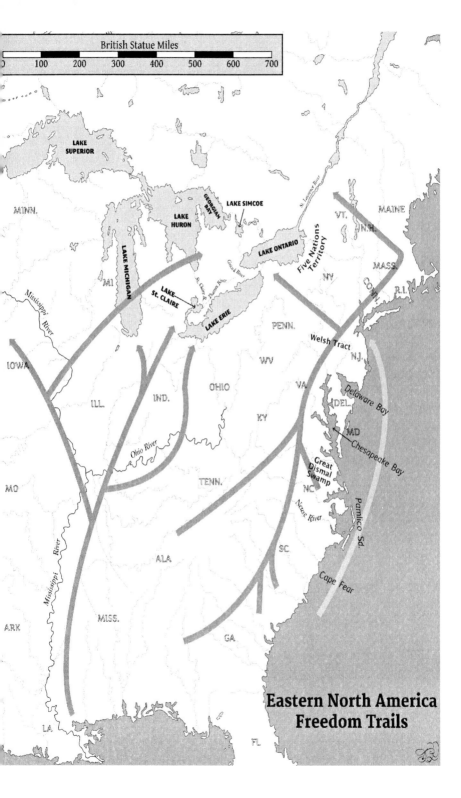

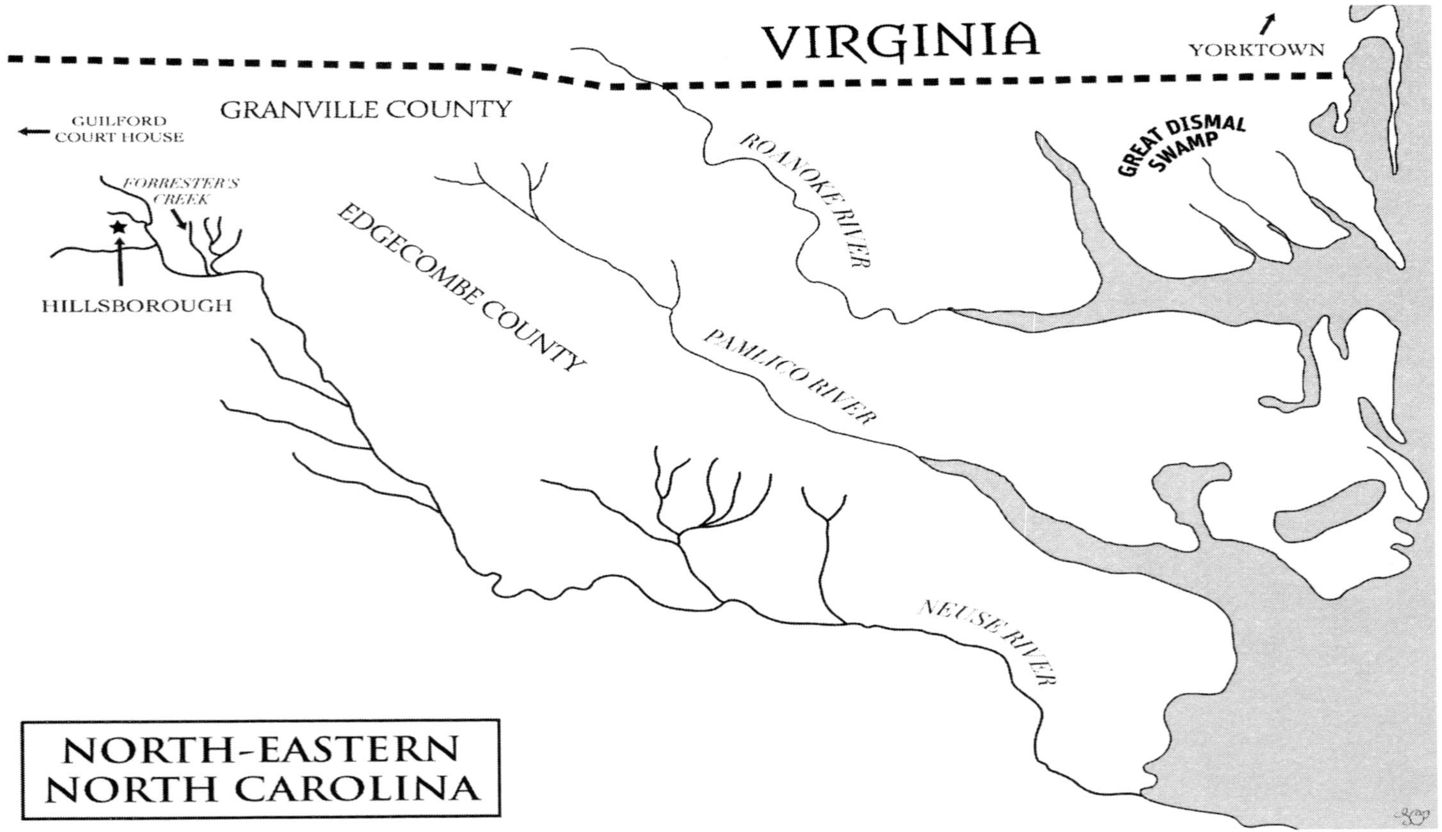

NORTH-EASTERN
NORTH CAROLINA

HILLSBOROUGH

GUILFORD
COURT HOUSE

FORRESTER'S
CREEK

GRANVILLE COUNTY

EDGECOMBE COUNTY

PAMLICO RIVER

ROANOKE RIVER

NEUSE RIVER

VIRGINIA

GREAT DISMAL
SWAMP

YORKTOWN

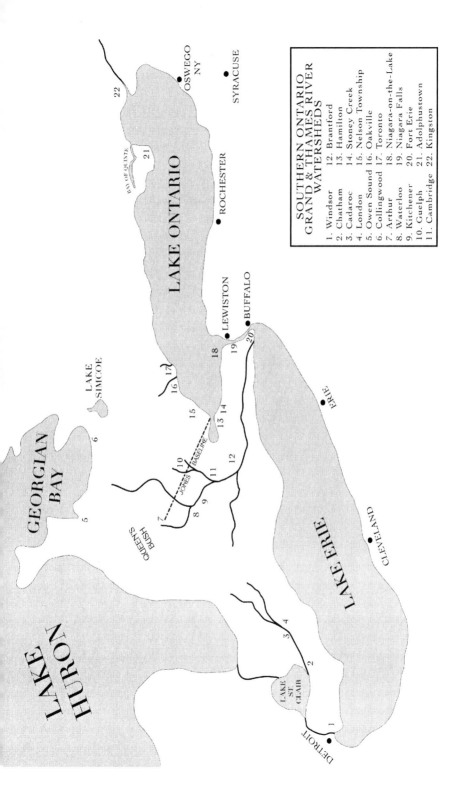

SOUTHERN ONTARIO
GRAND & THAMES RIVER
WATERSHEDS

1. Windsor   12. Brantford
2. Chatham   13. Hamilton
3. Cadaroc   14. Stoney Creek
4. London   15. Nelson Township
5. Owen Sound   16. Oakville
6. Collingwood   17. Toronto
7. Arthur   18. Niagara-on-the-Lake
8. Waterloo   19. Niagara Falls
9. Kitchener   20. Fort Erie
10. Guelph   21. Adolphustown
11. Cambridge   22. Kingston

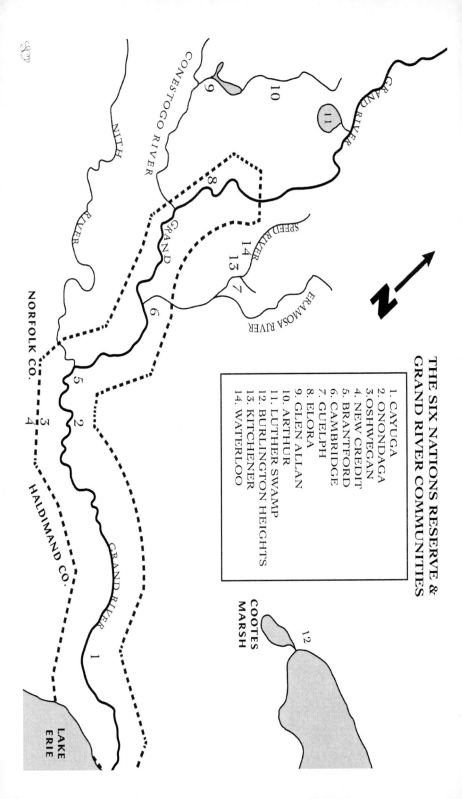

THE SIX NATIONS RESERVE &
GRAND RIVER COMMUNITIES

1. CAYUGA
2. ONONDAGA
3. OSHWEGAN
4. NEW CREDIT
5. BRANTFORD
6. CAMBRIDGE
7. GUELPH
8. ELORA
9. GLEN ALLAN
10. ARTHUR
11. LUTHER SWAMP
12. BURLINGTON HEIGHTS
13. KITCHENER
14. WATERLOO

COOTES MARSH

LAKE ERIE

NORFOLK CO.

HALDIMAND CO.

GRAND RIVER

CONESTOGO RIVER

NITH RIVER

GRAND RIVER

SPEED RIVER

ERAMOSA RIVER

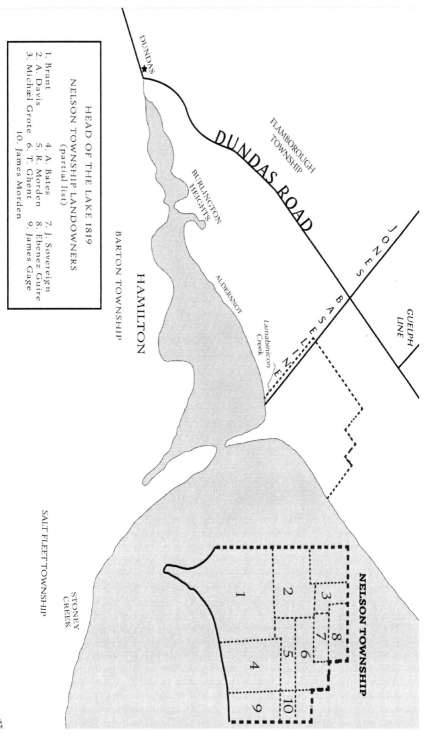

HEAD OF THE LAKE 1819
NELSON TOWNSHIP LANDOWNERS
(partial list)

1. Brant   4. A. Bates   7. J. Sovereign
2. A. Davis   5. R. Morden   8. Ebenez Guire
3. Michael Grote 6. T. Ghent   9. James Gage
10. James Morden

DUNDAS

FLAMBOROUGH
TOWNSHIP

DUNDAS ROAD

JONES

GUELPH
LINE

BURLINGTON
HEIGHTS

BASE LINE

ALDERSNOT

Lamabinicon
Creek

BARTON TOWNSHIP

HAMILTON

SALT FLEET TOWNSHIP

STONEY
CREEK

NELSON TOWNSHIP

1

2

3

4

5

6

7

8

9

10

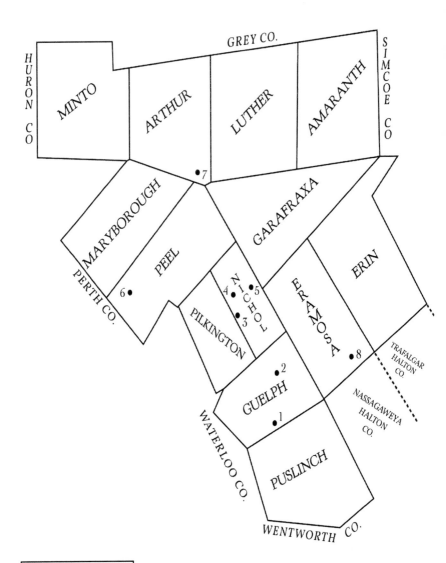

GREY CO.

HURON CO.

MINTO

ARTHUR

LUTHER

AMARANTH

SIMCOE CO.

MARYBOROUGH

PEEL

• 7

GARAFRAXA

ERIN

PERTH CO.

• 6

NICHOL

4 •
• 5

• 3

PILKINGTON

ERAMOSA

• 8

TRAFALGAR HALTON CO.

• 2

GUELPH

• 1

NASSAGAWEYA HALTON CO.

WATERLOO CO.

PUSLINCH

WENTWORTH CO.

TOWNS & VILLAGES

1. GUELPH
2. MARDEN
3. ELORA
4. SALEM
5. FERGUS
6. GLEN ALLAN
7. ARTHUR
8. ROCKWOOD

MAP OF
WELLINGTON COUNTY
Townships Circa 1880

*to reclaim property and family left behind. What resulted was a long, brutal struggle fought within and around what is now Schoharie County. *theoldstonefort.org*

As mentioned before, the name Chrysler has a connection to Michael of Nelson through his grandson James Chrysler, to whom he left Mike Sr.'s land. The above-named Chryslers not only appear to be the source of all white loyalists of that name in early Upper Canada, but blacks of that last name are also descended from their many slaves, more on which later.

Adam Crysler was a Butler's Ranger, and it was on behalf of his family that the Rangers were involved in a particularly savage set of attacks in Schoharie while under his command. The attacks were triggered when Balthus, the youngest of the Crysler brothers, was dragged out of his Schoharie home in front of his wife and soon after executed. The subsequent revenge massacre sullied the reputation of the Rangers, after which Crysler was warned to keep his native command in check, and which he subsequently did.

As for Simon Speck, he appears in a document called *Names Only But Much More* by Janet Carnochan, published in the Niagara Historical Society no. 27, where he is listed in the Muster Roll of Butler's Rangers, signed by Jacob Ball*, 1ˢᵗ *Lieut.*

1783, in which it is stated: Simon Speck Gone by express to Oswego in January of that year, ie, before the war ended.

(*Jacob Ball's son will make an appearance in book two, as a Guelph Presbyterian minister married to a sister of the abolitionist Globe newspaper editor, George Brown. (Balls Falls above Stoney Creek is named after the family.)

Speck was back in Upper Canada for the 1794 petition, and having failed to receive land, re-petitioned at Niagara on

27 May 1796 . . . "The Petition of Simon Speck – late of Butlers Rangers – who never received any Certificate but the one annexed– & never located any Land—Respectfully shews, That your petitioner is desirous to settle on the lands of the Crown in this Province, being in a condition to cultivate and improve the same. That he has taken the usual oaths, and subscribed the declaration, that he professes the Christian Religion, and obedience to the laws, and has lived inoffensively in the country. Prays your Excellency, would be pleased to grant him three Hundred acres of land in the

*township above the Delaware Village on the Thames, or such other
quantity of land as to your Excellency in your wisdom may think
meet. And your petitioner as in duty bound will ever pray."
[Unsigned] Read in the Executive Council on 13 Jul 1796. Ordered
recommended to be confirmed in 300 acres.*
[Upper Canada Land Petitions LAC "S" Bundle 2, Petition Number 38]Land Board
Ticket attached to the Upper Canada Land Petition of Simon Speck]

Not only was the petition confirmed, but Speck was granted
the three lots he sought:. *"Simon Speck Ranger Three Lotts Board
[Signed] P Frey"* [UC Land Petitions LAC "S" Bundle 2, Petition Number 56a]

P Frey, (Philip) who signed the petitions, was the Acting
Surveyor General, and the surveyor in charge of Niagara and
Detroit; Frey was also Augustus Jones' boss in the 1790's. It is
also possible that Phillip Frey may have been the former owner
and/or father of the free negro petitioner Tom Frey.

Simon Speck probably ended up living in Caradoc township
on the Thames where Mike Sr.'s probable son Simon
Grote/Groat eventually settled, but there appear to be no other
records of Speck, be they census, burial or other. There are
however, African-identified Speck's in the 1871 Census of the
St. Lawrence community of Cornwall, which has Mohawk
Reserves on either side of the river in Canada and the United
States. Since Speck had served in Oswego across the lake from
the river mouth, perhaps Simon ended up near Kingston.

Three other men on the 1794 petition were also Butler's
Rangers according to Nancy Butler in her 1993 work, *Slavery
and Freedom in Niagara*: John Baker, John Becker and John
Cesar. [Butler 17]

John Baker left a record of land petitions in which his name
is also spelled Becker, which makes the free negro petition
names Baker and Becker more fluid as well, and again, since I
have not seen the original 1794 petition, perhaps John
Becker/Baker is the same man.

The preamble of Baker's 1796 claim is identical to Speck's:
*Upper Canada Land Petition of John Becker [sic] dated at Niagara
on 12 May 1796 ... "The Petition of John Becker [sic], late a Private
Soldier in Butlers Rangers and who never received any Land—
Respectfully shews, That your petitioner is desirous to settle on the
lands of the Crown in this Province, being in a condition to cultivate*

*and improve the same. That he has taken the usual oaths, and ...
Prays your Excellency, would be pleased to grant him Three
Hundred acres of land as a discharged Ranger..." [Unsigned]
Received at the Executive Council Office on 30 May 1796 and read in
Council on 13 Jul 1796. Ordered it appearing from the papers
annexed that petitioner intends to sell his lands. It is presumed he
does not mean to become a settler. The Committee do not
recommend therefore the prayer of the petition. Read again in the
Executive Council on 14 Jul. Ordered recommended for 200 acres.*
[Upper Canada Land Petitions LAC "B" Bundle 2, Petition Number 9]

Ralfe Clench, Lieutenant of Butler's Rangers and others
attested to Baker/Becker's time with the unit. *"The Bearer John
Becker [sic] served as a Soldier in Capt Butlers Company of Butlers
Rangers, during the late American War—[Signed] R. Clench, Lt
Late Rangers, Thos Butler, Lt late Rangers, Andw Bradt Capt. Late
Rangers."* [UCLand Petitions LAC "B" Bundle 2, Petition Number 15]

Andrew Bradt, who supported Baker's claim, was the father
of George Bradt who married Abigail Guire, daughter of
Ebenezer and Jemima (Groat) - daughter of Mike Sr. . Michael
of Nelson also had a daughter named Jemima.

The Free Negro petitioner Peter Green left no trace of his
existence beyond his 1794 signature (that I have yet found.)

Pompadour on the other hand, while he has received less ink
than Pierpoint, otherwise has more words written about him in
history books (rather than petition records) than anyone else
who signed the 1794 document.

According to Adrienne Shadd, Pompadour was *a free Black
who worked for the family (of Peter Russell) for wages.* Peter Russell
was the Colonial Administrator in York from 1790 until his
death in 1808. *The Dictionary of Canadian Biography* begins
their article on Russell by stating: *...office
holder, politician, and judge; b. 11 June 1733 in Cork (Republic of
Ireland), only son of Richard Russell and his first wife, Elizabeth
Warnar; d. 30 Sept. 1808 in York (Toronto), Upper Canada... was
the son of an improvident Irish army officer who claimed without
much evidence to be related to the Duke of Bedford.*

Wikipedia introduces him by stating that he was *a gambler,
government official, politician and judge...* He joined the British
Army to serve in the *Seven Years War* against the French in

North America because of his gambling debts. By 1781, he was a captain at the time that Cornwallis was defeated in Yorktown, and the following year, was superintendent of the port of Charleston.

Peter Russell may have been in Charleston in 1782 after the collapse of the southern campaign, but he returned to England where, once again, he burdened himself with gambling debts. He was sent to Upper Canada in 1790 to help Simcoe administer the colony. Once here, Russell served on the Executive Council and in the Legislative Council, supporting the Lt. Governor's agenda.

Russell lived, (according to Chris Raible in *Scandal and Scurrility in Upper Canada*) in *a grand home... Russell Abbey,* which, like all the other buildings in York - future Toronto — was made out of wood, presumably with timbers of considerable size. In the Toronto publication *Share*, Murphy Browne goes on to say of Russell that he: *remained acting in the position of*
 administrator until 1799 when Simcoe's permanent replacement as Lieutenant Governor... was appointed.

Murphy Brown's comments also include this record and her comments: *"TO BE SOLD:A BLACK WOMAN, named Peggy aged*
 about forty years; and a Black boy her son, named JUPITER aged about fifteen years, both of them the property of the subscriber. The woman is a tolerable cook and washer woman and perfectly understands making soap and candles."
  The boy is tall and strong of his age, and has been employed in County business, but brought up principally as a House Servant - They are each of them Servants for life. The price for the Woman is one hundred and fifty Dollars - for the Boy two hundred Dollars, payable in three years with interest from the day of Sale and to be properly secured by Bond &c. - But one fourth less will be taken in ready Money. PETER RUSSELL York, Feb. 10, 1806

Russell's phrase *servants for life,* is disingenuous, since they were slaves and not indentured servants, but it suggests that he bought Peggy when he came to the colony in 1790, and that Jupiter was born the following year, two years before the anti-slavery act freed the children of slaves born after the act (once they were 25.) Jupiter must have been one of those unfortunates, who did not qualify for freedom except by manumission. That can't have made him a happy slave, so no wonder the family made Russell miserable.

According to Shadd, who published a letter from Russell to a slave agent who had been trying to sell Peggy to Joseph Brant for him, Peggy had just been released on bail paid by Peter, the bail included the stipulation that she *was not permitted by my Sister to enter this House.*

In Elizabeth Russell's diaries, *Peter's sister described Peggy, Pompadour and Milly as dirty, idle and insolent...* Shadd then postulates that *This was classic dissembling, known in today's parlance as "slave resistance," whereby slaves lied and invested in schemes or excuses to get their own way.* [Shadd p 48]

In Sept. 1803, Peggy ran off, forcing Russell to post a public notice so that the readers were *hereby cautioned from employing or harbouring her...* Shadd also suggests that for Peggy truancy became a way of life, a way to disappear but never for good. The reason for her constant returns, were the children.

Browne in *Share** concludes her comments on Pomadour's family with: *When Peter Russell died in 1808, his sister Elizabeth inherited his property, including the Pompadour family - Peggy and her children. Elizabeth Russell eventually gave away Peggy's child, Amy, to her goddaughter Elizabeth Denison as a gift.* [*Share News /

According to Natasha L. Henry in *Talking about Freedom, Celebrating Emancipation Day in Canada,* ... *The only known descendant of the Pompadour family is Amy's son, Duke Denison ...born in 1811... said to have lived until the mid-1800's.*

Duke does not appear in the 1842 or '52 census, unless he is using another name. There are also no African Denisons in the Canadian Census of 1871 (Ontario index.)

Of the rest of the men who signed the 1794 petition, at this point, only Adam Lewis has traceable history, but he will be discussed in a separate chapter because there may be a family link between the Lewises and the Groats. There were other free Loyalist blacks in the colony, but again, little is known about them.

The Lewis Family

Adam Lewis had filed a land petition in 1794 earlier than the one he signed with Mike Sr.. The fist was on Mar. 13 1794.

May it please your Excelency (sic) to take my Complaint into Consideration the people that Lives By me is Determined to Let me Clear No more Land the Land is Lying on the Lake Near the mouth of the thirty mile Creek it is Crown Land that I am Living on or What is Called Broken Land I have But 5 acres under improvement the people have a mind to Bind me up to that small Enclosure Which is to Small A Quantity for me to Subsist Upon I should take it as a great favour of his Excelency if he Would please to grant me some more of this Land. I am Sir your Humble petitioner [Signed] Adam Lewis" Received at the Executive Council Office on 27 May 1794. Ordered referred to the Surveyor General. [Upper Canada Land Petitions LAC "L" Bundle 1, Petition Number 17]

Adam's petition was read in Executive Council on 27 May 1794 and included supporters: *"We whose names are Subscribed Do Certify that the above Named Adam Lewis hath Lived in this Township this four years in wich (sic) time he hath Behaved himself Honestly and Soberly as witness our hands this 4th of March in the year 1794*

[Signed] Crist Buchner, John Adair, David Adair, John Matthews, Thos Matthews, Elias Anderson, Daniel Corson" Read in Council on 27 May 1794. Referred to the Surveyor General. Granted.

Adam Lewis wrote a response dated at Clinton on 26 Aug 1797 that details his origins and time in the province *"Humbly Sheweth – That your Petitioner came into this Province in the Year of 1788 And hath not received any Grant of Lands, And that he was Free Born, and brought a pass into this Country, that he applied to his Excellency John Graves Simcoe Esquire—Governor, and was ordered to enter his Lands in the Surveyor Generals Office, but was informed that the Land was entered to Frederic Willaker since Deceased, who Died without any Heir—that Your Petitioner hath Improved a Lot of Land And Humbly Prays Your Honor would be pleased to Confirm his Grant of Land unto him and Your Petitioner as in Duty bound will Ever Pray [Signed] Adam Lewis"*

Received at the Executive Council Office on 30 Aug 1797. Ordered people of the Petitioner's description are not granted lands unless they have military claims.

The last sentence is significant in two ways, the first is that some accounts claim that Lewis was a Butler's Ranger, when clearly he made no military claims, the second is the clause 'people of the Petitioner's description', presumably meaning that free-born blacks were not granted lands, which was the same result as the free negro petition later in the year.

The story of the 'free-born' Adam Lewis deepens through information in a petition file on his father, Levi Lewis Sr.

dated at Newark (Niagara-on-the-Lake) on 26 Jun 1795 "Humbly Sheweth—That your Petitioner was settled in the now State of New Jersey, on his own Farm, & that by his Industry and frugality had procured a considerable Estate, when the war between Great Britain & America commenced, & that by reason of his not complying with the requisitions of the new System of Government, he was imprisoned in Morris Town and lost great part of his substance;

That in the year 1789 he removed with his Family to this Province, & by reason of Sickness and other misfortunes, has lost the greatest part of what he brought with him; Therefore your Petitioner humbly prays your Excellency will grant him such portion of the vacant Lands of the Crown, as your Excellency in his wisdom may seem meet—And Your Petitioner as in Duty bound will ever pray— [Signed] Levi Lewis"

Postscript: "Your Petitioner also begs to observe that he has a family consisting of a wife and Five children under age and has received 250 acres of Land—he was imprisoned with Mr Pettit" Received at the Executive Council Office on 27 Jun 1795 and read in Council on 27 Jun. Ordered granted 200 acres in addition....

A certificate signed by Nathaniel Pettit and dated on 24 Jun 1795 at 40 Mile Pond was appended to the petition:

"This is to Certify that I was well acquainted with the berer mr Levi Lewis Snr in the State of New Jersey and that he was a man of Good Character and Esteemed an Industres honest man and had a Considerable property in Lands and other Effects in his hands and that by Reason of his attachment to the Crown and Constitution of Great Britain Lost Great part of what he (had)... *and that by a fall about four years past became a Criple and unable to Suport himself and family Certified by [Signed] Nathl Pettit" [Bundle 1, Petition 56]*

(Levis' daughter Hannah married a Saltfleet Pettit. The Pettits were Loyalist family of the Niagara Region. Nathaniel was born in Sussex County, New Jersey in 1724, and appointed a judge there on the court of common pleas in 1766. After 1776, he refused to pay taxes to the rebel government and was imprisoned by the patriots. Once he was released, he moved to the new colony two years before Lewis, where he became a judge and a member of the first Parliament of Upper Canada.)

Morristown, New Jersey where Lewis was from, is in the northeastern part of the state and was originally Lenape-Delaware territory, which immediately echoes the Ramapough and other "tri-racial isolates". The echoes are all we have however, since there is no evidence that the Lewis had anything to with that 'tribe". Levi Sr. was, as his petition notes, a free black imprisoned around the same time as Pettit.

As for Levi Sr.'s quest for land, there is a Townsend Township, Norfolk County document from April 5 1797 deferred to June with the information that land was finally given: *Levy Lewis, Senior Lot 1 Concession 13.* It came too late, however, since the file closed with a notation that 'Levy' had died. [Bundle 3, Petition 62] Clearly, however military claims were not the only ones the government responded to when it came to free-blacks.

Levi Jr., brother of Adam, lived in Saltfleet township and signed a petition dated at Niagara on *2 Sep 1796 "Respectfully shews- That your Petitioner has a Family consisting of a wife & four children, & has been in the Province nine years—That he has received Certificates from the Land Board for 200 acres for himself & 200 Acres family Lands & that he has located on Lots N^o1- in the 2nd& third Concessions of Saltfleet...*
[Upper Canada Land Petitions LAC "L" Bundle 2, Petition # 26]

There can be no doubt that the Saltfleet connection puts the Lewis family in the orbit of the Groats from the beginning.

The fact that the Lewises were free blacks (possibly mixed-race) living on their own land makes them, like the Groats, a natural magnet for the thousands of newly emancipated fugitives entering the colony before and after the establishment of the UGRR.

These Lewises may or may not be connected to the Groat family by marriage, but there are two Lewises who married Groats: Richard, who married Margaret, the daughter of John and Catherine Groat-Mike (She is the Margaret baptized by Reverend Jones alongside her brother Peter in 1833; the other is Mary A. Lewis, who married Simon Grote in the Queens Bush in 1847.) We will return to both couples. Mary however, is listed as German in census records, and Levi Jr.'s wife was a German-American named Mary Beemer, with whom he had a daughter named Mary, born in 1800. Levi appears to be the first 'coloured' politician in Upper Canada, since was elected to the Legislative Council in 1808, and was JP for Gore in 1818.

Groats and the War of 1812

For the Groats of Nelson township, the War of 1812 was certainly nothing compared to the events surrounding the Fall of Yorktown in 1781, however, the head of the lake was of critical importance to the defense of the colony, since Burlington Bay was a large sheltered harbour from which either combatant navy could control the west end of Lake Ontario. It was also through that Bay that the Americans hoped to move through the creeks of Coote's Marsh to the Dundas Road and west via the Governor's Road to Six Nations territory. If they'd won control of the Bay, they could have controlled the region.

The confederacy of First Nations that had fought for the British during the Revolutionary War played a defensive role during the War of 1812. The Americans started the conflict based on President Jefferson's promise that winning would only be a "matter of marching', so most of the actions of the war took place inside Canada, with the exception of retaliatory raids, one of which was aimed at the Lewiston Tuscarora, a story to which we'll return.

Christopher Densmore believes that the American Iroquois were influenced in their decision to avoid a war of aggression through their association with *The Society of Friends*.

The Quakers thought that their primary function among the Seneca was to teach agriculture, that is Euro-American agriculture as the Iroquois were already an agricultural people, and the mechanical arts. ...Quakers provided an ethical basis for minority group survival. The choice before the Iroquois was therefore not simply adopting or rejecting in total the white man's ways, but they could, like the Quakers, be selective in their choices.

Densmore goes on to note:

In September 1812, a Council of Oneida, Onondaga, Stockbridge and Tuscarora addressed the President of the United States on the subject of the war. They reminded the President that "it was the United States government under Washington that had advised them to refrain from shedding blood: this advice was good. Our good prophet of the Seneca tribe... (Handsome Lake) *has given us the same advice, and our tribes have entered into a league to follow that advice. We wish to hold fast to it, and not to take any part in the contest between your people and the British."*

In *Burlington Connections To The War of 1812* that city's museum staff posted original documents from the war relevant to the area's bi-centennial war celebrations, which provide an excellent overview of battles and Nelson township. The narratives in those texts, being first hand, tell themselves, so my focus will be to weave the role of the Groats through the conflicts for control of Burlington Bay and Port Nelson.

There can be no doubt that for loyalist mixed-black families led by men like Mike Sr., the old wounds of the Revolutionary War losses still ached. None of the generations of Six Nations Groats or Mississauga Groat Mikes were born yet, since the eldest of those, Abram, son of William and the Tuscarora Margaret Groat wouldn't be born until 1814, the year William's presumed younger brother Michael of Nelson turned nineteen.

Mike Sr. in Nelson and his probable older sons, William, Peter and Simon - brothers of his certain-son Michael and his youngest, probable son John - would have been as acutely aware of the importance of the head of the lake as anyone.

It's not surprising that when the conflict heated up in 1813, the farmers and orchard workers of Nelson who had been given militia training since the colony was created, constituted part of the 2nd York militia as patrolers of the Dundas Road.

Joseph Brant had died seven years before the start of the new war. His successor as Captain of the Confederate tribes was Chief John Norton. John Brant, Joseph's youngest son, was 19 years old and had since 1802 been living at what is now known as the Brant House on the shore of Port Nelson. John was about the same age as Michael of Nelson. After John's father had died, the old chief's last wife, Catherine Crogan, had stopped living along the shore but several of her children remained.

If Mike Sr. had been married to a Tuscarora, or had fathered at least some children with a Six Nation's woman, he needn't have been on the Grand River to do so, since the Brant home at Burlington was a centre of native activity. Mike's lands and his neighbours' properties were surrounded by Brant holdings.

There is no evidence of what Mike Sr. did during the War of 1812, but it is conceivable that if he had in fact served among the Tuscarora before the Revolutionary war, he may also have fought with the confederated tribes following the American invasions of Upper Canada, more on that in a moment.

The presence of the kinds of settlers that Joseph Brant had sold to in Nelson Township helped prevent US occupation, because Americans never took the head of the Lake, despite repeated efforts to do so by land and water. Thus, First Nations, loyalist and British military efforts at Port Nelson, Burlington Heights and Stoney Creek remain a touchstone of our existence as Canadians. The fact that American tribes largely stayed out of the war also meant that US plans for taking the Niagara Frontier required troops having to face loyalist warriors in their own turf without reciprocal help. And because the Grand was a long, winding, shallow river, they couldn't take Six Nations Territory without controlling Burlington Bay.

The Head of the Lake in War

The Burlington Museum's website, devoted to documenting local War of 1812 actions, begins by noting events at York (Toronto): *On April 27, 1813 the first offensive by the Americans at the western end of Lake Ontario took place at York. Fourteen American vessels and 1,700 soldiers landed... British forces, along with the allied natives and the local militia, were forced to retreat back across the Don River as the Americans occupied the town.*

For six days they exerted control over the local population, finally departing after destroying the Parliament buildings and pillaging and burning much of the city. Thus, the reality of an American invasion of Upper Canada was impressed on everyone's mind...

The website also notes that: *Burlington Heights would prove to be the backbone of defense... Brigadier General John Vincent (British commander in Niagara) reports to his superior Sir George Prevost in Montreal, describing the destruction of the King's Head Inn* (it stood on the Barton township side of the Bay): ..."*the American Flotilla after remaining at anchor at this harbour for three days..., proceeded down the Lake, and the wind being fair for Sackett's harbour it is probable its destination was to that place –*

Some of the smaller vessels remained and continued cruising for several days, between this post and York and previous to their final departure they landed a party of nearly two hundred men at the Head of the Lake for the Express purpose of destroying the Government House and out buildings *

[*Samuel Hatt – the man who bought Joseph Brant's slave Sarah Pooley the year before the old chief died - commanded the Government Inn on the south sandbar Beach in Barton:]

"*The Yankeys.....visited the Head of the Lake with two Schooners and I believe about 200 Men – Major Fitzgerald of the 49th was stationed there, he had about 14 Regulars and 25 Militia under his Command. I met him within two miles of the Beach with a reinforcement of about 30 choice Militia, but he, I think properly too, thought proper to retire to my station at Durand's. The Yankey's burnt the Government House, but did no other mischief, they sailed the next day.*

[The 'beach' referred to is the sand bar created by the silting of the Stoney Creek Delta washing north up the Barton sandbar, extending like a finger towards the Brant house across the mouth of the bay at Port Nelson.]

On May 27, 1813 the tide of war turned in favour of the invaders when the American general, Henry Dearborn, took Fort George on the Niagara River near where it enters Lake Ontario, across from old Fort Niagara.

[The old fort had been abandoned to the Americans by the Loyalists after the Jay Treaty in 1796.]

After the taking of Fort George, the British Commander, Brigadier General John Vincent retreated to Burlington Heights, after dispersing the loyalist militia of Niagara, who though dispersed, continued to report the movements of the Americans to the British. Vincent was followed part of the way by an American brigade commanded by Brigadier General Wm H. Winder, who went as far as 40 Mile Creek, but being outnumbered, waited for his commanding officer, Brigadier General John Chandler's arrival.) The combined strength of 3400 men then moved north up the lake shore to Stoney Creek, where they commandeered James Gage Jr.'s farm.

The British were well alerted by Norton's Mohawks. [Sweeney 137] (Billy Green, the 19 year old son of Loyalists from the plateau, appears to be the person most responsible for what followed since he got word to a Colonel Harvey about the position of the American forces below William Davis' lands.) Harvey in turn informed Vincent at Burlington (Heights) who then wrote to his commanding officer Governor General: *Prevost at Kingston dated*

> *Jun 6, 1813: ...Col. Harvey ...having advanced close to and accurately ascertain(ing) the Enemy's Position, sent back to propose to me a night attack on his Camp...*

[Burlington Heights is at the western end of the Bay overlooking the now widened entrance to Cootes Marsh: a delta of three creeks: Borers, Spencers and Chedoke, the outflow of which kept the original gap open.]

The last stand of the British army from Niagara had established a cantonment on a farm [near the spot where the Peter Jones had been born and on what is now the property of Dundurn Castle.] Vincent chose that site because it allowed him to guard the marsh access to the village of Dundas and the Governor's Road to the Six Nations. The Heights likewise gave him an advantage over American ships in Burlington Bay, though an assault by land *and* water would have surpassed him. Vincent states his case for his decision to Gov. Gen. Prevost on June 6:

> *Tho' strong for a large Body* (Burlington Heights) *is far too extensive for me to hope to make any successful stand in against the superior force understood to be advancing against me in three separate points, Viz: by the Lake, by the center road and by the Mountain on my right.*

(The center road was the road that led through the centre of Barton township (now Hamilton's Queen Street, the shortest route between the Heights and Stoney Creek. The *Mountain on my right* would have been Hamilton Mountain, because Green reported that some of the troops at Stoney Creek had gone up to the plateau at Mount Albion and might discover the way down behind the British position via the Sulphur Spring Valley.

The Attack I knew would not be delayed, I had neither time or inclination... to retreat from my position, I... embraced the proposition of... Harvey... an alternative not only worthy of the gallant Troops under my command, but as offering the best chance of crippling the Enemy, and disconcerting his plans, as well as gaining time for retreat, should that measure still be... necessary.

What followed, was in fact one of the most gallant raids in the War of 1812, its murder and mayhem notwithstanding; facing flight or defeat, Vincent chose instead an act of controlled abandon that must have thrilled every Blue-Eyed Indian among them on their 20 mile/stealth maneuver through the dark of the Barton Lowlands with Norton's Mohawks and Green in the lead. They arrived unannounced. *On the night of June 6, 1813 Colonel Harvey and General Vincent led five companies (700 men) forward against the Americans. [The remainder of his men stayed as a reserve force at the Heights]...When they got to Stoney Creek the sentries were silently subdued by bayonet. The British then stormed the camp taking the Americans by surprise. There was great confusion in the cover and darkness of night and though the Americans tried desperately to defend their position, the British charged the lines that held their guns. During the tumultuous fight two American generals (Chandler and Winder) were captured when their forces abandoned their guns and fell back.*

...The Enemy was completely surpriz'd & driven from his Camp... charged by our brave Troops, whose conduct throughout this brilliant enterprize was above all praise. The Action terminated before day-light... three Guns & one brass Howitzer with their Tumbrils, two Brig. Genls.,

By daybreak, the Americans - having escaped upland with five remaining guns onto the Davis lands of Saltfleet – realized that the British forces were withdrawing with their captured generals &

upwards of a 100 Officers, non commission'd Officers & Privates ... in our hands. Not conceiving it prudent to expose our small Force to the view of the Enemy, who, tho' routed & dispersed, was still formidable, as to numbers & position... the Troops were put in motion at day-break & marched back to the Cantonments.

It was only later that day that the Americans realized that they had outnumbered the British Troops five to one. Having lost most of their command however, US troops found themselves a long way from home without supplies or orders, and with the fear of Indians on the plateau dissolving their courage, they pulled back to Fort George. It would be nearly a month before the British command at Burlington Heights was challenged, this time by water.

Commodore Chauncey's Take

The Burlington Museum War of 1812 document collection also includes an American Naval report of the subsequent 'Battle' of Burlington Heights, written by Commodore Chauncey of the USS General Pike, on Aug 4, 1813:

SIR – After leaving Sackett's harbour, I stretched over for the enemy's shore, and from thence stood up the lake. The winds being light, I did not arrive off this port until the evening of the 27th ult. On the 24[th,] I fell in with the Lady of the Lake, on her return to Sacket's Harbor, with prisoners from Fort George.

I transferred the prisoners to the Raven, and ordered her to Sacket's Harbor; the lady of the lake, I despatched to Fort George for guides, for the head of the lake. Gen. Boyd having informed me, that the enemy had a considerable deposit of provisions & stores at Burlington Bay, I was determined to attempt their destruction. On the 25th I was joined by the Pert and on the 27th, by the Lady of the Lake, with guides and Capt. Crane's company of artillery, and Col Scott, who had very handsomely volunteered for the service.

After conversing with Col. Scott on the subject it was thought advisable to take on board 250 infantry – which were embarked by 6 o'clock next morning, and the fleet immediately proceeded for the head of the lake; but owing to light winds, and calms, we did not arrive to an anchorage before the evening of the 29th. We sent two parties on shore, and surprized (sic) and took some of the inhabitants; from whom we learned, that the enemy had received considerable reinforcements, within a day or two; and that his force, in regulars was from 600 to 800 men.

The landing was almost certainly in Barton, across the mouth of the Bay from the sandbar in the delta of La Mabinicon Creek, where the inhabitants, including the Groats, were mustered into active militia duty and backed up by the presence of large numbers of Confederacy of Tribes warriours.

We... landed the troops and marines and some sailors next morning and reconnoitered the enemy's position – found him posted upon a peninsula of very high ground, strongly entrenched, and his camp defended by about 8 pieces of cannon. In this situation, it was thought not advisable to attack him, with a force scarcely half his numbers, and without artillery; we were also deficient in boats, not having a sufficient number to cross the bay, with all the troops at the same time. The men were all reimbarked, in the course of the afternoon; and, in the evening we weighed and stood for York..."

So the 'Battle' of Burlington Heights wasn't, instead it was a show of force by British troops in the full strength of the victory of their night raid on Stoney Creek a month before, not to mention the three guns and howitzer seized during that battle.

The war at the head of the Lake had one more action to undergo, and that too was a naval conflict, during which the Nelson Township militia was patrolling the Road between Nelson and the Heights while natives camped on their lands.

The Burlington Races

By September of 1813, the American fleet under the command of Commodore Chauncey had already attacked and burned York twice – *once on April 16, 1813 and again on July 30th after an aborted attempt to attack Burlington Heights....*

Sir James Yeo of the British fleet had also wreaked havoc on the American side with his campaign at Sackett's Harbour... most of their engagements on Lake Ontario were...hit and run attacks... both sides knew that the preservation of the fleet was paramount in their continued efforts to defend their position on the lake.

A report from Yeo at the Head of the Lake to Admiral Warren in Halifax Sept 29, 1813: notes that the Americans: *immediately bore down, in a long extended line, our Squadron keeping their wind, under a press of sail, at 12 o'clock, the Pike, Commodore Chauncey's Ship, being nearly within Gun Shot, our Squadron Tack'd in succession, to close with the centre and rear of their line...*

In his own report to the Secretary of the US Navy dated Oct 1, 1813 Commodore Isaac Chauncey wrote about having...

reluctantly relinquished the pursuit of a beaten enemy; this ship was making so much water, that it required all our pumps to keep her free, the Governor Tompkins with her fore-mast gone, and the squadron within about six miles of the head of the lake, blowing a gale of wind from east and increasing with a heavy sea on... I considered if I chased the enemy to his anchorage at the head of the lake, I should be obliged to anchor also, and although we might succeed in driving him on shore, the probability was that we should go on shore also; he amongst friends, we amongst our enemies, and after the gale had abated, if he could succeed in getting off one or two vessels out of the two fleets it would give him as completely the command of the lake as if he had 20 vessels. Moreover, he was covered at his anchorage by a part of his army, and several small batteries thrown up for the purpose..."

What is revealing is the Commodore's assessment of how poorly his men would have done on land among the locals.

Dundas Road Patrolers

The Burlington Museum Document Collection includes a document entitled *A CALL TO DUTY – THE MILITIA*

By 1809, the combined population of Brant's Block, Nelson Township and East Flamborough (the borders of which coincide closely with present day Burlington) had reached 295 – 80 men, 70 women and 145 children.

By law, every man from age 16 to 60 who was capable of bearing arms was required to enroll in a militia company within the division in which he lived. In the case of "Burlington", residents would have served in either the 2nd York or the 5th Lincoln regiment.

The patriotism of the men in the Burlington area is shown in their service to the 1st and 2nd flank companies of the 2nd York regiment and the 2nd flank company of the 5th Lincoln.

Fred Blair began the Ancestry.com genealogical thread *War of 1812 Groat/Grote*, because he wanted to know who the Groats are that were named on the Dundas 'Street' patrol lists: namely William, Michael, Peter and Henry. Blair believes that Henry and a Caleb Groat in the Lincoln militia were both white Palatines. I think it probable that Henry was a son of Mike Sr.'s, since a Henry Groat lived beside "Michael Grote" (Mike Sr.) in the 1818 assessment records of Nelson township, and thus could easily have been related to Mike Sr. There was a Palatine white Henry Groat also from Halton, county in the next township east (Trafalgar) but whether he was living there or in Nelson in 1818 isn't known to me.) At the same time, Michael, Peter, William and Henry Groat each served together or in different groupings with their Nelson neighbours during September and October 1813. While they didn't see battle, they helped prevent the idea of landing on the north shore from seeming like a good one to the American Commander.

The question is, were William, Michael, Peter (and Henry) Groat the sons of Mike Sr. as they seem to be, and who were their neighbours who served with them on the Road patrol?

There is no specific evidence that they are all sons of Mike Sr.,since Mike's only certain son is Michael of Nelson, assuming that Michael was in fact born in 1795 and thus wasn't Mike Sr. himself.

Michael's 1842 census age of 47 being applied backwards to the Dundas Road patrol days, he would have been 18 in 1813, and more likely to have been the road patroler Michael Groat than his father, since Mike Sr. is known to have had First Nations forces living on his land during the same time period We will return to that subject momentarily, but it should be added that he was not only one with First Nations camped on his property. [Blair personal email]

As for the Groats on the road patrol, in the fall of 1813, Michael of Nelson, who didn't father William of Guelph until 1820, was probably though not necessarily, still single.

William of Tuscarora was born in 1783, so he would have been 30 if he was the William Groat serving on the road patrol, the son of Mike Sr. or not.

William's son, Abram, by the North Carolina Tuscarora Margaret, was born in 1814, and we know that the presence of Six Nations families in Nelson township was common before and after the death of Joseph Brant, but if other loyalist lands were used by war parties, the North Carolina connection through the Davis-Ghents and the Groats, may explain Margaret's presence and the birth of Abram following the autumn encampments at the Head of the Lake. It is unknown where Abram was born, perhaps at Mike Sr.'s, before or while the British and the First Nations were driving the Americans out of the Niagara Frontier.

Whether the mother of Mike's children was Mississauga, Tuscarora, black or white is not known, nor is it known if she was alive and on the farm or not. I think the scenario necessitates her being native, but that is not proof.

According to the research done by Fred Blair and sent to me by email: *On September 13, 1815, he* (Mike Sr.) *made a war claim as a resident of Nelson Twp. for losses to Indians encamped on his farm in the fall of 1813. He lost 400 rails, 175 sheafs of oats, eight sheep, a three year old steer, a three year old sow, three two year old hogs, and seventeen fowls, fifteen bushels of potatoes, thirty panels of pine, and 200 rails on another part of the farm. Ebenezer Guire, his son-in-law, certified the claim.*

The losses to Indians were losses of the same kind as those experienced by the Davis-Ghents when Cornwallis quartered his forces on their plantation in North Carolina. The warriors were probably led by Brant's son in-law William Kerr, husband of Catherine's daughter Elizabeth, more on whom shortly.

Blair also notes in his email that: *Unfortunately there were no funds available to pay claims after the war and this caused additional hardship for the settlers. Money was not available until about 1823 and then claims had to be resubmitted. There was no indication that Michael* (ie Mike Sr.) *had resubmitted his claim.*

It may be possible to make too much of the fact that First Nations were on Groat land but according to Blair,

Looking at the number of war claims while moving from York towards Niagara there were 5 claims in each of Toronto and Trafalgar Twp., 21 in Nelson Twp., and over 100 in Ancaster Twp . Most of the war claims in the Nelson Twp. and the townships where Hamilton is were for losses to Indians. After the loss of Tecumseth in 1813 many of his Native supporters retreated with the British to the Niagara area. [Blair, personal email Dec 26 2013]

With that evidence in mind, it strengthens to absolute certainty the fact that Mike Sr. was known to the tribes. And if the road patroler named Michael was Mike's son and not Mike, then Mike Sr.'s 1812 service may have been with the tribes.

Neither he nor they individually appear in any war service record. The presence of First Nations on his land leads to the probability of the presence of a Tuscarora camp helper named Margaret and may explain the 1814 birth of Abram and also how Abram and William ended up on the Six Nation's Reserve listed as Tuscarora warriors in 1842. It is not out of the question that Mike himself had been adopted by the Tuscarora and that Mike was the son of one of the original slaves the remnant Nation met when hiding in the Great Dismal swamp.

At the same time, if not on Groat land, then somewhere in Nelson, there would have been an encampment of Mississauga, also members of the Confederacy of tribes; which likewise, creates a theory for how John Groat-Mike ended up married to a pure blooded Mississauga named Caty. He may have only been ten or eleven during the war, but he and she were on the Credit River together by the mid 1820's, because their children were born there before moving to the Grand with Peter Jones.

The Brant family owned more acreage in Nelson township than anyone, so the fact that Mike Sr. and twenty others hosted portions of the native force should cause us to grasp the friendship advantage British sailors would have had on the north shore of the mouth of Burlington Bay. Also to be considered is that the Thames Nations diaspora (following the death of Tecumseh on Oct 15 1813) joined the combatants at the head of the Lake, and in fact, Captain Matthew Elliot of the Western District Rangers, and a man who had been allied to Tecumseh's people since the revolution, died in "Burlington" on May 1 1814. A story to which we will return, since one of Mike Sr.'s future son-in-laws served with the Rangers and the tribes.

But back to the Road Patrolers. In the 1830 assessment of Nelson there is a Pete Groat, who was on a farm in the vicinity of 'Michael Groat', living beside David Gant (1804-1875) a child of Thomas Ghent and Elizabeth Davis. David was the younger brother of William Ghent (who lived at Glen Allen in the Queen's Bush from the early 1820s until his death there in the 1848s.)

[Wm. Ghent had also been one of the road patrolers and lived in the same area of the Queen's Bush as Simon Groat did when Simon married there in 1847.]

Also on the 1813 patrol and still in the Nelson neighbourhood in 1830 were Nicholas Kern and Asahel Davis - the eldest son of William, and the man who rode from the mouth of the Genesee River with Thomas Ghent to get help from Simcoe back in 1793.

Since Pete Groat's age isn't given, it's hard to know who he is, but if he was the road patroler, he can't have been Michael of Nelson's son of the same name as identified in the 1846 will, by virtue of Michael's age in 1813. It seems most probable that Pete was a son of Mike Sr. The ages of the people on Pete's property in 1830, including him, were 2 males over 16, 4 under 16, 2 females over 16, and two under 16. Those ages could be for anyone, including Michael's family come from Saltfleet. William of Guelph was ten in 1830. Pete seems to vanish from the records after 1830, so perhaps he died, possibly in the cholera outbreak at the head of the lake/Hamilton in the early 1830's

The Henry Groat on both the road patrol and the 1818-1819 assessments of Nelson was one property away from Mike Sr., and beside Ebenezer Guire. As noted, Fred Blair suggests that Henry was part of a white Groat family who settled in Whitby, but since there was also a white Henry Groat family in Trafalgar and Nassagaweya, and they could have been living beside Mike Sr., but I still think Henry was a son of Mike's. Every last name on the Dundas Road patrol can be found in Port Nelson before and after the War.

Document 119 Apr. 25 to Oct. 24, 1813 Muster Roll and Pay List of a Detachment of Capt. James Mordan's Company of the 2nd Regiment of York Militia from the 25th of Sept. to the 24th of Oct. 1813 both Days inclusive... [Fred Blair]

All last names in those lists appear in loyalist records from Capt. Morden to Ensign George Chisholm, En. Thomas Lucas; Privates... Ralph Morden, Jacob, Nicholas & Nicholas Jr. Kerns, Robert Sovereen, David Morden, Thomas Mordan, Jacob Vanorman, Stephen Lucas, Asahel Davis, Augustus Bates, William Ghent, Elias Rambo, John Sovereign, Guire and the four Groats.

Ebenezer Guire and Abram Topp

Fred Blair discovered the link between between Jemima Groat and Ebenezer Guire, and his notes, sent to me by Guire-Bradt family researcher Tammy Mitchell, are as follows: *Private Ebenezer Guire (c1778-) In 1806 he purchased a lot in Brant's Block (BHS). In 1811, he owned part of Lot 22, Con. 2 SDS, Nelson Twp. (BC pg. 6). He served August 29 to September 9, 1812 (2Y293). He was absent September 25 to October 24, 1813 (2Y295). He worked on Dundas St. October 27 to 30, 1813 (2Y297). He was at Burlington Heights July 25 to August 5, 1814 and took part in the Battle of Lundy's Lane (2Y158). He was fined 5 Pounds between December 1, 1814 and March 1, 1815 (2Y10). On September 13, 1815, he certified Michael Groat's (Mike Sr.'s) war claim as his son-in-law (WC782).*

Blair also noted that Guire... *was recorded in the 1816 and 1818 Nelson Twp. Assessments with 100 acres (N16)(N18). The 1851 Census, Nelson Twp., recorded Ebenezer Guire, 75 years old ... and Jemiah, 66. The 1861 Census, Nelson Twp., recorded Ebenezer Guire at 82...(born) in the United States.*

According to Tammy Mitchell * *One of the daughters of Ebenezer Guire and Jemima Groat married the son of Lieut.-Col. Andrew Bradt (c1755-1830.)* (*private email) We met Bradt earlier as one of the men supporting the 1796 petition of John Baker. Andrew was a nephew of Captain Butler:

Bradt. served in Butler's Rangers (OBF pg. 82).

... On October 13, 1812, he was at the Battle of Queenston Heights (VBA pg. 270)...On July 23, 1814, he commanded the regiment at the Battle of Lundy's Lane (WRG pg. 262). .. He died at 15 Mile Creek in Louth Twp. at 75 (OBF pg. 82). (Blair ibid)

Andrew's grandson, Walter George Bradt married Abigail Guire, daughter of Ebenezer and Jemiah Groat. George also witnessed the will of Michael of Nelson in 1846.

The Groats and the Guires were two thirds of the core of the loyalist free black community in Nelson, a community that also included Abraham Top, whose family of ten are recorded as 'coloureds' on the same 1840 assessment page as the Guires (who were listed as family of 9 - all 'coloureds'.) Top was also one of the three 'subscribers' of Michael of Nelson's will. It was also he who served with the Western Rangers, under Capt.

Elliot's command, a small company of ten men who fought with the Shawnee and Chippewa. Topp would have joined the Rangers in Colchester township where the St. Clair River becomes the north shore of Lake Erie. It took until after the rebellion of 1837, but Topp was eventually given land in Nelson for his service during the war of 1812. (See Appendix 5)

Abraham is also known to have married a Margaret Groat, because their daughter Hannah Topp married Rev. Lindsey Anderson, the first the A.M.E. minister of Ottersville, Norwich Township in Oxford County, about 30 miles west of Brantford.

In the 1871 census of Norwich, Margaret is a 74 year old Canadian-born mulatto widow, which gives her an approximate birth year of 1797, which would make her Michael's younger sister. In the '61 census, Abram was 69, a Canadian-born farmer, given him a birth year of 1792. It is possible that the Topps had come to Canada with Captain Elliot after the Revolution since he is known to have brought 60 slaves with him to Amherstburg in 1783.

By 1861, Hannah, was 41 and married to the 41 year old American-born Anderson (known to have escaped slavery) They were all listed as mulattos and living near her parents and with her own family of seven, the eldest of whom was 1861 buts her birth in 1821 and the age of the eldest child suggests that she had been married Anderson since at least 1845.

Hannah's older brother, Abraham, was born in 1819, according to the same '61 census of Norwich. He was married to a woman named Jemima, with whom he had five children. All are listed as mulattos. Jemima is an Episcopal Methodist, but Abraham and the children are listed as Friends. Which means that the son of Abram Topp and Margaret Groat was a Hicksite, living in the south east corner of Oxford County, a day's walk of the Six Nations of the Grand River Reserve. Norwich was a home to a large Hicksite community, the best known of whom was the abolitionist Frederick Stover, the man responsible for using American Quaker funds to buy the land in Middlesex County that became the Wilberforce Settlement, more on which in future books.

It should also be noted that The Western District Rangers

fought at Lundy's Lane, one of the places Simon Groat also served. And given the presence of Thames first nations and Captain Elliot's unit in "Burlington' over the winter of 1813 1814, it's not hard to imagine how Topp would have met Margaret Groat.

The existence of black Quakers, African Methodist Episcopalians and a daughter of Mike Sr.'s married to yet another of the founding black families of Nelson Township/Burlington takes on significant proportions when the locality of Norwich relative to the nearby Thames River towns of Woodstock and Ingersoll are added into the equation, since both those communities became home to black populations. Ingersoll also has deep loyalist connections, since it was founded by the father of Laura Secord of War of 1812 fame.

The only other known black family from Nelson, that also appears in the same assessment as the Groats, the Guires and Abram Top, is the family of a man named Zecheriah Estrass (?) who had a 'coloured' family of 8 in Nelson. In the 1851 census, we learn that Zecheriah was 63, and born somewhere in the States in 1788, he was married to a 45 year old, US-born woman named Hannah, who may or may not be Michael's sister, but if she was, she may have come into the world just before or after Mike Sr. bought the land off Joseph Brant in 1806, assuming they weren't living in Canada before then. The eldest of the seven children, John, was 22 in the census, so they had been married since at least 1829. The only probable evidence of their existence after that, is that in the 1871 census, where there is a single record of a Sarah Estrees, 26, of African descent, working as a servant in St. Catherines, coinciding in age with the daughter Sarah of Zechariah and Hanna, who was 6 in 1851.

There were no Groats/Grotes or Groat-Mikes living in Nelson by 1852. James Chrysler, to whom Michael left the farm, was also gone. Michael's son William was living in Guelph by then, where he would have been listed in Wellington County with his wife Elizabeth and their first daughter, Hannah, but for the fact that the census of Guelph for that year no longer exists.)

By 1852, both Mike Sr. and Michael of Nelson were dead. Michael's children: Peter, Jemima, Margaret and Hannah, also named in Michael's will, also appear have to vanished, although Hannah may be buried in the Woodlawn cemetery in Guelph in a recorded but unmarked grave.

In 1852, there were however, at least 25 negroes/coloured persons living in Nelson township, including the Guire-Groats, and up to 50 Indians. The original Road Patrolers were dying off, and by 1850 their grandchildren were taking over. It was the year of the re-enactment of the Fugitive Slave Act in America; but whether that act was met with action by the Groat-Guires of Nelson or by the Groat-Adams of Guelph is not clear, action by the Tuscarora Groats is, however, more certain.

Groats, Brants and Property

In the *History of Brant County* 1883, there is a description of the origins of Tuscarora Township: *This political subdivision originally belonged to the County of Wentworth (1816), in the District of Gore. On the formation of Brant...in 1852 it was...bounded on the north by Onondaga Township; on the east by Oneida... Haldimand Co...on the south by...Walpole, Haldimand... Townsend, Norfolk... and on the west by the latter township and... Brantford....It has an area of 41,122 acres...*

The ownership of the Grand River was first proclaimed by Sir Frederick Haldimand (Governor of the conquered lands of former New France from 1778 to 1786.) He returned to England in 1784 after the loss of the Revolution, to plan new colonies north of the St. Lawrence and the lower Great Lakes.

The Haldimand Proclamation was issued on Oct, 25, 1784, three days after the Americans and Haudenosaunee signed the *Treaty of Fort Stanwix,* ending their own conflicts. It reads:
"Frederick Haldimand, Captain General and Governor General in Chief of the Province of Quebec and Territories depending thereon, General and Commander in Chief of His Majesty's Forces in said Province and the Frontiers thereof --
Whereas His Majesty having been pleased to direct that in consideration of the early attachment to his cause manifested by the Mohawk Indians, and of the loss of their settlement which they thereby sustained-- that a convenient tract of land under his

*protection should be chosen as a safe and comfortable retreat for
them and others of the Six Nations, who have either lost their
settlements within the Territory of the American States, or wish to
retire from them to the British -- I have at the earnest desire of
many of these His Majesty's faithful Allies purchased a tract of
land from the Indians situated between the Lakes Ontario, Erie and
Huron (the Mississauga Purchase) and I do hereby in His Majesty's
name authorize and permit the said Mohawk Nation and such
others of the Six Nation Indians as wish to settle in that quarter to
take possession of and settle upon the Banks of the River
commonly called Ours [Ouse] or Grand River, running into Lake
Erie, allotting to them for that purpose six miles deep from each
side of the river beginning at Lake Erie and extending in that
proportion to the head of the said river, which them and their
posterity are to enjoy for ever.*

*Given under my hand and seal at arms, at the Castle of St Lewis at
Quebec, this twenty-fifth day of October one thousand seven
hundred and eighty-four and in the twenty-fifth year of the reign of
Our Sovereign Lord George The Third by the Grace of God of Great
Britain, France and Ireland, King, Defender of the Faith and so
forth.   Fredk Haldimand By His Excellency's Command ...*

Perhaps if the King hadn't been in the throes of going mad
in the knowledge that thereafter history would teach that it
was during his reign that England lost America, George III
might have been of help to the First Nations and his colonial
subjects. As it was, in the real world of the newly created colony
during the decades of the king's distraction and then outright
madness; (and later in the decadence of the Regency of the
Prince of Wales) native lands, as well as crown ones, became
the source of wealth for the scavenger class that oversaw the
colony.

All that is left of Haldimand's Proclamation are the words
themselves and the interpretation of their meaning among the
tribes. The only other trace of Haldimand himself is the county
named after him, which sits due south of the one named after
Brant: a seal of the promise between the two men.

The Six Nations still hold to the view that the Proclamation
was an extension of the Royal Proclamation of 1763: a covenant
between sovereign peoples, while from the beginning Simcoe's

position was based on the theory that once the land had been bought from the Mississauga through Haldimand's agency on behalf of the crown, then the tract became crown land, and thus the transaction was not a gift in compensation for lands lost to rebels, but rather, the gift was a right to use the property and to enjoy its fruits, as per the laws of usufructuary.

The concept of the possession-less possession of crown-possessed land, seems like deconstructionist legalese, but Haldimand's language is not as clear as the Royal Proclamation.

The History of Brant tells the story of how the Haldimand Grant became crown owned and sold off to settlers, lands that previously had been described as Six Nations territory before becoming known as a reserve in the 1840's.

The following is a list of the principal surrenders that have been made by the Indians: January 15 and February 6, 1798.- The lands forming the Townships of Dumfries, Waterloo, Woolwich and Nichol extending downwards on both sides of the river, from the northern extremity of the reserve, (ie from the site of the town of Arthur as per Augustus Jones' surveyed Baseline and not the headwaters as proclaimed by Haldimand: *as well as the greater part of the Townships of Canboro and Moulton on the eastern side of the entrance of the Grand River, 352,707 acres.*

April 19, 1830.- The site of the Town of Brantford on the Grand River, 807 acres.

April 19, 1831.- The northern part of the Township of Cayuga, on the same part of the river, 20,670 acres.

February 8, 1834.- The residue of the Township of Cayuga, the Township of Dunn, and part of Canboro' and Moulton, 50,212 acres.

On March 26, 1835, all the surrenders made up to that time were confirmed.

January 18, 1841.- The residue of the lands, with the exception of a reserve of 20,000 acres, and the lands actually in the occupation of Indians, amounting to upwards of 220,000 acres.

In the *American Anthropologist Volume 68*, Issue 5, there is a book review of *The Valley of the Six Nations: A Collection of Documents on the Indian Lands of the Grand River* edited by Charles M. Johnston, and published by the Champlain Society, that notes: *Ironically, it was the Indian leader Joseph Brant, whom Johnston characterizes as "a considerably Europeanized entrepreneur," who insisted that Indian land had been given in fee simple and could consequently be alienated. Thus, he gave titles to over 350,000 acres to favorites of his, despite the fact that the Crown maintained that the land had been granted in leasehold only.*

Only the recognition of the Confederacy as a distinct national community, together with complete freedom over the land, asserted Brant, constituted adequate acknowledgment of his loyalty to the British Crown, and anything less might force him to reconsider his allegiance.

The Crown's position was rigidly enforced by Lt. Governor Simcoe (1791-1796), but after his resignation more timid governors and military commanders gladly appeased Brant. Further, the laxity of the Crown, the dereliction of the trustees of Indian lands, and the real pressure of the settlers made the alienations a fait accompli.

In 1835, all leases granted by Brant, plus almost 72,000 acres "sold" after his death, were officially conveyed to the purchasers. And, by 1841, the Lt. Governor had convinced himself that the only way to end trespassing by Whites on Indian lands was to have the Indians "surrender into the hands of the Government the whole tract, with the exception of such part of it as they may choose to occupy as a concentrated body. . . . " Thus, 220,000 more acres were conveyed...

In the end, Brant's role in all these matters was challenged from within the confederacy, because the idea of private property was an anathema to traditionalists, and from without, because crown trustee supporters thought Brant was a privateer of crown lands.

At the same time, there was the simpler reality that with their territories becoming surrounded by white settlers, it was becoming impossible for the tribes to sustain their hunting and fishing practices, they needed income streams, and Brant chose land sales.

In Brant's defense, I think he saw that his people would slowly but surely find themselves estranged among waves of people who didn't know them. Which is why I think he chose to surround himself and his people with those he knew would fight any attempt at American expansionism. Brant and his people had some very angry enemies in America, and not just in Schoharie NY. I believe he thought there was no hope of his people surviving as a people if they didn't have allies on the ground around them.

And of course, Brant was right, the ink on the international border maps was only 17 years dry before the Americans launched their War of 1812 attack on the colonies; an attack that came less than six years after Brant died. One thing is certain, he left the Grand River and the head of the lake full of people who fought back when the Americans came. The fact that natives camped on his old lands during the American attacks on the head of the lake proves the worth of his having sold land to Grote and company rather than waiting for the colonial administrators and their bagmen to speculate with it.

Mike Sr.'s Nelson township acreage was only one of the properties sold by Brant before he died. However all those transactions, ended up in legal limbo by the 1830's. In fact, there is a May 1833 land record discovered by Arlene Noble, in which Michael Groat (father or son?) transferred the land to William J. Kerr, followed eleven years later by a transaction on September 24 1844, in which the property was sold by the wife of William J. Kerr, back to Michael of Nelson.

From the 1833 date it would seem that the property was caught up in the above discussed issue of whether Brant had a right to sell the land or not, and thus Mike Sr.'s freehold may have been regarded as a leasehold, because the property reverted to the heir of Joseph Brant, who was in this case Elizabeth Kerr, wife of William Johnson Kerr, the grandson of Sir William Johnson and Molly Brant. Elizabeth, was the youngest daughter of Joseph Brant by his third wife Catherine Crogan - the daughter of a Scot's Irish Indian agent and of Catherine Tekarihoga, the head of the Mohawk Turtle Clan.

Kerr, his nephew John Brant and Chief John Norton were the three commanders of native troops at the Battle of Queenston Heights. Which is why I believe that Kerr may have been in command of the First Nations camped in Nelson. Kerr was also one of the early advocates of responsible government in Upper Canada, although he was later arrested for giving William Lyon Mackenzie a beating over 'The Little Firebrand's' activist stances against the Compact, of which Kerr had become an increasingly reactionary member.

In 1859, after the death of Joseph's son John Brant, Walter the old chief's grandson, and the son of Elizabeth and Kerr, became chief of the Mohawks because Elizabeth had, in 1837, inherited her mother's matriarchal role as head of the Turtle clan, and thus held the right to choose the chief, and so chose Walter. Catherine Crogan Brant (who had once scarred Brant's slave Sarah Pooley with a hatchet) had also left the 700 acre Brant Farm in Wellington Square to Elizabeth, so presumably in 1833, William J. Kerr was acting on behalf of Brant's dowager, while in 1844 Elizabeth, was acting on her own behalf, because Kerr was incapacitated.

William J. Kerr died in April of 1845; Elizabeth, two days later. There can be no doubt that the Groat family were well known to Kerr/Brants from day one. It is probable that the ownership of Mike Sr.'s land became an issue in the first place in 1833 because Mike Sr. may have died that year, and because of the issues related to Brant's land sales, so the title was only given to Michael of Nelson after the larger issues were resolved in the 1840's.

William Johnson Kerr

[The land for the oldest Anglican Church in Burlington was donated by the Kerrs, so like Brant, they were Church of England.]

Groats as Tuscarora Warriours

The most important set of facts to us now in C.M. Johnston's Six Nations document collection, are two entries: the first is the *Petition of the Tuscarora to Sir Charles Bagot, April 1842* (PAC Indian Affairs, Civil Control, VI 390-4). The second is from the same year and is a letter from the Anglican Missionary Reverend Adam Elliot (husband of Eliza Howells) to his boss, Bishop Strachan, head of the Church of England at Toronto.

[Rev. John Strachan had arrived in the colony in 1812, eventually becoming Bishop and the spiritual father of the Family Compact. He appears to have hated slavery as much as he hated dissenting religions and democracy. During the Blackburn extradition case in 1850 Strachan urged the Lieutenant Governor to grant asylum to the slaves, he also encouraged Anglican journals in their opposition to slavery, so presumably he knew who Eliza's father was.]

In Lord Durham's *Report on the Affairs of British North America* after the Rebellions in 1837-38, as recorded by C. M. Johnston, Durham makes mention again of the 'alienated lands that were privatized from the Six Nations by speculators':

Of the manner in which the large portion they have alienated was acquired by individuals into whose hands... it passed with the sanction of the government of the colony... It is, however, certain that the consideration paid for it was for the most part of merely temporary benefit to them. (The Six Nations.) *The government...in these instances... have neglected or violated its implied trust... not... careful in its capacity of trustees of these lands, than... its general administration of the Lands of the Province...*

The origins of the fortunes of many of Ontario's early families (and those in England, America and elsewhere) were rooted in government sanctioned pillaging of crown lands during the years of the Mad King's reign and those of his degenerate heir, George IV.

Lord Durham created the framework on which responsible government would be established in Upper and Lower Canada after the Rebellions. He was also one of the authors of the British Reform Act of 1832. King William IV, another son of the Mad King, had to dissolve the House of Lords in order to stop Lord Wellington from preventing the reform bill's passage.

Lord Durham was also a member of the Reform cabinet that passed the Emancipation Act of 1833-34 and so helped put an end to sanctioned slavery throughout the British Empire.

The Wellingtonian Protectorate that governed Upper Canada resisted implementing the Reforms within the colony long after the Rebellion.

Durham died a heroic outcast in 1840, beloved in England for his Reform work, and highly respected in the Canadas for his attempt to help, but in the end, the Compact realities of the colony remained fully functioning.

By 1842, Sir Charles Bagot, the man to whom the Tuscarora petition was addressed, was a career diplomat, having earlier in his career been named *Minister Plenipotentiary and Envoy Extraordinaire to the United States* after the War of 1812. He had also been part of the Lake-of-the-Woods to the Pacific Ocean border negotiations in 1818, after which he became British Ambassador to Russia dealing with the establishment of the Alaska border, which was then in Russian hands. Bagot was also active in the negotiations that created Belgium, after which he rested for ten years before coming out of retirement to serve the new conservative government in the colony's dealings with America. Bagot arrived in Upper Canada on January 10 1842, with orders from the Tory Prime Minister, Sir Robert Peel, to resist responsible government in the province. It was shortly after his arrival that the Tuscarora Baptist petition was submitted to him.

(The ellipses in the following quotes are those created by CM Johnston in the text of Champlain Society Publication that contains the documents.)

Petition of the Tuscarora to Sir Charles Bagot

May it please your excellency, We the Chiefs and Warriours of the Tuscarora Nation of Indians residing on the Grand River, beg leave to express our sincere respects to your excellency, and our thanks to our Great Mother, the Queen, for appointing your excellency to come over the Great Water and govern this part of her vast domains...

We would furthermore inform your Excellency that whereas many of us have seen proper to differ only in the form of our Worship of the only wise God and our Saviour from others of the the Six Nations Indians, and have left the Church of England and united ourselves to the Baptist Church, our Chiefs have been deposed from their office and we are threatened farther oppression in consequences of differing with them in matters of conscience.

We beg leave to inquire of your Excellency, and wish your Excellency to inform us, if, in doing as we have, we in any respect have transgressed the laws, or shall in any way suffer any losses as it respects our rights to presents, &c. from the Government. We cannot bring ourselves to believe that the threats which have been thrown out in respect to this, will ever be put in execution, but as

there are many among us who are fearful, we hope your Excellency
will merely inform us in writing whether we shall be deprived of our
privileges as Indians because we have thought proper to act
"according to the dictates of our consciences" in merely changing
the form of our Religious Worship...
Signed by Chiefs William Johnson...William Green... John Silver...
and warriors Cornelius Owen   Cornelius Otter   Nicholas Smith
Jacob Thomas   Adam Longface   Isaac Whitby Levi Turkey   Abram
Groat   William Groat Sr William Groat Jr.   John Sherry   Henry
Dickson   Augustus Johnson   Powerless (aka Powlos) Silver   Jacob
William   James Dagget Aaron Hill John Douglass John Denna
William Ash   pgs 264-65

There, unequivocally, is proof that within the Tuscarora, the
long history of native-African American intermarriages was
part of the fabric of the tribe, and that William Groat Sr.,
Abram Groat and his brother William, and their half brother
Isaac Whitby were regarded by the Tuscarora chiefs as
warriors (sic.) More on Whitby below.

There was more going on in the petition than meets the eye
of course, including the fact that the remnant of the lands
granted under Haldimand's defunct Proclamation had been
consolidated only the year before and the new gift payments to
members had been established using the interest acruing in the
land sale fund. The right to keep receiving those payments was
what the Petitioners were partially concerned about.

It would seem that the Baptist congregation was originally
an outgrowth of the Temperance Society founded by James
Cusik in Brantford *the first pastor ordained in 1836 when the new*
denomination was admitted to fellowship in the   area's White
Baptist Association, according to Anthony. F. C. Wallace in
Tribal Worlds: Critical Studies in American Indian Nation
Building [p 93]

Wallace also makes this point about the Baptist faith, which
was, in his opinion: *more appealing to the Tuscarora and Tonawanda*
Senecas for several reasons. First of all...the ordained ministers, the
licensed preachers, the deacons, and other church officials were
Haudenosaunee, Tuscarora, or Seneca kinsmen ...

According to the *Haudenosaunee Project*, Rev. James

Nicholas Cusik (who's native name was Gee-Me) was born on either the Six Nations Reserve in 1816, or, by the evidence of two of his grandsons in their Kansas Land Claims, in Lewiston, NY and died there on May 6 1861. Cusik's father Nicholas was a chief named Ka-nat-soyh, and his mother was named Rebecca.

Evidence of Baptists and American Tuscarora can be found in this 1839, *Memoir of the Late Rev. Lemuel Covell, Missionary To The Tuscarora Indians and the Province of Upper Canada...Up to the Time of Mr. Covell's Decease In 1806.*

> Until 1802, nothing of the kind had been attempted among us in systematic form. A Baptist missionary, the Rev. Elkanah Holmes, had been previously established among the Seneca and Tuscarora Indians; but I am informed he was sent out by the New York Missionary Society, composed of different denominations, but mostly of the Presbyterian. Baptists had not then become sufficiently numerous, or sufficiently endowed, to do more than supply their own immediate territory.

The fact that the mixed-race Groats in Nelson township were originally Presbyterian should not be lost on us, and it is evident from the Tuscarora petition, that before 1842, the Groats there were originally Anglicans and that some had been Wesleyan Methodists since at least 1833.

It would appear from Covell's account that the Congregationalists also had an oar in the waters of the Tuscarora. On the Access Genealogy web site, there is document titled *Missionary Work: A record of the Congregational Church in the Tuscarora Reservation The*

> church in the Tuscarora Reservation was organized in the year 1805, embracing six members only, under the care of the New York Missionary Society. Rev. Elkanah Holmes, first missionary, from 1805 to 1808.

> Members of the Church were Sacarissa, a Sachem, and his wife; Nicholas (James Nicholas) Cusik, an interpreter, and his wife; Apollas Jacobs and Mary Pempleton.

In the *Christian Review, Volume 12*, edited by Rev S.F. Smith, and dated December 1847, the author notes that Cusik was converted in early life, and *joined the Paedobaptist mission church about 1823. His Presbyterian brethren sent him to an academy at Lewistown.* So here we have Presbyterians, Baptists and Congregationalists working together without need of credit.

Cusik had been baptized as an adult in the Niagara River in 1833, as was his 81 year old father (born in the Mohawk valley to a white father and a full blooded Tuscarora mother and educated at Johnson Hall [home of the Sir William Johnson] though he fought with the rebels in the Revolutionary War. Nicholas Sr.'s influence ... *led Father Holmes to the village.)* We will return to the Baptists.

Reverend Adam Elliot's Version

The Anglican Church on the Tuscarora Reserve was the church of Brant, Chief John Norton, Rev. Lugger, Rev. Abram Nelles - the mentor of Adam Elliot and Bishop Strachan.

Robert Nelles, father of Abram Nelles was a Palatine German from the Mohawk Valley of Upper New York, a Brant-allied, land negotiator, profiteer and Revolutionary War expression of outrage against the rebels in battles and skirmishes alongside the tribes.

Reverend Abram Nelles (b.25 Dec 1806 d.23 Dec 1884) was more of a pastoral care worker for the tribes than a force of nature like his father Robert.

There is a curious account of Reverend Nelles' father and brother Robert in the *Dictionary of Canadian Biography* that notes: *On one of these murderous missions in 1780 Nelles "recovered" his teenage son Robert, who joined him at Fort Niagara (near Youngstown, N.Y.) as a lieutenant in the Indian Department. Robert proved as energetic and resourceful at frontier terrorism as his father, leading raids in 1781 and 1782 with a cool fury. He returned in modest triumph from the 1782 campaign with "a parcel of negroes & wenches" in tow, for which he found a ready market in Niagara.*

That *parcel of negroes and wenches* arriving as it does with the Butler's Rangers in 1782 at Fort Niagara, is one of the undoubted sources of loyalist-era African American slaves who, along with free black soldiers, crossed into the newly created colony of Upper Canada for good after the Jay Treaty defined the international border. Reverend Abram Nelles was not his father or his brother however, he *became a noted Church of England missionary to the Six Nations Indians. This appointment served to mark the great change that had taken place over the generations in the relative fortunes of the Nelles family and their Indian neighbours. Abram, a professional man from a well-off family, ministered to the poor and confined population of a reservation, descendants of the warriors his father and grandfather had fought alongside in three wars, whose friendship had so generously endowed the family with land.*

As members of the state church of the new colony, Anglicans were the only church allowed on the Six Nations Reserve until the mid 1820s, but Nelles had grown up among the Confederated Tribes, so this was not missionary work in the sense of the ministers going to live among the Tuscarora of Lewiston, though it is closer to Cusik among his own people. Robert Nelles Sr. had been given a large tract of land by Joseph Brant on the lower Grand River about 25 miles up its winding way from Lake Erie. Presumably, Brant thought Nelles a personal and tribal friend on the river.

It is also possible from the perspective of this book, that the Reverend Nelles was the man responsible for establishing anti-slavery activities on the Grand. Slavery split families; at the start of the colony his brother had no compunctions against selling stolen slaves, but the Reverend may have held different views and acted on them during his years on the Reserve.

Back to Reverend Elliot, there is a letter written by the Anglican missionary to Bishop Strachan about his side of the story of the events described in the petition above, which was also published by the Champlain Society in CM Johnston's *Valley of the Six Nations*. Elliot wrote his letter from the Tuscarora village on June 9 1842: *On reaching this place above four years ago I considered that such of the Indians as had become Christians first claimed my attention. Though most of the Tuscarora had been baptized the congregation was not as numerous as might have been expected... this was principally to be attributed to the inconvenience of the place in which they then assembled... By the munificence of the New England Company (they erected) a church (through) the united efforts of their missionaries*

(Nelles and Lugger)... *Nearly all the Tuscarora and Onondagas were attracted to the Methodists...*

(Rev. Peter Jones had begun his 1826-29 mission with his Mississauga on the property of Mohawk Chief Thomas Davis but Elliot says they *returned to our Communion* (presumably after Jones and co. returned to the Credit River.)

While the divisions of authority in an aristocratic society and a community of worship like the Church of England did not sit well with Methodists, Baptists and Presbyterians, it is also obvious that they did not bother Reverend Elliot:

Three members of the Church, whom we believe to be sincere Christians, were encouraged by John Obadiah to assist him in my absence to exhort and instruct the people on religious subjects. One of these was from the United States and had formerly belonged to the Baptists, another is a Chief of the Tuscarora Nation, and the other also a Tuscarora, who joined the Methodists, but returned to the Church...

Adam Elliot continues: *Not long after I had reason to regret that so much notice had been taken of these individuals. They soon began to be extremely assuming, considering themselves regularly appointed catechists, and evincing too much solicitude for making speeches in the church... I frequently tried to reconcile the catechist (Obadiah) with his assistants... he would suggest some improvements which he thought might be made... he considered it best for me when administering the Sacrament...to call him and his assistants to come forward first and partake of the Holy Communion before the rest of their brethren...*

The one who had been attached to the Methodists told me that when he had belonged to that Society he had been encouraged to make speeches and did not approve of laymen being excluded from the pulpit... though my refusal was stated in the mildest manner of which I was capable, they replied with rudeness... even threatened me with schism in the congregation... John Obadiah appeared at length to be convinced of his error...The other three not only separated themselves from our Communion, but endeavor to persuade all within reach to follow their example.

Through the influence of two or three of the Indians from the United States a Minister of the Baptist Persuasion was suddenly introduced among the members of the Church... who... regularly visited our settlement for above three months... a very considerable number have been induced to desert the Church and join them. These consist partly of persons who many years ago seceeded from the Church, but had returned to our Communion, others of them are from the U. States of a mixed breed, having parents of Indian and African extraction. [Johnson p 265-267]

(The Groats and Whitbys appear to have become the bane of Rev. Elliot's existence.)

It is not possible to pinpoint who exactly who was a Methodist or a Baptist and an America, but there is an 1845 report on events in 1840-44 written for the New England Company (which was paying for the Anglican mission):

the Bishop of Toronto held a confirmation in the Tuscarora Church last September (1841) *and fifty-eight persons were confirmed, all Indians except one, who is a coloured man.* [Richardson p. 15]

Later is is noted that: *Among the congregation I discovered several coloured people, both male and female, who are connected with, and live on terms of great amity with the Indians. Twenty-five persons were confirmed, and amongst the number, meekly kneeling by the side of Africans, and Indians, was the wife of the faithful Missionary.* (Eliza Howells Elliot) [Richardson p. 87]

As for the result of the 1842 petition, according to *Father Theo's Blog: Chronicle of Canadian Aboriginal Policy, 1828 to 1876*, posted on Feb. 28, 2011, *The Bagot Commission...issued a report in 1844...problems with squatters on Indian lands; poor land records; poor administration of band funds by officials; shrinking hunting territories; and alcohol abuse among Aboriginal people.*

It recommended centralizing control and taking official control of band lists; persuading Indians to take up farming and other trades; establishing boarding schools to counter parental values and promote Christianity. (Training and tools ...would replace treaty payments.) They also suggested... Indians be encouraged to adopt individual ownership of land under a ... land registry system, to buy and sell plots of land among themselves, but with no sales to non-Indians permitted.

As noted before, the Nelson land record in which Elizabeth Kerr transferred the land back to the Groats was a probable consequence of the report.

The above chapter also shows that the Brantford UEL

tradition of Baptist Tuscarora being responsible for the blacks in that community (necessitating the 1830's settling of the Queen's Bush) cannot be credited to the Baptists until after 1842, when their church becomes *the* alternative to the Church of England, but then the baptists leave for Kansas, only to return a few years later much worse for the wear, after which many - like Abram Groat's family – leave to escape harassment. The UEL may be referring to individuals later known as Baptists. Bishop Strachan's ardent anti-slavery sentiments however suggest that the Anglicans remained active.

Isaac Whitby

In 2013, a Mohawk/Tuscarora Groat descendant named George Beaver, whose grandmother, Caroline was the granddaughter of Abram Groat, posted the following in *Haudenosaunee Social Dancing: Who We Are*: *She was born in a little log house at Six Nations in 1931. My Mohawk grandmother was the midwife who delivered me as well as most of my nine sisters and brothers. She came to visit for about a week from her home on Sixth Line by the Grand River. My Tuscarora grandmother lived just up the road on First Line. Most of our neighbours... were Tuscaroras.*

George Beaver also notes: *Seven generations ago some of my Tuscarora ancestors were still in North Carolina... notarized documents at the Tuscarora Reservation in New York State ... trace my grandmother Caroline Beaver's ancestry through her grandmother and great-grandmother's line in the 1700s to Margaret Groat of North Carolina.*

According to the *Haudenosaunee Project*, Caroline Beaver's *Kansas Land Claim : lists Margaret Groat of North Carolina as the mother of Abram Groat. She also lists Isaac Whitby as the half-brother of the children of her grandparents.*

Caroline's mother was Levina/Revina Groat, daughter of Abram, so her mother can't have been a half sister to Isaac Whitby, since Isaac Whitby was 45 in the 1852 census, (where the name is listed as Witby) which means he was born in 1807, making him 7 years older than Abram Groat. Isaac Whitby was therefor a half brother of Abram's. *The Haudenosaunee*

Project goes on to note that Caroline: *further mentions her great grandmother Molly Turner who lived in North Carolina, migrated to New York and then Canada where she died. Molly Turner married a man named Smith.*

A grandson of Isaac's named Levi Whitby (born 1870) also filed a Kansas Land Claim and he too *lists Molly Turner,.. as his great grandmother.* Levi thus places Molly in the same generation as Abram's mother, Margaret Groat. The marriage to Mr. Smith veers us toward Abram's stepmother, Amelia (Emily) Smith. The mother of all of William of Tuscarora's other children. However, since Molly is a diminutive of Amelia, it is conceivable that Molly Turner married a Mr. Smith, who must have died, after which she could then have married William Groat of Tuscarora.. The fact that Isaac was born in 1807 to the former Mrs. Smith, means he was born before Abram was born to Margaret, making him the eldest of William's children with Emily/Molly, which is not impossible for a people that practiced bigamy like Augustus Jones had with his Mohawk and Mississauga wives.

Isaac Whitby was married to Sarah Stiskaw - born in the Bay of Quinte in eastern Ontario. She was probably from the Six Nations Reserve there and may have also been Tuscarora. Their son John was married to Martha Thompson (born in Tuscarora (village) in 1845. Both Martha and John are listed as Indians in the 1852 census. Levi Whitby was their child.

The 1852 census record lists Isaac Whitby as being from Philadelphia. On the *North Carolina History* website there is a possible explanation for how a mixed race Tuscarora named Isaac Whitby could have been born in Philadelphia in 1807: according to historian Carl Waldman, *approximately 400 Tuscarora were sold into slavery, and some as far north as Philadelphia...*

After the Tuscarora Wars and a few decades before the Revolution, Tuscarora slaves in Philadelphia could have turned into the Whitbys after Pennsylvania abolished slavery in 1780.

The Native Heritage Project also notes that the Tuscarora were present at councils held at Philadelphia in 1742, a hundred years before the Baptist petition to Sir Charles Bagot.

In 1797, the tribe was living with the Seneca in Upper New

York state not far from Philadelphia so it is not impossible to imagine Isaac Whitby being born there ten years later.

The migration patterns of the Groat-Whitbys make them central - and until now - hidden players within UEL lore about how fugitive slaves came to Brantford, because Baptists, Anglicans or Methodists, they are the only identifiable, inter-married blacks among the Tuscarora, and therefor, the most likely people involved in the aiding and abetting of fugitives.

A Note About Kansas Land Claims

On Eric Jansen's Haudenosaunee Project, there is an essay called *Kansas Land Claims and the Buffalo Creek Treaty of 1838* which states that the treaty: *... called for the removal of all Haudenosaunee from the state of New York... Land in the Kansas Territory was set aside awaiting their... arrival.*

A small number of Haudenosaunee left for Kansas about 1846... That no Haudenosaunee remained in Kansas (afterward) was an indication of the total unsuitability of the land... The Six Nations... requested compensation...

After years of court proceedings the federal government was ordered to pay the survivors and descendants ... It took another seven years for the bureaucracy to produce the forms we know today (as) the Kansas Land Claims. (November 1901.)

A Kansas Land Claim was a four page form that attempted to identity the rightful heirs of the signers of the 1838 treaty. As such, genealogical information was required in considerable detail. Parents, children, grandparents, uncles, aunts and cousins were listed by age, gender, tribal membership, dates and places of and death. In many cases the applicant filled out the claim in his/her own handwriting.

Tuscarora Baptists in Kansas

Anthony F. C. Wallace in *Tribal Worlds: Critical Studies in American Indian Nation Building*, in talking about the Kansas land offer to the Six Nations notes that: *The readiness of the Temperance Society, and of the newly formed Baptist congregation to sign the treaties and set forth for Kansas can probably best be characterized as part of the policy of accommodation...ideological rather than financial... the majority of the Tuscarora residents were still followers of their 'native religion' and a move to Kansas might have seemed... an opportunity.*

In 1846, the Baptist Minister James Cusik led most of his congregation of eighty or so westward to the new lands promised them...The expedition was a disaster: a third of the wanderers died and the survivors, many of them sick, returned to a hostile community... [Wallace p 93-94]

It is unclear whether William Groat Senior or Junior. went to Kansas with Cusik, and then returned to face hostility, but Abram Groat almost certainly did, because it was his descendents who filed the land claim.

Abram can't have been in Kansas long, since his daughter Lydia was born in Tuscarora in 1848, and another child in 1850, so presumably it didn't take much more than a year for disaster to strike and the whirlwind catastrophe of it all to dump the remnant back on the Grand.

Abram and his family left the Tuscarora village shortly after 1852 and ended up on the Chippewa Reserve in Middlesex County, where he was much later identified by Chief John Henry as not being *an Indian but a negro.*

Groats, Williams and Smiths

William of Tuscarora, the Baptist father of Abram Groat, was born in 1783 according to his 1852 Tuscarora township census record. As a presumed son of Mike Sr. and an unnamed mother on the Grand River in 1783, William may have been the son of a Tuscarora woman, since Mike Sr. was regarded as a free negro in the 1794 petition, and therefor William's existence in the 1842 petition as a Tuscarora 'warriour', could have been in keeping with either Haudenosaunee maternal clan lines or tribal adoption practices.

On the *Haudenosaunee Project*, William of Tuscarora's son by Margaret Groat, Abram, is listed as having married Sarah Ann Williams, born on the Tuscarora Reservation in Lewiston, New York. She was the daughter of John Williams and an unknown mother, and about whom nothing else is known except that Sarah had a brother named Jacob. There were other native William families living on the Grand.

In the 1852 census of Tuscarora township, 36 year old Jacob Williams is married to a 31 year old Sarah born in Onondaga township. He is listed as a negro, as is their 11 year old daughter Christeena, while the rest of their four children are listed as Indians like their mother. There are in fact 36 Williams listed in Tuscarora township in the 1852 census, the eldest of whom is a 76 year old New York state-born Baptist Indian, a likely relation of Sarah Williams Groat.

The presence of Jacob Williams, a negro Baptist born in Tuscarora in 1816, leads us back to probable early role of the Groat Williams Whitbys in the movement of American fugitive slaves to Brantford.

Further to that, is the 1852 information for William of Tuscarora and Emily Smith his wife: William is by then regarded as an Upper Canadian-born, 69 year old negro, Emily (Amelia) is a 63 year old South Carolina Indian, and they are living in a log shanty with an unnamed three year old Groat child, and two negro couples, James and Margaret Carpenter (born: NY 1816 and SC 1802) and Henry (1830) and Margaret Thompson (1834), both from Ohio, both Church of England.

Thus two people with a decade long association to the Tuscarora Baptist church and well beyond, are living with US-born African Americans from three different states, one of which states was the same one as the one in which Emily was born. It should be remembered from the chapter on the Tuscarora of North Carolina that some of them went into South Carolina before heading north again.

Emily and William of Tuscarora remained on the reserve the rest of their lives, they were never asked to leave, even though the 1852 census defines them both as coloured/negroes, so presumably they might both have been mixed race. It may be that Emily was one of the black women identified in the 1844 report of the New England Company, and that she herself was a mixed-marriage Tuscarora.

There are numerous Six Nation's Smiths listed in the *Haudenosaunee Project*, none of them born in either of the Carolinas: most were born in Canada, or Lewiston, Cattauraugus or Buffalo Creek, New York. There also 29 native

Smiths in Tuscarora township in 1852: three were born at the Credit River, a few were born in Brantford, or at the Mohawk village; most were born on the Grand River, none are of the generations that came from the Carolinas. There is one colored-negro Smith family living in Cayuga South township, Haldimand Co. but they were newcomers: their 8 year old was born in the US, while their 6 year old was born in Canada West.

By the 1850's, the native Groat-Smith-Williams could not easily be separated from the blacks, except by the not so genetically useful tool of appearance. My guess is, therefor, that those who looked black were recorded as black, and those who looked native were identified as Indian, with only the coloured-negro definition to shade the reality.

Blacks in Brant and Haldimand

The 1852 census shows that there were 17 coloured-negroes in Onondaga township, 75 in Cayuga South, 40 in Cayuga North, 4 in Oneida, 90 in Brantford, and 40 in Tuscarora (22 of whom are Groat 'Witbys' or Groat Mikes.)

Among the 90 blacks in Brantford was John Van Patten; the son of Prince Van Patten – an old slave of Joseph Brant's; John had also lived in the Queen's Bush and in the Pierpoint settlement before the creation of Fergus (northeast of Guelph) beginning in the 1820's.

Also in Brantford in 1852 were the O'Banyons. Simon, the father, was one of the founders of that community's African Methodist Episcopal Church, and Josephus, his eldest son, was also an A.M.E. Minister; leader of a famous Jubilee Choir and chief celebrant during the 1880 B.M.E cornerstone setting ceremony in Guelph. Josephus was also a close ally of Bishop Randolph Disney and a brother-in-law to Bishop Albert Johnson of Oakville. The O'Banyons/Obanyouns will be much discussed in book three, Blood in the Mortar.

Also in the 1852 same census page with Isaac Witby were 47 year old Polly Brant, and her daughters Eliza, 15 and Mary, 6. Polly was born at Stoney Creek, while her children were born at the Credit River. She was the wife of Jacob Brant Jr.

and the half-sister of Peter Jones. Polly's brother Henry also lived near in Tuscarora. All were Wesleyan Methodist Mohawks.

There was also a negro family named Wilson living near the Witby's, the father's name is given as Mr. and his wife as Mrs; but he was born in New York State and she and the children were born at the Grand River.

William Groat the Younger

The fourth individual from the 1842 Tuscarora petition that concerns us here is William Groat Jr., the son of William and Emily, was born in 1822 in a village called Boston on the Grand River reserve. The village had been so-named by someone passing through in the first decade of the 19th century who had noticed that the first four settlers (squatters) were people from Boston, Massachusetts.

According to the 1852 census, Mary, the 19 year old wife of William the Younger, was born in Onondaga township, but he, she and their children are all listed as coloured-negroes. Thus, like his parents, William the Younger was not acknowledged as native even if they were Tuscarora band members..

William's 3 year old daughter Peggy was born in that township, while their one and a half year old son Mike was born in 'Boston'. Also living with them were three of William's sisters, Elizabeth, 33, Sarah, 20, and Hannah 17. The first was also born in Boston, the other two in Tuscarora village. All adults were Baptists and may have been to Kansas.

Having said all that, it is now evident that not only did the extended Baptist Groat-Whitby families live in a mixed community with Six Nations, Mississauga, as well as 'coloured-negro' neighbours in 1852, they had been doing so for decades.

Emancipation and the Groats

Having established who the black Baptist Tuscarora were and when they became Baptists, and having shown that the Six Nations Groats lived among African Americans in the 1852 census, we can assume, if not state categorically, that they must be the Tuscarora Baptists remembered by Brantford

Loyalists.

The fact that three Groats were among the Tuscarora petitioning the new Governor General for help in their troubles with the Anglicans, begs questions for which I have no answers: were Groat-Whitbys the only mixed-race Tuscarora; were others involved in abolitionist activities among the *Six Nations*?

The Mississauga Groat-Mikes became Wesleyan Methodists early in the ministry of the Reverend Chief Peter Jones, who baptized two children of John and Caty's on the Grand in 1833. They stayed on the Reserve when Jones and co. went back to the Credit. Were John and Caty, as Methodists, active abolitionists; or just good neighbours to blacks moving inland from *The Crossing*? John and Caty were on the River in the days the Hicksites created the Underground Railroad, they lived through the rebellions of 1837-38, when the troubles disrupted the flow of fugitive slaves. John and Caty were nearby when William of Tuscarora and his sons were named warriors, they were on the Grand when the Baptists went to Kansas, they were there when Cusik and co returned, there after the 1850 re-enactment of the Fugitive Slave Act, there beyond the Civil War, but who knows if they were anti-slavers like many Methodists, however probable it might seem.

As for the North Carolina connections, they seem to neatly tie up in a bow of Loyalist ribbons from the War of 1812 road patrol days before and after. NC is the tie that holds the name of William Groat - the probable eldest son of Mike Sr. - to Saltfleet and Nelson Presbyterians and the Davis-Ghents, they tie-in the company of Presbyterian Congregationalists, and Baptist Tuscarora of Lewiston, NY; tie the Grand into the flow of free blacks confronted with the passing of America's 1793 Fugitive Slave Act, tie the past to Lincoln's Emancipation Proclamation seventy years later.

All questions come down to *Who else* from Loyalist times is more likely to have led fugitive slaves into the Queen's Bush Settlement, than mixed race Canadian First Nations? If the answer is no one, then no one was better placed over their decades on the Grand than the Groat-Whitbys.

As for the destination of many slaves, the Queen's Bush, whether by accident or purpose they would have met men like North Carolina-born Presbyterian William Ghent, son of William Davis' daughter and a peer of Michael of Nelson's, who lived in the Bush from the early 1820's until his death in the 1850's, making him not only one of the earliest squatters on the clergy reserve, but also a potential aider and abettor of American Fugitive slaves coming to the bush every decade of his time there.

Simon Groat, the last probable son of Mike Sr.'s whose story we will come to shortly, was married in the Queen's Bush in 1847; he and his wife ended up in the census records of Caradoc Township, Middlesex County in the 1860's and '70's. Caradoc was not only home to Chippewa and Delaware reserves on the banks of the Thames River near London, it is also where Abram Groat came to live after abandoning the Grand River because of the malice of the Anglicans when they got back from Kansas.

Simon's presence there also echoes the reason Munsee elder Leroy Dolsen supported the claim of the Ramapough in 1995, even if the dots can't yet be connected and he knows only the names DeGroat/DeGroot. Something in common is going on.

Abram's Children in Caradoc

According to records we will come to, Abram Groat took up land on the Caradoc Reserve around 1854, and moved there with his wife Sarah and their family. Their daughter Lydia later married David Beeswax, a Chippewa from that Reserve. In the 1852 census of Caradoc, David Beeswax is a 17 year old Chippewa farmer, born on the River Thames, living with his 56 year old Thames-born mother Maria (1795), and his 55 year old, American-born farmer father Wahtringa Beeswax (1796).

In the 1871 census, there is a 37 year old, Ontario-born Anglican named William Groat, listed as being Indian, living in Caradoc. The township at the time contained a portion of the Caradoc Indian Reserve, which began life as an Industrial School for First Nations created by the Methodists in 1849 on 200 acres of the township. A remnant of Munsee-Delaware, have their own reserve in the township and attended the school.

Assuming the age he gave, 37, was correct, William of Caradoc is ten years younger than William Groat-Mike, son of John and Caty, and four years older than William of Guelph. He was almost certainly the son of Abram Groat and Sarah Williams, who had by 1871, had returned to the Grand River.

Curiously, in the 1852 Census of Caradoc, there is also an 18 year old native Wesleyan Methodist scholar named Jane Amanda Mike, presumably at the Church's Industrial School. She is the only non German-born, non-Lutheran Mike in the province outside of Tuscarora township, Brant County. She was either the grand daughter of William of Tuscarora through his son Henry, or she was the daughter of the Mississauga, Caty. If she was the latter, she later married a man named George Hoag of Oneida township, Haldimand county. (Hoag appears to have been the son of Hosea Hoag (1786-1856) a Quaker from Pine Plains New York and Elizabeth Stewart – both of whom died in a house fire in Brantford in 1856. Since Elizabeth was not a Quaker, it is possible that Hosea had been shunned from the Society, but still regarded himself as a Friend.

[Cheryl-Gasiewski/WEBSITE-0001/UHP-0069.html]

It is unclear where Abram Groat was, since his name does not appear in the 1852 census or any community in the province. However, his whereabouts and that of his family can be deduced from a series of documents that the Archives of Canada posted online, entitled, *Caradoc Agency – Correspondence Regarding the Claim of the Daughters of the Late Mrs. Abraham Groat to Lot 9 Concession 3 Longwood Road on the Caradoc Reserve.* (In 1871, Simon Groat lived in Caradoc on lot 18, concession 3, so he wasn't far away.)

Clearly there was some reason for Abram to chose Caradoc, and it may well have been Simon's presence there. In my assessment of the family of Mike Sr., Simon would have been Abram's uncle, because he was a probable brother of William of Tuscarora. It should also be remembered that Mike Sr.'s old peer ,Simon Speck, was also given land in the area.

The archived file is a series of letters, the first was sent from the Grand River Reserve's Ohsewkan Council House on *April*

4th 1894, to the Superintendent Generals of Indian Affairs, Sirs
Some forty years ago, (1854) Abram Groat and his wife who was a
member of the Six Nations, sold their improvements on the north
1/2 of lot no 14 concession 5 Tuscarora, and took the proceeds and
moved away to Munceytown after they were allowed to stay there
and were adopted into the band. Abram Groat purchased some land
on no. 8 side line, lot No 9 3rd range south of Longwood Caradock
Reserve, and after they have been there for many years they came
back to Grand River Reserve on a visit and left the home at
Caradock in charge of John Henry Indian.

After they were here (Grand River) they were restored on the pay
list of the Six Nations, that act induced them to stay, and sometime
after that Mrs. Groat died and never returned to Munceytown to
dispose of the place.

The gist of the files is that the daughters of Sarah Williams
were hoping to be compensated for their father's improvements
to the land on the Chippewa reserve in Caradoc, which is why
Josiah Hill, secretary of the Grand River band, wrote the
Department to have them oversee a resolution of the issue.

The old man Abram Groat is alife (sic) and would be able to give

the whole history of the matter. (Since Abram was born in 1814,
he would have been 80 in 1894.) The issue was put into the
hands of the department's agent in Strathroy, Mr. Gordon, and
received the following response.)

With respect to the letter sent to Ottawa by Josiah Hill... on behalf
of Mr. A Groat's daughter who left her husband and moved to
Grand River with instructions not to come back again... I bought
the lot from John Simon who died many years ago... this is well
known by my band. Ex-chief John Henry

April 28th [In my letter to you yesterday I forgot to tell you that Mr.
A Groat's wife never did belong to our band but their daughter who
married a Chippewa named David Beeswax he too is alive Many
years ago (sic) and I cannot see what claim they could have after
forsaking her husband. Her parents had no right to buy land on the
Caradoc Reserve- her father is a colored man not an Indian,
J Henry

While the Chippewa, Chief Henry, seems to render tribal
adoption meaningless and strips Abram of his Tuscarora
status, it is clear from the above, that Abram and Sarah and

the Tuscarora had been reconciled on the Grand, probably due to the emergence of the Baptist church as the accepted dissenting church, and thus, the fact that Abram was restored to the pay list, meant that Abram was legally regarded as Tuscarora even under the new laws.

Lydia was gone from Caradoc by 1871, but she is not listed in that census as being anywhere else in the province, so who knows where she went, although did have four husbands.

As for Abram Groat, in the 1901 census of Brant, (Abraham) Groat is an 87 year old Indian, born in 1814, living with his 53 year old son Henry, Henry's family, and a housekeeper named Lucy Williams. Both men were widows; all seven in the house were Baptist Indians; as were their next door neighbours, 31 year old Levi Whitby and his 25 year old wife Althea.

Lydia's son Samson and an Edward Groat are named on lists of Six Nations World War One veterans.

In 1898 Samson Groat got into a property issue on lot 13 concession 2, Tuscarora township with his brother-in-law, Joab Hill, married to his sister Christine, in which their brother Henry was witness, there was no issue of his race or band status. Thus, however bumpy the ride, in the end, the Groats remained *Tuscarora warriors* long after they had left the Church of England.

The truth of where that status began may yet be traceable, since, as George Beaver noted on his blog, *The Beaver clan is one of the eight clans of the Tuscarora Nation, which is perhaps the root of my surname of Beaver... My Tuscarora father was of the Bear Clan but I belong to the Turtle Clan because of my mother and grandmother.*

As always when it comes to family history, clan genealogists might suddenly appear with traces of Groats through the Tuscaroran ages and thus open up new lines of inquiry into their not so *isolate* mixed-race history.

The Long Road to the Longwood Road

Just down the concession in Caradoc from where Abram Groat and his family settled in 1854, his presumed uncle Simon lived out the rest of his life after leaving the Queen's Bush.

According to the census of 1871, (in which he is listed as 'African') Simon was born in the US in 1801. However, 1801 is clearly not the year of his birth since Simon is one of four Longwood, Middlesex Co. residents listed in 1877 as still living, and thus still qualifying to receive a pension in recognition for their services as militiamen during the War of 1812; something Simon probably didn't do as a boy of 11. There is better evidence that he was born in 1793, to which we will return.

According to an online article posted by the Niagara Historical Museum, all who applied for the pension were checked against old records to determine whether they could participate in a gratuity voted to veterans by Parliament in 1875, as contained on page 40 in volume 7 of the Sessional Papers of 1876. Curiously, there is also a Dolsen named.

Electoral Dist.	PostOffice	Case#	Militiaman	Amount/eremarks
MIDDLESEX	Longwood	3176	Dolsen, Isaac	No return
MIDDLESEX	Longwood	1601	Grote, Simon	20.00
MIDDLESEX	Longwood	3177	King, George	20.00
MIDDLESEX	Longwood	3178	Snake, Thomas	20.00

In *The History of the County of Middlesex, Canada* by Daniel Brock with an Index by Muriel Moon, Brock notes that

Simon Grote of Longwood (colored) could not remember his age, but that he enlisted at the beginning of the war and served through it all; thought the name of his Colonel was Clause ... regiment composed of colored men... at Lundy's Lane, Queenston, and St. Davids. He got a hundred acres of land from the government. pg 147

Colonel Claus would have been William Clause, a maternal grandson of Sir William Johnson and Molly Brant. In 1796, Claus replaced the just deceased Captain John Butler, as commander of Fort Niagara, and was eventually appointed Deputy Superintendent of Indian Lands. Claus was one of Chief Norton's main opponents in his efforts to get the British government to agree with Joseph Brant about the rights of the Indians to sell their lands. Claus in part sided with the native traditionalists who believed the lands belonged to the tribe (though he regarded the lands as held in trust by the crown.)

During the War of 1812, Claus was in command of the troops at Fort George and Queenston Heights. The Coloured Corp, of which Simon Grote was a member, was commanded by a white man named Runchey, although the idea for it was put forward by Mike Sr.'s old friend Richard Pierpoint. Pierpoint, with his Butler's Ranger's Revolutionary War prestige and status as one of the most important free blacks in Upper Canada, was the magnet that drew other free negroes and indentured black servants into the Corps.

Simon's own evidence that he joined at the start of the war and served throughout the conflict, makes sense for someone born into the loyalist circles in which Simon would have been raised, and explains why he wasn't in Nelson township in 1813 to patrol the Dundas Road.

According to ancestry.com, in Vol. 26 of *Canadian Veterans of the War of 1812,* Simon Grote's birth year is given as 1793, which would make him two years or so older than Michael of Nelson (c. 1795); both are listed in census records as being born in the United States - Michael in the 1842 census that gives his age as 47, and Simon in the 1861,'71 Caradoc township census records, in which he misled the census taker about his age (in 1861 Simon claims to have been born in 1814, and in 1871, he claimed to have been born in 1801. Maybe his real age was catching up with him, since he was not around for the 1881 census.

It is my assumption that at the start of the war he was 19 years old and living in Nelson with the rest of the family; and that he signed up with the Coloured Corps as did many blacks, because he was concerned that victory for the Americans would lead to the re-establishment of untempered slavery in Canada.

And once again, the fact that both Simon Grote and Isaac Dolsen served as militiamen (in different units) suggests that the Dolsens may have long regarded Simon as at least partially Munsee, even though he never belonged to the band.

There are a number of white Palatine Groats in other parts of Middlesex County but they are unrelated.

Simon and The Coloured Corps

After 1813, the company became a unit of the Provincial Corps of Artificers, working for the Royal Sappers and Miners. its field of activities in both manifestations was the Niagara frontier. The Niagara frontier was also where the Provincial Colored Corps was when the men were released from duty after the Americans officially conceded that the existing international boundary would remain in force.

In a submission report to the *Historic Sites and Monuments Board of Canada*, entitled *The Colored Corps (1812-1815)* by Gareth Newfield and Maryann D'Abramo, they note that from...*July 1812 to 24 March 1815 ... An all African-Canadian military*
corps formed in Upper Canada to defend Britain during the War of
1812 ...at least two sources claim it (the Colored Corps) fought in
the climactic Battle of Lundy's Lane on 25 July 1814.

If Simon (like Ebenezer Guire) was at the battle of Lundy's Lane, he was lucky to have survived it, for it was the bloodiest conflicts of the war, with Upper Canadian, American and Native losses reaching into the thousands. The three battles the company unquestionably participated in were the Battle of Fort George, the Battle of Queenston Heights (in which Chief Norton's military prowess was proven) and at the Siege of Fort Erie. Those three conflicts were a war's worth of heavy service and would have left their marks on Simon Groat.

The Marriage of Simon and Mary

There is no evidence of anything done by Simon Grote after the war until his Oct. 11 1847 marriage to Mary A. Lewis, *both of Peel* (township) conducted by a Baptist Minister named James Sims in the Queen's Bush Settlement and witnessed by an Isaac Lewis and Chauncy Simons. The fact that it was a Baptist service is of interest since that is around the time the Tuscarora Baptists went to Kansas. The Lewis connections conjure up Adam and the Levi Lewises, while the Queen's Bush setting places them squarely in the most important fugitive slave settlement in the province. 1847 was probably the peak year - population-wise - for African-American fugitives squatting on those Clergy Reserve lands.

Using Linda Brown-Kubisch's work *The Queen's Bush Settlement (1839-1865)* as a means of providing local context for Simon and Mary's marriage, the white American abolitionist and educator Fidelia Coburn Brooks was in the community exchanging letters with the American anti-slavery leader Lewis Tappan about her work and life, which was rewarding, difficult and underfed.

(Tappan, it should be remembered, was an ally and mentor of Theodore Weld's.)

1847 was also the year an Irishman arrived in the township after a four day wagon trip from Toronto with his family; they came across a black logger named Keath in a shanty who had no food to share, but who sheltered them, a story Brown-Kubisch supplies as evidence that the former slaves made good neighbours. (Keath was probably Thomas Keith who lived on Concession 1: in 1846 Thomas Keeth was listed as 'admitted on trial' as a minister-to-be of the British Methodist Episcopal Church at the Canadian Conference held that year in the Queen's Bush. It is unclear if he was ever ordained.)

In the same paragraph as the good neighbour story, Brown-Kubisch also mentions that: *William Ghent, another early white settler, had constructed his new home with the help of his black neighbours, whom he praised as reliable and honest.*

As stated previously, William Ghent was the eldest son of Thomas Ghent and Elizabeth Davis. Ghent was born in Saltfleet township in 1796. His wife, Mary Fonger, was born in Aldershot (East Flamborough) in 1803. Burlington historians believe the Fonger family were the first settlers in the community, back in 1783, when the place was known as Browns Wharf.

Ghent and Fonger married in 1819 and had eight children, most of whom were born in Glen Allen, Peel township, Wellington County, a village on the banks of the Conestoga River, a tributary of the Grand. Their daughter Harriet was born there in 1823, so they were among the earliest settlers, black or white in the area. William Ghent died on April 15 1848, and is buried in the Glen Allen cemetery. Glen Allen was one of the cornerstones of the Queen's Bush Settlement, and scores of black families with deep roots in the underground railroad would have known the Ghents.

The Ontario Heritage Trust historical plaque for the Queen's Bush makes note of Glen Allen.

THE QUEEN'S BUSH SETTLEMENT, 1820-1867

In the early 19th century the vast unsettled area between Waterloo County and Lake Huron was known as the "Queen's Bush." More than 1,500 free and formerly enslaved Blacks pioneered scattered farms throughout the Queen's Bush, starting in about 1820. Many settled along the Peel and Wellesley Township border, with Glen Allan, Hawkesville and Wallenstein as important centers. Working together, these industrious and self-reliant settlers built churches, schools, and a strong and vibrant community life. American missionaries taught local Black children at the Mount Hope and Mount Pleasant Schools.

In the 1840s the government ordered the district surveyed and many of the settlers could not afford to purchase the land they had laboured so hard to clear. By 1850 migration out of the Queen's Bush had begun.

The fact that Simon Grote was living in the settlement at the same time as William Ghent may just be coincidence, however, it may not be. Ghent was born a Welsh Presbyterian, and we know the Presbyterians had been anti-slavery activists and allies of the Tuscarora for decades. The Methodist Church also had a mission in Glen Allen from 1832 on, so perhaps William Ghent and Mary Fonger had gone to the Queen's Bush as a force for good. Maybe they went because she was sixteen or seventeen when she married him. The fact is, they stayed, and like William's father Thomas Ghent, William had no problems being friends with free blacks or self-emancipated ones. Was he an abolitionist? Probably, but even better perhaps, he appears to have been a good neighbour.

The most important event in the Queen's Bush in 1847, was a petition in which a large number of black squatters prayed to be granted the lands on which they lived, in recognition for their having "improved" them for agriculture, the petition was not the first, and the blacks were not the only petitioners. It was those petitions however, that triggered the decision by the government to sell and organize the Queen's Bush by township

and county, with some of the African American settlers soon
after buying lands they had improved.

The problem for many of the Queen's Bush squatters,
however, was a lack of buying power, which meant that most of
them had to abandon their lands, triggering the dispersal of
most of the former fugitives away from the Bush.

That same year, as mentioned in connection to Thomas
Keeth, the African Methodist Episcopal Church held the second
of three annual general conferences in the Queen's Bush. (The
first was 1844, the last was in 1853.)

The man who married Simon Groat and Mary Lewis, the
Reverend James Sims, was the first Baptist in the settlement.
Whether he married them because the couple were Baptists, or
because the Reverend's church (his house) was the closest place
of worship isn't clear. Sims and his family had settled as
farmers, so he and Simon and Mary may have been neighbours.
The Baptists never became a large presence in the Queen's
Bush however.

So who was Mary Lewis? Considering that one of the
marriage witnesses was an Isaac Lewis, then it should be noted
that in a survey of Peel Township in 1843 there is an Isaac
Lewis listed as living on Concession 2; Brown-Kubisch notes:
*Isaac Lewis moved to Peel Township in October 1843 east half of lot 13
Concession 2... built a house... cleared six acres.. registered claim at
Elora and then deferred payment until Jan 1847* (p 214.) He also signed
the 1843 Queen's Bush petition, as did a Henson Lewis. (p 239)
Both men are identified as black by Brown-Kubisch, Henson
Lewis is from Maryland, Isaac's origins are unknown. In 1845 a
Thomas Lewis registered a claim on the same property as
Isaac. (p. 214) Both are identified in the 1852 census as Germans.
(Mary is listed as being German in the 1871 census of
Caradoc.)

Mike Sr.'s peer, Levi Lewis Jr. and his wife Mary Beemer
had a daughter named Mary, who thus had both black and
German heritage, so perhaps she is the woman Simon married,
perhaps not. [canon/research-topic-misc-blackhist.html]

Brown-Kubisch makes no mention of Simon or Mary in the
settlement, and they don't appear in the census of 1852. No

direct link can be made from Mary to Isaac or Hanson.

As for the other wedding witness, Chancy Simons, his name was spelled Chauncey in a now offline virtual exhibit about the community of Priceville, Ontario, called *Echoes of the Old Durham Road*

When the census taker came through in 1851, the Simons family were ...from the United States and may have come to the Durham Road by way of the Queen's Bush settlement on the Garafraxa Road. Chauncey was 47 years old...

Chauncey Simons' role in the life of James Henson, the man who wrote the story of his own life is described in: *Broken Shackles: Old Man Henson From Slavery to Freedom* :

While living in Lockport, NY*, he (Henson) was visited by Chauncey Simons who had gone to the United States to convince fellow Black refugees to come to Artemesia Township** in Grey County where he resided. This was in 1853. According to Henson, Chauncey gave a glowing report of life in the township:

...Chauncey accompanied Henson to Owen Sound, arriving there on St. Patrick's Day, 1854.

*Henson had escaped to upper New York State from Maryland several years before Simons found him. Lockport, is about 20 miles south of Niagara Falls and was home to a large Quaker community. An African Methodist Episcopal Church was founded there in 1839.
**Artemesia is the second township south of Owen Sound; Glenelg, the first, was the pseudonym used by Henson when he published his book in 1889.

Simons himself is listed in the 1852 census of Artemesia, along with his wife and ten year old daughter Rosel: all were born in the US, which means that Chauncey came to Canada after 1842 (Isaac Lewis came to the Queen's Bush in 1843.)

Chauncey's trip to Lockport NY in 1853 may have been a singular event, or part of a long commitment to anti-slavery activities.

Thus, while it may be possible to make too much of the fact that Simons served as a witness to the marriage of Simon Groat and Mary Lewis, it is not impossible that Groat not only shared some of Chauncey's efforts, but as a free negro with deep roots in the pre-Underground Railroad, Loyalist black community of Port Nelson, Simon Groat might have been more of an activist than Simons.

Certainly, if Isaac Lewis was Mary's witness, Chauncey was almost certainly Simon's.

Just when Mary and Simon left the Queen's Bush is unknown, perhaps around the same time as Chauncey Simons. By 1861 they were living in Caradoc, Middlesex County.

By 1871, Simon Groat listed himself as a 70 year old, African farm labourer on the 3rd concession, lot 18, of that township; Mary is listed as 64 year old German, born in 1807. By 1871, many mixed race individuals who could pass for white, were doing so in increasing numbers: the Jim Crow world of racial intolerance that started emanating from the south after the American Civil War was slowly drifting north.

On the Caradoc township website there is a driving tour that includes the following directions to the Longwood Road...

At the bottom of the steep bank is the Thames River, and on the other side is the Oneida Settlement, which began in 1840. Early South Caradoc pioneers recall that many families had dugout boats made by the Oneida craftsmen. Fishing and boating on the Thames were part of pioneer life...

For whatever reasons, Simon and Mary moved to a township in which - and around which - there were three First Nations reserves: Oneida, Delaware/Lenape-Munsee and Chippewa, the latter was also the reserve on which Abram and Sarah Groat settled with their young family after the debacle in Kansas.

The History of Middlesex County notes: *The Missions of the Canadian Wesleyan Conference among the Indians were instituted in 1822, two years before the Missionary Society was formed at Grand River, Brant County, Ont., with Rev. Alvin Torry, preacher.* (The man who baptized the Reverend Peter Jones.) *In 1828, a mission among the Otchipwes, Oneidas and Munceys of Caradoc and Delaware was commenced, the membership being 15, increased in 1873 to 123.*

The population of Middlesex county in 1861 was: 30,702 English-speaking, and 77 French-speaking, 312 negroes and 1,182 Indians. Of the latter, 643 resided in Caradoc ; 531 in Delaware ; 2 in London ; and 6 in Westminster.

There were only four self-identifying Africans in Middlesex

County in 1871, three other besides Simon; one is a 10 year old, Ontario-born, Christian Brethren named Hugh Groat who was a servant in Caradoc, (presumably working for Moravian Delaware Indians or their German-American relations.) In the same census of the same township there is yet another Michael Groat (the 19 year old son of Abram's brother Henry), who was an Ontario-born Methodist Episcopal, and was a servant, living in a home not his own.

The fourth African was a 57 year old man named Joseph Harris, born in Ontario circa 1814, and also a Wesleyan Methodist. It is tempting to believe that Hugh was a son of Mary and Simon Groat, but there is no evidence for it, which of course, doesn't make it not true.

The question that comes to mind, is what – if any - is the connection between Mary Lewis Groat, Isaac (and the other Queen's Bush Lewises) and the Richard Lewis who married Margaret Groat Mike daughter of John and Caty Mike, and do any of them have anything to do with the Black Loyalist Lewises, Adam and Levi senior and junior? It would seem that almost none of those questions can be answered, yet.

Not Indian Enough 1. Margaret Groat Mike

Back on the New Credit Reserve in Tuscarora township, Margaret Groat Mike married Richard Lewis in 1849. In the 1852 census Margaret is listed as a 25 year old Indian. Her husband is 30, and described as coloured-negro, which again may imply mixed race. They were both Wesleyan Methodists living on the Grand River. She is the Margaret who was baptized with her brother Peter by Reverend Jones in Tuscarora village in 1833. In the 1861 census she and Richard are listed as Baptists.

The next we hear of Margaret is in June of 1883, when a petition on behalf of the Mississauga Council was sent to Sir John A. MacDonald requesting *a commissioner to investigate the rights and privileges of a number of persons residing on our lands and receiving interest money from our funds, who are not entitled to same according to law.*

Margaret is the subject of this digitized *Collections*

Canada website file – *New Credit Agency –Indian Agent P.E. JONES is transmitting the minutes of the council of the Mississauga of the Credit held on the 21st of March and the 15th of May regarding various matters.*

May 15th 1889 The case of Margt. Lewis's claim for compensation for improvements on N12 Lot 12 concession 2 Tuscarora... Mar 21st 1889 She had Mr. Aug. Jones and Rev. B Anthony to urge her claim.

May 20 1889 Margt Lewis is one of the Mike family, she was married to a negro, and was allowed by old chief Joseph Sawyer to squat upon lot mentioned over thirty years ago. After living there for several years and claiming some land they were ordered to leave and failing to do so, were sheriffed off. After a lapse of nearly thirty years, she now lays claim to the respectable sum of $955.00 which I think the Council very properly disallowed. PE Jones

(Chief Joseph Sawyer "Nawuhjegeezhegwabe" was an uncle of the Reverend Peter Jones and was known as Sloping Sky. He was a member of the Eagle clan *and d. 3 Nov 1863, aged 80 ys.*
[localities.northam.canada.ontario.brant/9569.2/mb.ashx]
PE Jones was a doctor and the third son of Peter and Eliza Fields Jones. Augustus Jones was probably Charles Augustus Jones, PE's brother, although John Jones also had a son with Augustus as a middle name.)

Since Catherine Mike was alive and was a full-blooded Mississauga, the only difference between Margaret Lewis and Rev. Chief Peter Jones, whose mother was also a pure blood Mississauga, is that Margaret's father was part African. Under the laws of the day, native status was derived from the father, which made things difficult for the matriarchal Six Nations, the Mississauga on the other hand, were traditionally patriarchal. Reverend Peter Jones would never have been recognized as a chief of the Mississauga in the years the Mikes were being driven off the reserve. PE Jones was the son of a half white father and a fully white mother, and did not face the harassment faced by the Groat Mikes, but then he lived on the reserve because he worked for the department of Indian Affairs.

Not Indian Enough 2. Margaret's Brothers

The *Collections Canada* website also contains a series of letters starting in 1882, that are part of a file involving Wm David McDougal of the Chippewa on the Mississauga Reserve at Hagersville, Haldimand County, regarding yet another a parcel of land. (see Appendix Three for Map)

In a letter also addressed to Sir John A. MacDonald, Superintendent General of Indian Affairs, (he was also the Prime Minister at the same time.) *About eighteen years ago I purchased from one William Mike whose proper surname is Groat, a Coloured man (who is married to an American white woman.)* (Presumably Adeline Jones.) *His improvements made of the North 1/2 of Lot 6 on 1st concession of the township of Oneida, a portion of the lot belonging to the Indians on the Grand River Reserve. The sum of two hundred dollars, all of which account has been paid since. I then came into possession of the 50 acres.*

Without getting into all the details about the land deal in that file, what interests us here, is that William Groat Mike, son of John and Caty, had legitimately owned an 'interest' in land he held and sold in 1862, that he was identified by a Mississauga, Wm. MacDougal as a coloured man, and that William was married to American white woman.

Again however, the only difference between Reverend Chief Peter Jones and William Groat Mike, is that William's father was part black and Jones' father was white, otherwise both mothers were full blooded Mississauga. It would appear that the Mississauga, a people on the edge of extinction at the start of the loyalist period, later punished those who married blacks, something that did not occur among the Tuscarora.

In 1882, William, Henry and Peter Mike each requisitioned and received approval for money from the Mississauga band's capital account for land improvements, *less the cost of the timber sold, notwithstanding their uncertain tenure of the lands they occupy... Mike, signing a transfer of the lot... (when the other man) was drunk and advantage taken.. but Mike said he got it fairly The department can take no action... After their removal, the band may, I suppose give the farms to members of the Band, or lease them for the benefit of the Band... they appear to have some grain sown, if so, they may fairly be allowed to remain until reaped.*

The Indian agent agreed with the decision of the Band Council, and gave them until Oct 31 to vacate the premises, despite the fact that they had the support of various band leaders.

Henry Mike's claim had been supported by Reverend David

Sawyer, Oneida Township, Haldimand,who noted *I am well acquainted with Henry Mike the petitioner... and his mother Catherine Mike and other members of his family for fifty years (1832) I am an Indian and a recognized member of the New Credit Band of Mississauga... formerly a chief and further I know that the Mother of said Henry Mike was a full blooded Indian woman of the Mississauga...*

Henry's petition was also supported by Jacob Johnson, *a member of the New Credit reserve well acquainted with the petitioner Henry Mike and his mother Catherine Mike and other members of this family for over forty years (circa 1840)... the said Henry Mike is a sober industrious man a good citizen. He has not been guilty of any improper conduct and I think he ought to be allowed to remain possession of the said lands.*

Likewise Jacob Herkimer's support of Henry Mike's petition began with) *I am a member of the New Credit Band of Mississauga Indians, one of the chiefs of the said band,* (he noted that he had known the family for thirty five years) *and I wish hereby to represent to the Superintendent General of Indian Affairs that I consider this a case in which it would be unjust to enforce the order of Mr. Gilkison.*

(Gilkison wanted to get rid of them in order to conform the band membership with the Indian Act of 1876. According to Ian Getty in *As Long as the sun shines and waters flows* Jaspar T. Gilkison* was removed by MacDonald from his position in 1891 because of heavy handedness, so perhaps the Groats are once again central to a transformative conflict on one of the reserves. [Getty p. 112] [*Gilkinson was a favourite of Pauline Johnson's - Keller p 24]

Henry's statement of facts supported by both Johnson and Herkimer included: *That your petitioner's mother whose name was Catherine Mike was up to the time of her death which occurred in 1877* a recognized member of the said New Credit Band of*

Mississauga Indians and was on the pay list and continued to draw up to the time of her death the regular payments from the Indian department... and had a parcel of the said Indian Reserve allotted to her upon which she resided at the time of her death.

Your petitioners' father whose name was John Mike, the legal husband of the said Catherine Mike was not an Indian.

Your petitioner when a child was on this pay list of the members of the said Band while it was located at the Credit.

(*Caty Mike aka Catharine Groat Mike, an aged and much respected woman died on September 30th 1877... interred Oct. 2nd 1877 by the New Credit Missionary, William Cross.)

Henry Groat Mike lived with the band in the Etobikoke area before the creation of the New Credit reserve. Which also means that John Groat, his father, lived with the family there.

And subsequently after being moved to Oneida while your petitioner was still young... he with the other children of the said Catherine Mike were struck off the pay list of said band but for no misconduct of your petitioner... it is not the wish of the band that he shall be turned off his lands he has so long occupied... your petitioner submits... that the facts are that your petitioners wife is an Indian woman and all the members of his family have all their associates among the said band... to remove him and his family, all Indians, with Indian associations only... your petitioner submits that his case is quite distinct from that of white men who have either squatted or leased or otherwise unlawfully got possession of Indian land...

The Mississauga band voted to give Henry money for his improvements, and gave him and his brothers until the spring of 1883 to get off the land. Gilkison visited them in the spring and discovered him still there... *on reaching William Mike's, his wife, a white... were not ready and had no intention to ever...* (vacate the land.)

Henry Mike sent a letter to Sir John A. in January of 1883, in which he noted that *From the information you gave at our interview I must acknowledge that as the law now stands I have no claim to occupy lands in the Indian reserve on account of my father being a mulatto... land I have occupied for the past 34 years (since 1859.)*

What is informative in that letter, is that Henry says that his father was a mulatto, and not just black, which suggests that John Groat Mike's mother was either white or native. My assumption is that his mother was Tuscarora.

In Peter Groat Mike's petition, filed during during the same time period, it is noted that: *This man has a Six Nations woman (not married) for many years, has family of children, for which she was – years ago – erased from the list by the Council.*

That Six Nations woman was Hannah/Anne Claus, the probable daughter of the Mohawk Chief Powless Claus. The fact that she was erased from the membership list because she was unmarried and had a family with the mixed-race Peter, is a telling insight into the way undesirables on the reserve were culled for reasons other than race. Which may in fact be the real issue with the Mikes, some of them had become undesirable. Family researcher Arlene Noble has a Aug 11 1851 marriage record for Peter Mike and a woman named Sophie Belleville conducted by Reverend Adam Elliot, so they were both presumably Anglicans at the time. It isn't clear if she was native.

By May of 1883, further letters were sent suggesting that the Band was unhappy with the deal made by the Department because the file notes that: *the Mikes are unpopular*. There is of course, a disconnect between the support letters of some of the chiefs, and the statement that the Mikes were unpopular. It could of course be racism of some individuals, since the constant refrain in the attacks on them is that they were negroes not Indians. At the same time, it may have been a line of attack best suited to getting rid of them on moral grounds.

By October of 1883 orders to vacate the land were once again issued, while lands were found for William, who was apparently one of the more acceptable members of the family, and thereafter leased property from a Mrs. Russell.

By December 3, the police were on hand to ensure that they left their various properties, at which point the Groat Mikes were finally removed from the New Credit Reserve.

William received compensation for his improvements to the land in 1886. It took Peter Mike until 1893 to get money from the band for the improvements to his property,.

There is a newspaper clipping in the file, dated October 21st

1885, no publication is named, however. It is titled *Indian Laws, Mike vs. Gilkinson* and goes on to describe William Mike's claim of having Indian blood through his mother, *A large amount of evidence was given by the plaintiff. The archives of the Indian Tribe of the Mississauga were unearthed, the ancient records of the Indians of the Credit were once again exposed to the light of day and the scrutiny of the court...*

It could have been that particular event that triggered Gilkison's removal, since the evidence of their place on the community rolls would have been found.

Ironically, perhaps, in July 1896, Peter E. Jones, son of the long dead reverend, revealed in the last document of the file that he was trying to get Henry the money he was owed for improvements because Henry was by that point about *68 years of age, and is a sober and quiet man, he does odd jobs about the village..... he has abandoned his immoral way of life, which made his removal so necessary... he had repented of his stubborness and now humbly appeals...*

There is a Henry Groat on the death index of the Brantford Library's *Expositor* newspaper collection for April 27 1917.

The Groat Mikes' troubles underline the fact that in the patriarchal societies of both the dominant white society and the Mississauga, racial purity was a split hair parted on the side of the father. As long as the pure blooded Caty Mike was alive, some of her children were acceptable, but after she died in 1877, things changed, but that was also because she died the year after the paternalistic membership law came into effect. At the same time, the larger family was interwoven with marriages to Mohawks, Oneida and Mississauga.

While the Tuscarora Groats were driven out of the tribe because they'd become Baptists, only to eventually return to the tribe, some Mississauga Groat Mikes were driven from the New Credit reserve for moral concerns while others weren't, so while racism may have played a role, it wasn't the issue.

Nelson Township Groats

Mike Sr. is not named in the 1842 census of Nelson township, Halton County, because only the head of the house is named, and in this case, the Michael Groat listed, is 47 years old, ie born circa 1795. It may also be that in the '42 census we see Michael of Nelson for the first time as himself. Not knowing the death date of Mike Sr., at no time before that census can we be so certain that the Michael Grote associated with the 1806 property in Nelson is *not* the 1794 free negro petitioner.

There may, however, have been a trace of Mike Sr. evident in that census, since that record does note the existence of a married male, 'over 60' living on the premises. If that was Mike Sr., and Mike was the father of William of Tuscarora born in 1783, the year the Revolution ended, whatever number of years Mike Sr. was 'over 60' in 1842, then he wouldn't have had to have been more than 16 or 17 to have fathered a child in 1783, putting his birth in the mid 1760's, and making him in his early eighties in 1842. (William of Guelph died at 80 in 1900.)

Michael is listed as being a coloured-negro in the 1842 census, so whether that means he was black or mixed marriage isn't clear. Michael's son, William of Guelph was likewise identified in various census records and local histories as mulatto, coloured-negro and African, so assuming he was mixed race, the question is, was his mother white, black or native?

Upper Canada/Canada West/Ontario census takers did not have distinctions as clear as the 1705 Henigs Statues of Virginia to define 'colored-negro', a term meant to include everyone not white or native, including Asians and East Indians, of which there were some.

[A Lancaster Regiment that served in Aboukir Bay, Egypt against Napoleon in 1803 came to the head of the lake in 1806 and served at Stoney Creek/Burlington Heights, so Arabs might also have followed; and used the *coloured-negro designation* without us knowing they existed except perhaps by name-analysis. It must have been Lancaster Regiment soldiers who re-named an indigenous trail that ran north from Dundas to Guelph, the Aboukir Road, because that was the name of the trail/path used by Puslinch and Guelph pioneers until it was planked in the 1840's and re-named the Brock Road.

One of the backers of the planking was Thomas Sandilands, who, by 1852 was also a Vice President of the Anti-Slavery Society of Canada representing Guelph, as well as a banker and political reformer we will meet again in Exodus and Arrival.]

William Groat came to Guelph in 1842, when the Brock

Road was being planked; those who knew him in Marden knew him as an axeman, so perhaps William worked the road north.

It seems improbable that Thomas Sandilands, the man who helped spear head the planking of that road would not have known William of Guelph or talked to him about the old days at the Head of the Lake, tales that only William could have known.

For me, Sandilands and Groat are the key and the keyhole to the door of the abolitionist movement in Guelph, and yet all I have is circumstantial evidence. Sandilands, a Scot, had come to Guelph in 1832; thus he was in the community almost from the start; he was also a peer of George Brown and other members of the Glasgow Anti-Slavery Society who arrived in Canada West shortly after the passing of the Emancipation Act. Sandilands must have known about the vanishing loyalist world of the Groats, the world of the first Fugitive Slave Act, when blacks, whites and natives had each other's backs, before the days of the naming of Aboukir Road.

It is possible that Michael of Nelson inherited the farm in 1833 and that Mike Sr.'s death brought the ownership of Brant lands to a crisis not resolved until 1844, two years after William left for Guelph, two years before Michael's death. In any event, we have only one Nelson story left to tell, that of James Chrysler, grandson of Michael of Nelson.

Groats Among the Cryslers

In the 1846 will of Michael of Nelson (see *Appendix 2*), Michael states that *Firstly, I give to my grandson James Chrysler the farm on which I live his heirs & forever assign.* Presumably, if Mike Sr. had been alive in 1842, by 1846 he too was dead.

There are three James Chrysler land registry records, the first in November 1847, in which he registered the land; then two more when he sold his inheritance in portions, the first in November 1849 to Daniel F. Sovereign, the second in February 1850 to Gilbert Davis (son of Asahel and grandson of William.) Both men were long-time loyalist neighbours.

Beyond those two records, James Chrysler seems to disappear, largely because of the uncertainty about who he was, since neither parent is known.

The most likely person is a James W. Chrysler married to a Sarah Addley, who had several children born in Nelson township/Wellington Square (several of whom later married into the Groat-Mike family, through the children of Henry Mike, son of John (1803) and Caty (1804-1877), Henry was one of the brothers removed from New Credit; three of his grandchildren married children of James and Sarah.)

```
4 Henry Groat (MIKE), Tuscarora township, Brant Co.
  m Ellen Taylor (the "white American woman")
  5 Margaret m. John Crysler
    6 Henry Groat Mike m Mary Groat Mike see 6 *
  5 Michael m Emily Chrysler
  5 William m Hannah Chrysler
  5 James m Annie Green
    6 *Mary m. Henry Groat Mike
```

Leaving aside the kissing cousins, Sarah Addley's ancestry is unknown, but both she and James W. Chrysler (born 1817) are listed as mulattoes in the 1861 Canadian census. (In the 1871 census James W. gives his 'origins' as German.) With a birth year of 1817, James W. is three years younger than William of Guelph, and is thus is an unlikely candidate for Michael's grandson. (Unless Michael wasn't actually 47 in 1842, and thus, there is/was only one Michael, ie. Mike Sr.)

James W. Chrysler and Sarah Addley had a son named James H. but he wasn't born until 1861. If James W. had an earlier son, also named James, he can't be Sarah's since she wasn't born until 1837, and thus can't be the mother of a child in an 1846 will. In that scenario, James W. could have fathered a child named James with one of Michael or Mike Sr.'s daughters, but there is no evidence of that birth, although the name James wasn't re-used by James W. until 1861, so perhaps the first James, was a Groat-Chrysler who had died by then. Maybe.

Four of the children of James and a by-then 19 year old Sarah were born in Wellington Square in the later 1850's. The fact is, however, that James W. was the only James Chrysler with black blood living in Nelson township in the years in question, so, problems of parentage aside, he is the most likely candidate, for the father of Michael's grandson James. We'll return to the second possible father shortly.

Besides James Chrysler, Michael's will also names William, Peter, Jemime, Margaret and Hannah as his children, but it does not say that they are his only offspring. The will also says nothing about whether the women were married or mothers. William was left a yoke and pair of oxen; the rest got a shilling.

There was a John Chrysler, who married Mary Ann Gage, who also lived in Nelson township; they had a son named James Gerrard Chrysler but he was *Born in Wellington Square ...on 23 Sep 1857...* so that too, is too late a birth for the will.

Mary Anne was the daughter of Asahel Gage and Nancy McCollum (Asahel, was the son of James Gage Jr. and Mary Davis.) On genealogical sites Nancy McCollum's father is John McCollum. In the 1852 census for Nelson there is a Canadian born John S McCollum who was listed as native, while his wife and mother, were not, though his children were. In the same census for Tuscarora there are a number of Credit River-born Indians between the ages of 6 to 50 named McCollum, John's wife is Eliza. On Peter Jones' 1855 New Credit census , John McCollum's wife calls herself Betsy, which, like Eliza, is a diminutive of Elizabeth. Mary Anne Gage Chrysler was both half native, and part of the loyalist head of the lake heritage .

Two of Nancy and Asahel Gage's sons, (brothers of Mary Anne) John and Asahel Jr., died during the American Civil War, fighting for the north in Sterling County, Iowa.)

Having gotten no closer to James Chrysler the Grandson, necessity requires us to delve more deeply into loyalist lore. The Chryslers have a mythical stature in Upper Canadian bravado, rooted as they are in their own mythos of the Blue-eyed Indians of Schoharie, New York, via Adam Crysler, captain of the Butler's Rangers and his four brothers. They fought alongside the confederacy of tribes in some of the most excessive fighting of the Revolutionary War. Adam was the uncle of John Crysler who later moved to the Morrisburg, Ontario farm on the St. Lawrence River on which was fought the 1813 battle now being marketed by that town as *The Battle that Saved Canada.*

Cryslers and the Upper Canadian Slave Trade

In *The Journey from Tollgate to Parkway: African Canadians in Hamilton,* Adrienne Shadd notes about the Chryslers that: *It is not known how many slaves the family ultimately possessed. What is intriguing is that Chryslers of African descent pop up in Wentworth archival records decades later...*

Shadd identifies Thomas, one of the black Cryslers of Ancaster, as a hotel waiter. What is not in her book however, is an appearance that Thomas makes in Nelson township history, to which we will return, as a possible candidate for father of James Chrysler.

Earlier in her book, Shadd discussed *an Agreement of sale between Adam Vrooman and Adam Crysler regarding a slave named Tom, August 25, 1792...* [p 229]

John Crysler (not the husband of Mary Ann Gage but the son of Adam) received a receipt from a man named Tom Blackman for being given his freedom by John in 1800. Blackman had been the slave Tom, purchased by Adam Crysler in 1792.

Received May the 3ʳᵈ 1800

From Mr John Crysler My former Master Twenty-five Dollars in Cash and a new suit of clothes and every other demand agreeable to my instructions Witness Present David Secord, His Tom x Blackman mark.

The closest we can come to connecting Tom Blackman the freed slave of Adam Chrysler to Michael of Nelson, is this 1847 District of Gore Sessional Committee report on road petitions:

In reference to... the Petition of Thomas Chrysler and others, for a new Road, south of the Dundas Street in the Township of Nelson...

And whereas, having duly considered the Petition of Thomas Chrysler and others, for altering and opening up a Public Highway in the township of Nelson, commencing at the south side of Dundas Street, at the limit between the townships of Nelson and East Flamboro';

and whereas a survey of said road having been duly made by James Cleaver, Esq., Road Surveyor, a description of which is as follows, that is to say: commencing at the south side of Dundas Street aforesaid, on the limit between said townships; thence south forty-five degrees, east on said limit forty-three chains fifty links, more or less, to the break of the mountain; then north thirty-seven degrees, east six chains down the said mountain; then south eighty-four degrees, east 23 chains ninety links; then south 45 deg. east, 18 chains, 50 links; then north 72° east ten chains 67 links; thence south 45 deg., east eight chains ninety links; thence south seventy degrees, east eighteen chains thirty links; thence south fifty-five degrees; east fifty-one chains and five links) more or less, to the laid out road in front of Freeman Sovereign's land; the said new road to be forty feet wide, that is, twenty foot on each side of the above description.

And be it enacted by the authority aforesaid, That the before mentioned description of road be established as a public highway to all intents and purposes.

And be it enacted by the authority aforesaid, That none of the general funds of the District be applied for payment of damages sustained by reason of the said road crossing the private property of any individual.

Passed by the Council SAMUEL CLARKE, Warden COUNCIL CHAMBER, Hamilton, 10th Nov. 1847. JAMES DURAND, D. Clerk, pg 76-77

What that means of course, is that in 1847, the year after Mike Sr.'s land became the property of James Crysler, a man named Thomas Crysler had a road extended to the property line that the Groats had shared with the Sovereign family for nearly forty years. (It was also to a Sovereign that James Chrysler sold part of Mike Sr.'s land two years later.)

In the 1852 census for Ancaster, Thomas Chrysler is a 25 year old coloured-negro servant with no creed, born in Canada West in 1826, living and working in Margaret Roy's Inn with another colored-negro named Julian Frazer. At 25, Thomas can at best be a son of Shadd's proposed Tom (Blackman) Crysler, born in Blackman's first year of freedom. Unfortunately, Thomas Chrysler of Nelson/Ancaster is not in the 1861 or 1871 census records. He would have been 20 in 1847, so perhaps his name was James Thomas, a son by one of Michael's three daughters, Jemime, Margaret or Hannah. Beyond that, nothing else is known, so it's all in the way you want it imagined.

William of Guelph's only son was also named James, but he died young and is buried in an unmarked grave in Woodlawn.

William Moves to Guelph

Four years before his father's death, William Groat "migrated" to Guelph, in Wellington Co. The same year, his wife-to-be, Elizabeth Adams came to stay in Guelph with an aunt and uncle, Mary Ann and William Archibald.

In a post on the genealogy blog of Arlene Noble's cousin, Sharon Hewlett, called *Long Tweed Skirts, Warm Sweaters and Small Crofts*, dated June 20. 2011 Hewlett notes that:

Elizabeth Adams, age 8 and Hannah Doherty, age 25 left... Bovagh... Aghadowey Parish, Londonderry, Ireland in 1835 for Canada .

Rumor or family lore, told to me by Frances Herren, of Arvada, Colorado, (four of the Groat-Adam's daughters ended up in Colorado) *now deceased, says that Elizabeth Hannah Doherty became pregnant by the Lord of the Manor, or someone of that stature and she was paid off and sent somewhere, maybe Scotland or Ireland to have the child or to relocate...The child would have been Elizabeth Adams. ... her mother had first gone to Quebec, or so her obituary reads, and then she to Ontario with her aunt and uncle William and Mary Ann Archibald. They settled in Peel Township.*

Immediately next door to the Archibalds in the Queen's Bush was *the William Docherty family - born in Scotland and immediately next to them was William Docherty Sr. born in Ireland, the probable brother & father of Mary Ann Docherty Archibald.*

Elizabeth Adams came to Guelph from the Queen's Bush with her aunt and uncle in 1846 and almost immediately married William Groat. In the 1852 Census of Peel township William Archibald and his wife Maryann are both back in the Queen's Bush, so they can't have stayed long in Guelph after Elizabeth married.

It may be possible to make too much of the direct link of Elizabeth's coming of age in the largest settlement of former fugitive slaves in the province or of her marrying a free-born black in Guelph with roots to the Baptist Tuscarora, because sometimes, a coincidence is just a coincidence.

None of the Archibalds or Dochertys are mentioned by Linda Brown-Kubisch in her study of the black pioneers of that

Settlement. Not that such an omission - of itself - means anything. Whether Adams knew the Ghents or not isn't known.

All that is clear is that Elizabeth Adams lived in the Queen's Bush during the height of the black settlement; and then married a mixed-race man, which meant that she had no qualms about race, so if she wasn't an abolitionist, she was emancipated enough to marry freely. She lived among Scots too, so perhaps she knew Thomas Sandilands.

The 1852 Guelph census does not exist anymore, so the next evidence of William's life (and by extension hers) is in the Ontario Directory for 1857, p37 when the family was living on concession 1 lot 15 in Guelph township (the village of Marden). What is curious in that, is that William Groat also owned or leased land in Puslinch at the same time, because there is a William Groat listed on Concession 10 lot 21 (front). Perhaps he had been able to parlay the team of oxen willed to him by his father in 1846 into a logger's life, since he was later known as a man who split 4000 cords of wood.

In the 1861 census for Guelph, William is listed as 40 years old, Elizabeth as 30, Hannah is 11, Mary Jane 9, Eliza 6, Louisa 5, and Abigail 2: all but Elizabeth were listed as mulattoes.

There is a nine year old named Rebecca Groat, born in 1862, who must have died by the 1871 census. Harriet was born in 1871. James Groat lived and died then too. In the Woodlawn cemetery there is an Archibald family plot, so maybe James is buried with them. Curiously, according to the cemetery records, there is also a Hannah Groat buried in an unmarked grave: she may have been William's sister, since his daughter's married name was Hannah Lillie. (There are other Groats in the Guelph cemetery but they are white Palatines from Lobo township in Middlesex County.)

Like William, Elizabeth Adams was originally Presbyterian but became a Methodist. It seems probable that there was some kind of return to church going, because all the daughters and James were baptized on April 20 1867 by Reverend John S. Carroll in Guelph. Rev. Carroll was the man who wrote about James Gage Jr. being a liberal supporter of Methodist activities.

In August 1874, William bought 1 acre on the southeast corner of Lot 15, Concession 1, Division D, on the Atkinson farm from George Atkinson (the property listed in the directory of 1857.)

According to Stephen Thorning in his January 4 2013 *Wellington Advertiser* column *Valuing Our History*, there were three hotels in Marden before the coming of the railway to Guelph in 1856, which is when Guelph became a shipping point. (The Brock Road from Dundas to Guelph had, by 1842, been extended north through what became Marden to Fergus and Arthur; as had the road to Elora, which branched northwest off the Fergus road about a mile north of Marden, so that the village became the preferred point for farmers to stop for the night; the teamsters would travel the last four miles into Guelph in the morning to transact whatever business they had.)

William Groat is referred to in A.E. Byerly's *The Beginning of Things in Wellington and Waterloo Counties*: *Richard Knowles ... who was born near Marden... wrote his reminiscences for me... "There were several others in that neighbourhood who never owned farms. Some of them mechanics, some labourers, all useful men... William Grote (colored), the Marden man in history, who chopped, split, and piled about 4,000 standard cords of hardwood. On putting up his two cords each day, he shouldered his axe and went home."* [Byerly p 67]

Two full cords a day for four thousand cords is two thousand days, six days a week with a rest on the sabbath and who knows what other delays and down times, equals seven years at the most, so perhaps he also felled trees and cut roads (a trade he would have learned on the fruit plantations of Wellington Square.) It seems probable that William Groat's 1857 presence on the land in Puslinch and Marden/Guelph township was connected to the railroad: 4000 cords was steam engine fuel.

There is, thus, better evidence of his playing a role in the actual railroad than there is for his role in the underground one, but every step of his way, he was man to whom fugitive blacks would have turned, in Guelph he must have been a touch stone, a rarity, a truly free black Canadian; in Marden he could tell Queen's Bush bound blacks heading north out of Guelph how to get where they wanted. All he had to be was a good Samaritan to those who knew less about freedom than he did to have helped more than many could have. He was 'a useful man', one who went home shouldering his axe until his natural health faltered and failed, after which his mind collapsed from the daily indignities indigence imposes on those struggling for daily bread in old age.

Let us hope William Groat had memory, and fond ones, because once he bought the property in Marden in 1874, he must have been able to make the purchase because of the stability of the cord word market. They may have been his best years, and he may have survived them for a time as a steady working man. His collapse may have been quick though his poverty was probably well advanced. They may have been good years for Elizabeth and William, despite the missing James and Rebecca. It would be from Marden that his daughters would marry and move away in turn. The one that matters most for the sake of this narrative is their first, *Hannah, born (in Guelph) December 28 1850, married Thomas Lillie (1842) and died in Salem, Wellington County* (now part of Elora) *on October 24 1934, she was the mother of 5 children....* [Hewlett] See Groat Family Tree, Appendix 1.

Thomas Lillie, Hannah's husband, was the son of George Lillie, a man who makes an appearance in *Exodus & Arrival* as a member of the Guelph Reform movement within Canada West grit-liberal circles. George Lillie was thus a peer of Thomas Sandilands, manager of the Gore Bank, Brock Road planker and Vice President, Guelph, of the Anti-Slavery Society of Canada as recorded in their Second Annual Report. There were other blacks in Salem, which is a story told in *Exodus and Arrival.*

In the 1891 Census William is listed as Methodist and living in Guelph. The now defunct Guelph Museum webpage where we began this book first noted that:

William Groat died on August 27, 1900 at the House of Industry... where he spent his last three years. William was 80 years old when he died and is buried in the Belsyde Cemetery in Fergus.

Elizabeth Adams Groat was 67 when her husband became an inmate of the House of Industry, 70 when he died. (William Groat, as his death record notes, died of apoplexy, a word that during his day meant a loss of consciousness caused by a blood hemorrhage, leading to immediate death - blood losses that are nowadays specified as to the organ that ruptures.)

[House of Industry records]

In July 1905, his widow Elizabeth sold (the Marden lot) to Charles Atkinson. She then lived with her eldest daughter Hannah in Salem until her death in 1909. [Guelph Museum]

If Elizabeth Adams Groat was 8 years old when she left Ireland in 1835, she was born in 1827, and thus was 78-79 years old when she died. She was buried in the Woodlawn Cemetery, Guelph, perhaps with James and Rebecca, or William's sister Hanna, or all three, while William was still interred among the House of Industry dead on a shoulder of the hill above the small gorge on the Grand River not far from Elora or the old Pierpoint settlement itself buried in new Fergus.

But was William forgotten? And how did he end up in the Belsyde cemetery House of Industry? Inmates were allowed visitors and the Lillies were nearby in Elora/Salem, so perhaps his time in the institution had had its pleasant moments. In the end, it is his last record that answers both the above questions and brings resolution to his beginnings: in the *House of Industry* accounts researched by Karen Wagner at the Archive, it is recorded that his body was removed from the cemetery by Mrs. C Farley in 1925, and then re-interred in Belsyde, Fergus. Mrs. C Farley was Hannah's daughter, William's grand daughter. It seems redemptive and fitting to me, that family loyalty should retrieve him from among the displaced; that his memory was cherished, inspiring generations of his descendants to go looking for a man they only knew by name.

Hannah Groat Lillie courtesy of the family

Conclusion

It seems to me, that while I cannot prove that William Groat was involved in abolitionist activities, the spirit of his life was ultimately emancipationist by virtue of his grand daughter's freeing him from ignominy of the poor house graveyard.

The Groats of Nelson and Guelph would have made perfect termini agents of the Underground Railroad; they had extensive links to the loyalist free-black and fugitive communities at the head of the lake from Stoney Creek to Port Nelson and Oakville, and they had Tuscarora Baptist and Mississauga Methodist relations. And if the Margaret Groat who married Abram Topp and had a son of the same name who was a Norwich township Quaker, while his sister Hannah was married to the AME/BME minister in Ottersville, Norwich, then perhaps everything that needed to be in place was in place. And yet that is not proof of involvement.

William arrived in Guelph as a 22 year old in 1842, a time when Thomas Sandilands had been in South Wellington for a decade, doing who knows what if anything about abolition until 1852, when he is listed as an Anti-Slavery Society of Canada vice president for Guelph. The Groat family stayed in Guelph for 15 years or so before moving to Marden by 1857.

Sandilands backed other roads and rail projects. It's not hard to see how his own business property in Guelph's Market Square could have been used in anti-slavery activities, carts and wagons coming and going at all hours in all directions.

William Groat was known from Nelson and Oakville to Guelph, Hamilton, the Grand River and beyond to the reserves of the Thames at Caradoc and to the Queen's Bush. He would have been sought by blacks passing through Guelph in the days when south Wellington was losing its wilderness to settlement, when native trails became Sandilands' roads until they were squared up by concession lines and block-crossed by side roads.

William Groat may have been the first and only free-born adult black in south Wellington County when he arrived in 1842 but there is evidence of local free-born children of African Americans earlier in Puslinch and Eramosa. Those times, places and people form the milieu of *Exodus and Arrival.*

The most extraordinary part of this research is that what began as an investigation into the history of a stone building in Guelph, continuously turned inward to reveal the shape of the native anti-slavery movement from Loyalist times and through a single family.

I was amazed at how following every turn of the story brought us back to Wayne Smythe's twin mandates to me, find proof that native trails were the beds of the Underground Railroad, and that those who traveled on them were aided, abetted and succoured by people of good faith, from all denominations, white, black and native, and to whom credit must be given.

For myself, I was surprised to find a family at the heart of it, and in the traces of it. A family whose story contained its own emancipationist ending. A family whose story turned the telling of the building of a British Methodist Episcopal church in Guelph into a search for fugitives arriving in the colony from 1793 on, which turned abolition into a Loyalist story.

However, just as the Groats surprised me during the research of *Laying the Bed*, so I continue to be surprised by people whose stories I've found during the research of *Exodus and Arrival: Fugitive Roads to Guelph* and found for its sequel, *Blood in the Mortar: September 17 1880*.

It's a big story about people – some of whom - were called terrorists in their own time, people working in common cause to end a tyrannical economic system, people who helped others become and stay, free. It's a story I like because 19th century evangelical Christianity makes 21st century Christianity seem like the Whore of Babylon working the temples of Babylon, pimped by Mammon. They knew something about Christ in the 19th century that 21st century Christians appear to dislike. The people in these pages need to be celebrated. They aren't perfect, but they knew injustice when they saw, it, and they did something about it, together and alone., on many fronts

Slavery still exists, the same kind of people run the system for the same reasons. We need generations who understand that *Let my people go* means Let my people go *now and forever.* Somebody say Amen.

Appendix 1
Groat Family Tree

1 Mike Sr. Michael GROTE African GROAT b.NC(?)d.UC
(1794 free negro petition Nelson township assessments)
+ unknown wife
.... 2 William GROAT-Tuscarora Negro
1783 - 1852
.....................+ 1st 'marriage' Margaret Tuscarora N.C.
...........................3 Abram GROAT -Tuscarora/Negro
1814 – 1904
+ Sarah Ann Williams Tuscarora
b. Lewiston NY (Haud Proj) died 1868
dau of John Williams, sister of Jacob
.... 4 Wm. Groat b.1834 Grand River, (c)Caradoc
...........................4 John Groat named *Haudenosaunee Project*
...........................4 Abram Groat name in Haud Proj
.... 4 Lydia Groat + 1ˢᵗ David Beeswax
Caradoc Chippewa
...........................4 Henry G. Groat (MIKE) b. S. 16 48, Tusc,
m Ellen Taylor
5 Margaret m. John Crysler
6 Henry Groat Mike m * Mary Groat Mike
5 Michael m Emily Chrysler
5 William m Hannah Chrysler
5 James m Annie Green
6 *Mary m. Henry Groat Mike
..........................4 Samson Groat , b 1850 Ont
..........................4 Levina(Revina) b S. 17 1852-1927 Tusc Brant
.... + Chief Solomon -Tusc- NASH 1836 - 1927
.... +2nd Husband of Levina
David WEBSTER 1836 - 1901
.... + 3rd Husband of Levina -
.... Joseph -Chippewa- BEAVER 1840 – 1918
5 Caroline Beaver (George's gg)
.... + 4th Husband of Levina
Nicholas -Tuscarora- OWENS 1868 - 1935
.................+ 2nd marriage Wm Groat = Amelia (Emily) SMITH
1789–1871 (mother? Molly Turner; m. Mr . Smith*)
*Haudenosaunee Project1819 - 1852
.... 3 William -Tuscarora- GROAT 1822 - 1852
.... +Mary w -Tuscarora-1832 - 1852
.... 4 Peggy GROAT 1849 - 1852
.... 4 Mike GROAT 1850 - 1852
.... 3 Sarah -Tuscarora- GROAT 1832 - 1852
.... 3 John -Tuscarora- GROTE GROAT 1833 - 1852
.... 3 Hannah -Tuscarora- GROAT 1835 - 1852
.............2 Jemiah b. (c) 1784 UC + Ebenezer Guire   1777 US
.............2 Simon Groat 1793-1880? b. US died Caradoc, On
+ Mary Ann Lewis (m. 1847)

....   3 William 19 1871   parents?
....   3 Hugh   10 1871   parents ?
...............2 Michael GROAT 1795-1846 (Nelson, m. unknown)
...................3 William (1820-1901) born Saltfleet, lived Nelson,
            Guelph, Marden m Elizabeth ADAMS 1826 – 1909
.........................4 Hannah Groat 1850 - 1932
...........................+Thomas LILLIE 1842 - 1890
.........................4 Mary Jane Groat 1851 - 1930
.... 4 Edith Elizabeth Groat 1854 - 1867
.........................4 Louisa Groat 1856 - 1943
.........................4 Abigail Groat 1859 - 1939
...........................+Thomas Hackett FENNELL 1856 - 1935
.........................4 Rebecca Groat 1862
.........................4 James Groat 1864-
.........................4 Henrietta Cecilia Groat 1865
.........................4 Harriet Alice Groat 1870 - 1870
.........................4 Winnifred Groat 1871 - 1959
.........................4 Martha Groat 1872 - 1881
...................3 Peter
...................3 Jemime
...................3 Margaret
...................3 Hannah
...............2 Margaret GROAT b.US 1797 + Abram TOPP b US 1788 (Michael's will)
...................3 Abram TOPP b UC 1819 Quaker, 1861 census = Jemima? Norwich
...................3   Hannah TOPP b UC 1821 + Rev. Lindsey Anderson AME?BME "
...............2 Peter GROAT   1813 Dundas Rd patrol
            'Pete Groat' 1830 Nelson assessment
...............2 Henry Groat   1813 Dundas Road patrol
.... 2 John GROAT Mike 1801
                    +Catherine (Mississauga). b. Credit River
          3 Peter   + Sophie Bellevue
          3 Margaret + Richard Lewis
          3 Henry   + Ellen Taylor
          3 William   + Anna Claus

Appendix 2
The Will of Michael Groat 1 of 3

388

In the name of God Amen _____ August [?] one thousand
eight hundred forty six _____ I Michael Groat of
the township of Nelson and District of
Gore and Province of Canada, Yeoman, being
very sick, and weak of body but of perfect mind
and memory thanks be given to God, therefore
calling unto mind the mortality of my body knowing
that it is appointed unto all men once to die
do make and ordain this my last will and testa[ment]
that is to say, principally and first of all, I give
and recommend my soul into the hands of Almighty
God that gave it and my body to the earth
to be bured in decent christian burial, at the
discretion of my executors, nothing doubting, but at
the general resurrection I shall receive the same
again by the almighty power of God And as touchi[ng]
such worldly estate, wherewith it hath pleased go[d]
to bless me in this life I give, demise, and dispose
of the same in the following manner and form.

Firstly I give to my Grand Son James
Chrysler the farm on which I live his heirs & Assig[ns]
Also I give to my Son William Groat one yoke
of oxen and one heifer. Also I give to my daughter
Jemima Margarett and Hannah the sum of
five shillings each Also I give to my Son
Peter Grout the sum of five Shilling[s]

continued

The Will of Michael Groat 2 of 3

do make and ordain this my last will and testa[ment]
that is to say. principally and first of all, I give
and recommend my soul into the hands of Almighty
God that gave it and my body to the earth
to be buried in decent christian burial, at the
discretion of my executors. nothing doubting. but at
the general resurrection I shall receive the san
again by the almighty power of God And as touchen
such worldly estate, wherewith it hath pleased god
to bless me in this life I give. demise, and dispose
of the same in the following manner and form

Firstly I give to my Grand Son James
Chrysler the farm on which I live his heirs & Ass[igns]
2 Also I give to my Son William Groat one Yoke
of oxen and one heifer. Also I give to my daughthte[r]
Jemime Margarett and Hannah the Sum of
five shillings each Also I give to my Son
Peter Groat the sum of five Shilling
Also the rest of my pursonall property I leave
in the hands of my executors to be Sold by them
and to pay the legaties and funeral expences an
any other debts that my accure

I likewise constitute, make, and ordain
Henry Guyre and William Davis my Sole executors of
this my last will and testament And I do hereby
3 utterly disallow revoke, and disannull all and every other
former testaments. wills. legacies, bequests, and executors

continued

The Will of Michael Groat 3 of 3

Gilbert Davis
George Bradt
Abram Top signatures

Appendix 3: The Groat-Mike Lands Outside of Hagersville

Appendix 4
Two Letters Henry C. Howells to Milo Townsend

Letter 66

from Henry C. HowellR.B. Union, Perth Amboy Decr 31, 1854

My dear friend Townsend,

More than three long-- no, short, very short months have passed away since I commingled with the happy spirits that form the pleasant circle at New Brighton.

There is yourself, your lovely and interesting wife, your beloved and venerable parents who like myself are almost on the confines of a better, happier world, then our honest friend Ewen with his amiable wife and lovely and interesting girls, then that sweet little gem of a woman opposite you who gave me Gurney's hymns, and lastly your good neighbor Mr. Higby. I have thought of you all a thousand times, and had I been disrobed of mortality I would surely have been with you as often or at least as often as I could have spared from other visits of love.

My intention was to write to you at a much earlier period, but my time has been so fully occupied that I too long neglected a correspondence even with my children. However I can now write to you concerning this place with more satisfaction to my own mind. I must first promise and set you and all my dear friends at N. Brighton (for to you all this letter comes) on your guard, that I generally look at the bright and hopeful and progressive side of every subject which concerns the extension of light, love, and blessedness in this our world. For our Father, God, and His Truth must triumph over all.

This is a lovely spot of retirement, beauty, and great capabilities of being made to promote human wants and happiness. The society includes a school of the first order conducted by Mr. T .D. Weld, consists of more than 150 persons and the most part of very intelligent and congenial minds, kind and Christian with a variety of religious theories tho for the most part Spiritualists. The families here live apart and can cook for themselves or take their meals at the public table. There is a large handsome palace-like-looking unitary dwelling and the old Mansion. In the latter we live which commands most beautiful country.

Jany 22nd. Just one month since I began this letter, which I could not finish, so fully is my time occupied. I now wish you all a most happy new year, a year in which you will prosper more than ever you have done in all that is just, true, lovely, and of good report. That you may be the better prepared, by the indwelling spirit of the Holy, lowly Jesus, and thus be the better fitted for an inheritance with the spirits of the just made perfect.

I have just been reading that interesting Spiritual Telegraph of yesterday. How much of precious truth it contains. Poor Doctor Dodds. "Saul among the prophets"! That is an excellent joke, if there was no such thing as conscience.

We have a meeting here every first day morning pretty much like friends' meeting except that sometimes we read scripture or other works and generally sing once or twice. The speakers are various men and women. Theodore D. Weld is the master spirit, a mind of the most spiritual and powerful order. If you come this way come and see us.

The Steamer John Potter connected with Perth Amboy, stops at Perth Amboy, which is only one mile from Raritan Bay Union.

The winter is passing away. The snow and frost will soon be gone, the flowers will soon appear, the birds return and resume their song and the voice of the turtle dove be heard in our land. Oh! This is a world of beauty. But what to the bright world to which we go.

Every first day evening we have a discussion in the Welds's school room of some reformatory subject in which all may take a part. This has been the most happy and merry Christmas I ever had a portion in in the way of music and dancing. Both are delightful and innocent amusements and good for health of body and soul. See the beautiful parable of the prodigal son's return and the joy of angels over him.

This is the 28 of Janr. I could not close this before.

With the kindest love of my heart to you all, I am your friend and Brother

Henry C. Howells

Adieu!

Let us hear from you soon.

Letter 97
from Henry C. Howells
Eagleswood, March. 26/57
Milo Townsend

My Dear friend:
As I am indebted to you a letter which I have not been able to answer heretofore, & believing that the brotherly affection which has long existed between us is undying, I think it well, though from much weakness I am compelled to use the hand of a dear friend, to write you a few lines from the borders of that happy spirit land to which I am hastening. My complaint being dropsy & asthma combined, I think it not unlikely that my stay will be very short.

I am indebted to you, my dear friend, for having first called my attention to the glorious realities of Spiritualism, which being in harmony with the spirit & love of Jesus, cheers my heart and elevates my hopes-- There are two mistakes which the world is making, one is the bold assertion that the whole Bible is the word of God and must be received as such on peril of salvation-- This conflicting with common sense & the best principles of our natures, has led other minds -- because they will not be trammeled, to reject the whole of Scriptures as unworthy of their regard. Now dear friend, if God has ever revealed his mind to man, most precious revelations will be found in the prophets, the psalms, the teachings of Jesus & the writings of the Apostles-- I am thankful, very thankful, that now in my weakness when unable to read, or to hear much, that the dew-drops of divine love are brought fresh into my soul, both by day & during the sleepless hours of night, in the form of precious portions from Scripture--

Give my kindest love to your venerable father & mother, to your beloved wife, to the widow Townsend & her family-- To the honest millwright whose name I forget, and his dear family-- To the dear little Quaker dame (whose name I also forget) that gave me the hymn book. And through her to dear little Sallie Jordan.Dear friends, Adieu, till we meet all in glory. May every blessing in time and eternity rest upon you all.   Henry C. Howells

First Published in *Milo Adams Townsend and Social Movements of the Nineteenth Century.* Townsend (1817-1877)

Appendix 5
Abraham Topp's Nelson Township Land Grant
for having Serving in the Western District Rangers
3rd from the top

Acknowledgments

First off, there are six Groat family researchers to thank: the first is Arlene Noble of North Bay, descended from William of Guelph's daughter Hannah, whose genealogical postings and emails gave me a way into William's father's family.

The second and third family researchers are Eric Jensen who compiled the *Haudenosaunee Project* based on his analysis of the Kansas Land Claim files; as well as Andrew Timlek, whose own studies came complete with a family tree of the native Groats of the Six Nations Reserve, supplemented by Jensen's work.

The fourth Groat researcher requiring thanks, is Sharon Hewlett of Utah, a distant cousin of Arlene's, who researched the Docherty/Archibald family and how they came to be in the Queen's Bush and Guelph.

Fifthly, there is George Beaver, the Tuscarora Mohawk writer from the Six Nations Reserve whose blog writings gave me another key to this work via the name of Margaret Groat of North Carolina, mother of Abram Groat, one of the Tuscarora Baptist Warriors from the 1842 petition. George died in the summer of 2013, he wasn't feeling well when I spoke with him a months or so before, I'm glad I did.

And lastly, Fred Blair, a man whose postings on the York Militia and the role played by the Groat family on the Dundas Road patrol during the War of 1812 provided the key to the interconnectedness of the black/native loyalist Groats, Guires and Topps.

Also of help in the creation of this book, was the Guelph Library, which provides access to ancestry.com, a site that allowed me to study the families contained in this book. The library also holds census and assessment records of Nelson township, a crucial source of information for understanding the Groat family and its loyalist roots. It was from those records that I began to disentangle the native Groats from the African ones, and to eventually thread them all into a whole.

I am also indebted to professional genealogist Hilary Dawson for sending me in the direction of Abram Topp, Margaret Groat their daughter Hannah and her husband the

AME/BME minister of Ottersville, after which I found Hannah's brother, the Norwich township Quaker, Abram, which allowed me to connect the dots to Abram Top who signed the will of Michael of Nelson.

Karen's Wagner's *House of Industry* researches at the Wellington County Museum were also a great help.

Likewise, without family historians, genealogists, and their online communities focused on their inter-related ancestors helping one another find evidence behind family legends and rumours, I could never have written this book.

United Empire Loyalist websites and their considerable resources were also invaluable including the writings of John A. Aikman and Paul L. Bingle who both gave me clues about where to find the Groats' back story via on the Davis-Ghent families during the Revolutionary War in North Carolina.

I likewise want to thank the Burlington Museum for their collection of historical documents from the War of 1812 and events involving Burlington Bay, which were of help in understanding the world in which William of Guelph's father Michael - and his grandfather Mike Sr. - lived.

I want to conclude by thanking John Leacock for his heart, Denise Richards for her friendship, Marva Wisdom for her commitment; Geneva Neale for food and her point of view, Rosemary Sadlier for preparing the way; Rochelle Bush for her trust and Wayne F. Smythe for sending me off to find what still can be found of this extraordinary story.

The last three years of research have been a labour of love for those who fled this way and the people who helped them where ever and whenever help was needed. The Guelph Black Heritage Society was conceived in that spirit, and is why Marva Wisdom and her board have laboured to save the church.

My last set of thanks go to my partner Morvern McNie, whose patience with my obsessions is gratefully and humbly received even if I am too stubborn some times for my own good; I'd also like to thank her son Brenan Pangborn for his cover design and his willingness to fine tune as it evolved, and finally, my own son James Campbell Prager for his maps and acerbic commentaries on earlier drafts of the book.

Jerry Prager, Elora, Ontario February 4 2014

Index

Works Cited
Books

Allen, Thomas B. *Tories: Fighting For the King in America's First Civil War*
    Harper Collins, New York 2010

Applegate, Debby; *The Most Famous Man in America: The Biography of*
    Henry Ward Beecher, New York, Doubleday 2006

Brock, Daniel. *The History of the County of Middlesex, Canada.*
    Facsimile edition Mika Studio, Bellevile 1972

Brown, Mrs. DC; *Memoir of the Late Rev. Lemeul Covell, Missionary To The*
    Tuscarora Indians and the Province of Upper Canada...Up to the
    Time of Mr. Covell's Decease In 1806; Brandon 1839

Brown, Leslie Christopher; Morgan, Philip D. *Arming Slaves: From*
    Classical Times to the Modern Age

Brown-Kubisch, Linda; *The Queen's Bush Settlement (1839-1865)*
    Natural Heritage/National History Inc. Toronto. 2004

Byerly, AE *The Beginning of Things in Wellington and Waterloo Counties,*
    Guelph Publishing Company, 1935 (Reprinted).

Clark, June Murtie *Loyalists in the Southern Campaign of the*
    Revolutionary War , Baltimore, Genealogical Publishing Co 1981

Christian, John T; *Baptist History Throughout the Ages,* Vol 11;
    New Orleans, Louisiana

Chrysler, Don. *The Blue-Eyed Indians, The Story of Adam Crysler and His*
    Brothers in the Revolutionary War. Zephyrhills, FL: Don Chrysler
    Books 1999

Cruikshank, Ernest. *Compiled From The Municipal Records Of the County*
    of Welland, Part I. 1792-1841; Welland Tribune 1892-93

Craig, Martha *The Garden of Canada, Burlington, Oakville and District,*
    Toronto, William Briggs Press 1902

Davis, David Brion, *Slavery and Freedom in American History and Memory*
    Yale, 2008

Densmore, Christopher *Migrating Quakers, Fugitive Slaves and Indians:*
    The Quaker Ties of New York and Upper Canada

Dorland, Arthur G. *History of the Society of Friends in Canada*
    MacMillan Canada, 1927, Toronto

Garrison, Wm Lloyd, *The Letters of William Lloyd Garrison,* Harvard Press

Gray, Charlotte. Flint and Feather: The Life and Times of E. Pauline
    Johnson, Tekahionwake Phyliss Bruce Books 2003

Hawkins, JJ; *Early Days in Brantford;* Brant Historical Society Papers, 1911

Henry, Natasha L. *Taking about Freedom, Celebrating Emancipation Day in*
    Canada. Dundurn Press Toronto 2010

Henson, James (Glenelg); *Broken Shackles: Old Man Henson From Slavery*
    to Freedom. Toronto 1889

Hosmer, Brian; Nesper, Larry, editors: *Tribal Worlds: Critical Studies in*
    American Indian Nation Building State U of NY Press 2013

Hood, Rev James Walker; *One Hundred Years of the African Methodist*
    Episcopal Zion Church; or, The Centennial of African Methodism:

Klinck; C. F. Talman JJ, editors: *The Journal of Major John Norton, 1816,*

Champlain Society, Toronto, 1970)

Johnasen, Bruce, Prtizker, Barry, *Encyclopedia of American Indian History*
ABC Clio, 2007

Johnson, Bruce E. Editor *Native Americans Today, A Biographical Dictionary,* Greenwood Publishing

Johnston, Charles M., ed. *Ontario Series VII, The Valley of the Six Nations: A Collection of Documents on the Indian Lands of the Grand River* pub. Champlain Society, University of Toronto Press, 1964

Keller, Betty, *Pauline: a Biography of Pauline Johnson* Douglas & McIntyre, Vancouver, British Columbia 1981

Kelsay, Isabel, *Joseph Brant 1743-1780 Man of Two Worlds*, 1984,

Landon, Fred, *Ontario's African-Canadian Heritage: Collected Writings* editors: Karolyn Smardz Frost, Bryan Walls, Hilary Bates Neary Frederick H. Armstrong; Natural Heritage Books 2009, Toronto

Louguen, JW. *The Rev. J. W. Loguen, as a Slave and as a Freeman. A Narrative of Real Life ;* Syracuse, NY JGK Truair & Co. 1859

Mafirici, Thomas B, and August, Elizabeth A; Images *of America: Cicero* Arcadia Publishing 2012

Marriage Register of Rev. Black 1828-1842 Districts of Gore & Niagara *Historical record of the posterity of William Black*

Martin, John H. *Saints, Sinners and Reformers: The Burned-Over District Re-Visited 2005*

Matthews, Hazel, *Oakville and the Sixteen, The History of an Ontario Port.* Oakville (Ont.) University of Toronto Press, 1953

McCoy, Ted ; *Hard Time, Reforming the Penitentiary in Nineteenth-Century Canada*, Athabaska University Press, 2012

Meyler, David and Peter *A Stolen Life: Searching for Richard Pierpoint* Natural Heritage 1999

Meyler, Peter (editor) *Broken Shackles: Old Man Henson From Slavery to Freedom,* Natural Heritage Books, Toronto 2001

O'Dell, William F. *Twelve Families: An American Experience* William F. Baltimore, Gateway Press 1981

Oliver, Peter *Terror to Evil-Doers: Prisons and Punishments in Nineteenth-Century Ontario O*sgoode Society for Legal History 1st edition, 1998

Ontario Directory for 1857 with a Gazetteer, Lambertville, New Jersey, USA: Hunterdon House, 1987.

Royal Colony of North Carolina: Henry McCulloch, Esq. - A Man of Mystery Uncovered

Ruoff, A. Lavonne Brown. Johnson, E Pauline *The Moccasin Maker 1913*

Shadd, Adrienne *The Journey from Tollgate to Parkway: African Canadians in Hamilton,* Dundurn Press, Hamilton 2010

Siebert, William *The Underground Railroad, Slavery to Freedom,* MacMillian, 1898

Simms, Jeptha R, *History of Schoharie County and Border Border Wars of New York.* Munsell & Tanner Albany NY 1845

Smith, Donald B.; *Sacred Feathers*, U of T Pub., Toronto 2nd edition 2013

Souffer, Allen P. *Light of Nature and the Law of God, Anti-Slavery in*

Ontario, 1833-1877 McGill-Queen's University Press 1992

Strong-Boag, Veronica Jane; Gerson, Carole. *Paddling Her Own Canoe: The Times and Texts of E. Pauline Johnson (Tekahionwake)* . University of Toronto Press, Scholarly Publishing Division (2000)

Sweeney, Allistair. Fire Along the Frontier: Great Battles of the War of 1812: Dundurn Press, Hamilton, 2012

Torry, Alvin; *The Autobiography of Alvin Torry;* WJ Moses, Auburn NY 1869

Townsend, Charles walker III, Peggy Jean, Arlene Ruth *Milo Adams Townsend and Social Movements of the Nineteenth Century.* 1994

Various Authors, The History of the County Brant County 1883, Toronto; Warner Beers & Co. 1883

Winks, Robin, *Blacks in Canada* McGill-Queen's University Press, 1997

Journals/Newspapers

American Anthropologist Volume 68, Issue 5

Bladen Journal, Steven Weaver

Canadian Quaker History, Vol 58

Christian Review, Volume 12 , edited by Rev S.F. Smith, December 1847

Crooked Lake Review, Fall 2005

Hamilton Spectator

Inside Halton, Helen Langford, New Findings

Journal of Negro History Vol. IV—January, 1919—No. 1, *chapter* IV
       The Royal Adventurers and the Plantations Riddell, William.

Names Only But Much More, Niagara Historical Society no 27, Carnochan, Janet.

Proceedings of the New Jersey Historical Society, Vol 68 No 1
       Maud Honeyman Green, Raritan Bay Union, Eagleswood, Jan. 1950

Number 1 Company, Niagara, Niagara Historical Society no 27, Ascher, Mrs. E

Proceedings of the Ohio Anti-Slavery Society 1835

Report by a Committee of the Corporation Commonly called the New England Company of their Proceedings for the the Civilization and Conversion of the Indians Printed for Circulation Among the Members of the Company According to the Resolution of the General Court held 15 July 1845, London, Printed by J. Gibson, Aldermanbury

Wellington Advertiser: Valuing our History Thorning, Stephen

Websites

- Ancestry.com, various users, Maya Harris, Bryan Norris,, Fred Blair, Arlene Noble, Sharon Hewlett, Tammy Mitchell . Surnames: Groat, Adams, Phillips Davis, Mike, Chrysler etc. canon/research-topic-misc-blackhist.html] *1998-2013 ;* localities.northam.canada.ontario.brant/9569.2/mb.ashx *Web 2011-13*
- Aikman, John A., William Davis and Thomas Ghent, United Empire *Loyalists' Association of Canada, Hamilton Branch,* web Nov 2013
- Angela, EM , Remembering African Canadian Settlement in Brantford, , Branches Newsletter v11 United Empire Loyalists' Association of Canada, Web Dec 2012
- Black Loyalists s in Upper Canada, United Empire Loyalists' Association *Western resource, undated, Web. Jan 2013*

- British Legion James' Troop, The Online Institute for Advanced Loyalist Studies, Web. Nov. 2013
- *Canadian Census of 1852, Ontario Genealogical Society. Web. Jan-Nov 2013*
- Clark, Walter .The State Records of North Carolina, Vol.XX11 Archive. Org *Web. June 1013*
- *Dictionary of Canadian Biography,* entries John Norton, Robert Lugger, Augustus Jones, Peter Jones, Peter Russell, John White, Robert Nelles Sr., James Gage, Reverend John Saltkill Carroll, David W. Smith Web June 2013
- Encyclopedia Britannica *Tuscarora, William Johnson* Web. May 2013
- Family tree legends beastybob/1 /data/1481 Edward Gant Web Dec 2013
  Cheryl-Gasiewski/WEBSITE-0001/UHP-0069.html Dec 2013
- Find a Grave, Ancestry.com Web. 2012-2013
- Fletcher, Freeman, The Travelling Tuscarora, Native Heritage Project Nov 2013
- Free pages, Genealogy, Rootsweb, surnames: Web. 2012-1013
- Genforum, Dorchester messages, Hazel Davis Clark, Web. Spring 2013
- Gibb, Carson, Abstracts of Wills, abstracted from Prerogative County 1746-1748 Web June 2013
- Journal of Negro History, Various Authors, Vol. 4 1919. e book 2007 Project Gutenberg Web 2013
- Kelly, Gerry, Irish Slavery In America, Scoilgailge Language School. Web Jan 2013
- Matilda Joslyn Gage Foundation, Underground Railroad Room/ Haudenosaunee Room/Women's Room Web Apr. 2013
- Mestern Pat, Poor House, Web June 2013
- Mulkewich, Jane; Sarah Pooley's Story, Dundas Valley Historical Society, Web Nov. 2013
- Muster Books and Pay Lists: Queen's Rangers 1783-1800, The Loyalist Collection, War Office Great Britain, Web. May 2013
- O'Connor, Jeff, Days of the Flockey, 2002 Schoharie Historical Society, Old Stone Fort Museum. Web. Mar 2013
- Ontario Cemetery Finding Aid, Ontario Genealogical Society, Web 2011-2013
- Petition of Free Negroes; Upper Canada Land Petitions Web. Sept. 2013
- Pensions in 1877 to Militiamen of the War of 1812-1815, Province of Ontario,
- Powell, Wm. S. Tuscarora War, North Carolina History Project, Web Apr 2013
- Putnam Historic District, Aboard the Underground Railroad, National Park Service, US Department of the Interior. WEB. May 2013
- Riddell, William R. The Slave in Upper Canada 1919 scribd.com Web Apr 2013
- Summary Under the Criteria and Evidence for Proposed Finding, Ramapough Mountain Indians, Inc. 1993 US Department of the Interior. Nov 2013
- Thomas, Robert K, A report on Research of Lumbee Origins, Part 18, Native Heritage Project, web Nov 2013
- Wagner, Sally Roesch, Matilda Josyln Gage, Web. Dec. 2013
- Warrick, Gary Grand Action/Grand Strategy newsletter, Summer 2004, Grand River Conservation Authority, Web. June 2013
- Wilson, William R. An Act to Prevent the Further Introduction of Slaves, Historical Narratives of Early Canada, Web. 2013
- YourDictionary , Matilda Joslyn Gage, Web 2013